The Presidents'
First Ladies

RAE LINDSAY

The Presidents'
First Ladies

Gilmour House
Englewood Cliffs, New Jersey

Published by Gilmour House,
A Division of R & R Writers/Agents, Inc.
364 Mauro Road
Englewood Cliffs, NJ 07632

Web: **www.first-ladies.net**
E-mail: info@first-ladies.net

Revised, Expanded Edition

304 pages; $24.95.

Printed in the United States of America

Design by Alex Lindsay

To the best men in my life:

My sons, Alex and Rob,
And my son-in-law, Loren

With my special thanks and myriad hugs, kisses and love
to Alex for his enduring patience in shepherding me through this book,
over a distance of 3,000 miles and a minefield of
winzips, pixels, 300dpi's, "burnt" cd's, Ventura 8,
computer disasters and national disasters…
gently propelling me technologically into the 21st century
for my 21st book, The Presidents' First Ladies.

CONTENTS

INTRODUCTION

The position of First Lady has been called the "world's hardest job." Eleanor Roosevelt, the woman who was First Lady longer than any other President's wife, once said, "Any woman who goes into public life has to have a hide like a rhinoceros."

Another first hand observer, J.B. West, who served as Chief Usher in the White House for thirty years, summed up the role: "As First Ladies of the land, these women filled the most demanding volunteer job in America. They were not elected; they were legally responsible to no one except the man with whom they had exchanged marriage vows. They had no official title. *First Lady* was a term popularized by a newswoman many years ago, but it has remained the only designation given to the woman who is married to the man we call 'Mr. President.'"

Americans usually think of the most celebrated and, generally, quite contemporary First Ladies as representative of the Presidents' wives. Eleanor Roosevelt is a history book legend, Jacqueline Kennedy remains a national favorite, Betty Ford is known for her forthrightness and her rehabilitation clinic, Rosalynn Carter continues to be a vital part of the Jimmy-Rosalynn team, Nancy Reagan stepped away from the headlines to care for her Alzheimer's stricken husband…and Hillary Clinton became the first former First Lady to win elected office on her own as New York's junior Senator.

Few of us know much about early First Ladies and their surrogates, the original members of a corps of some forty-plus women who served in an unelected, unpaid, highly visible position. These "pioneer" First Ladies were sometimes greatly admired, sometimes scorned and derided, as Americans judged not only the actions of their President, but those of his wife and family as well. All of the First Ladies make up a very diverse group, the only common denominator is that they married Presidents or were their daughters, daughters-in-law, sisters, nieces, or friends.

Many of the First Ladies were better educated, richer, and more socially prominent than the men they married, not surprising if you consider that an ambitious man who chooses a political career and strives for the highest elected position in the nation will tend to "marry up." George Washington married Martha Dandridge Custis, the richest widow in Virginia; John Adams's wife, Abigail Smith Adams, was a member of one of New England's first families; James Monroe married Elizabeth Kortright, a beautiful and wealthy New Yorker. Abraham Lincoln chose Mary Todd, the pretty, sophisticated, and rich daughter of a wealthy Kentucky family, and Andrew Johnson was forever indebted to his wife, Eliza McCardle Johnson, who taught the President-to-be to *read*. The choice of Warren Gamaliel Harding was a wealthy widow—some sources say divorcée—who lent her money and influence to help Harding become first a successful newspaper owner, and then a successful politician.

Harry Truman's Bess Wallace was *the* belle of Independence, Missouri; her father had been mayor, and her relatives looked down on Truman even after he became President. Dwight David Eisenhower married small-town deb Mamie Doud, the daughter of prosperous parents, and John Fitzgerald Kennedy courted Jacqueline Bouvier, who had social status the Irish Kennedys lacked. Lyndon Baines Johnson wooed Claudia Alta "Lady Bird" Taylor, who had the money; all he had was ambition. Ronald Reagan chose Nancy Davis as his second wife; her surgeon stepfather gave her polish, debutante status, and an enviable Smith education. The first President Bush also married a Smith graduate, while George W. chose a respectable librarian, perhaps to help change his reputation as a playboy. Bill Clinton married a Wellesley/Yale Law School grad, arguably as smart as he. When he became President, he announced "You have two for the price of one," a statement not appreciated by either the public or Congress.

Some future Presidents, perhaps in their haste to get where they were going *quickly*, asked their ladies to marry them on their first or second date. Although the more limited coverage of the time gives us little input about the earliest Presidents, we do know that Calvin Coolidge asked the very popular Grace Goodhue to marry him early on and reportedly "outsat everybody else." Harry Truman fell in

2

love with his Bess when she was only six years old (he was seven), and finally married her twenty-nine years later. Lyndon Baines Johnson asked "Lady Bird" to marry him on their first date, and they married two years later. Richard Nixon proposed on his first meeting with Pat Ryan but had to wait two years before she said yes. Gerald Ford was another first date suitor, and Betty Bloomer acquiesced shortly afterwards. George Bush and Laura Welch became engaged three weeks after they met.

Few of the First Ladies would be "kindred spirits" if they were to meet today. The renowned hostesses might enjoy comparing parties and celebrities; a few others, the political activists, could talk about national and international policies they had influenced; and more than a few might converse about the strains and stresses on their husbands and themselves which made being First Lady a nightmare. Only five or six might have specifically chosen to be First Lady, and most of the three dozen "official" First Ladies weren't prepared for such a role. Yet, especially in recent years, every President's wife's public actions or private problems have become grist for the media mill—their health, friends, clothes, speeches, interests, children, even their hairdressers. Everything about them is considered fair game.

In this book to bring some order to such disparate personalities, we have categorized the women of the White House according to the major role they played as First Ladies. It would be unfair, though, to regiment these women too rigidly. Most of them, like most women today, played several roles. For example, Jacqueline Kennedy Onassis, who is identified as a spokeswoman, could also be categorized as a First Lady who experienced "Private Pain," and was undeniably an "Elegant Entertainer."

When Pat Nixon was "running" for the job in 1960, the Republican National Committee wrote, "when you elect a President, you are also electing a First Lady, whose job is more than glamour. The First Lady has a working assignment. She represents America to all the world."

THE
PIONEERS

Martha Dandridge Custis Washington
1731-1802

Abigail Smith Adams
1744-1818

Martha "Patsy" Jefferson Randolph
1772-1836

Dolly Payne Todd Madison
1768-1849

Elizabeth Kortright Monroe
1763-1830

Louisa Johnson Adams
1775-1852

In the late eighteenth century, America was a very new country, a nation breaking away from the protective and restrictive domination of the United Kingdom, a raw country, with no real political precedents, and very few guidelines to follow. For years the "Founding Fathers," worked at framing a constitution for this "Brave New World" to follow, one that would give equal rights to everyone, a government by the people, for the people. While Benjamin Franklin, Thomas Jefferson, Alexander Hamilton, John Adams, George Washington and the other drafters and signers of the Declaration of Independence and later, the Constitution, worked so diligently in Philadelphia, even the most liberated had no idea that in the next few centuries, the women who were married to the "First Men" would have a major influence on our country as well.

Nor did those early statesmen make any provisions to help those women carry out this challenging, uncharted position. The new democracy, promising equal rights to everyone, would have to come to grips with the status of a person "without portfolio," a woman with no voting power, no clout, but certainly some important responsibilities to her country.

Unlike other countries where, should a woman become Queen, there were specific ceremonial routes to follow, the first women to serve as "First Lady" had no precedents to guide them. The term "First Lady" was first used by a journalist in 1877 to describe Lucy Hayes when her husband, Rutherford B. Hayes, was inaugurated. The first six First Ladies courageously went their own way, fulfilled their obligations as the wife of "The President," and laid the groundwork for the more than thirty women who would follow in their place.

Martha Washington, for example, never lived in the White House, but as a wealthy plantation-owner, she was able to act as an effective hostess for George Washington. Abigail Smith Adams was the first to live in the Mansion, which at the time was nothing much more than a very large building under endless construction. Although she hung the family wash in the East Room, she segued out of her washerwoman role and freely, volubly gave her husband advice about running the country. Dolley Todd Madison had been raised as a Quaker, but after her first husband died, she married James Madison, and became a brilliant hostess for widower Thomas Jefferson. Then, after James Madison was elected, Dolley set a standard for White House entertaining. Eliza Kortright Monroe, the wife of James Monroe, was a little more aristocratic, reportedly somewhat "snobbish" and not quite so willing to play the First Lady role. She was succeeded by Louisa Johnson Adams, the wife of the sixth President, John Quincy Adams, and Louisa had the unenviable position of following the act of her very strong and vocal mother-in-law, Abigail.

MARTHA DANDRIDGE CUSTIS WASHINGTON

Martha Dandridge Custis Washington was born in June, 1731, into a wealthy Tidewater, Virginia, family with prominent social credentials. She was called "Patsy," and reputed to be a tomboy, she once rode her horse up the stairs of her uncle's house. According to period paintings, Martha was not a classic beauty, but she was petite, brown–haired, big–eyed, rosy–cheeked, vivacious, and "cute." She wasn't formally educated (there weren't any schools for young women in Virginia at that time), knew only a little reading, writing and arithmetic, and was, by her own admission, a poor speller. But she knew about managing a house and servants, could play the spinet and dance, and was skilled at embroidery and knitting.

At 17, she married Daniel Parke Custis (then in his mid–thirties), whose father was the wealthiest man in the Tidewater area. Prophetically, the newlyweds' home was known as "The White House." The couple had four children, two of whom died in infancy. In 1757, Custis died, and his widow, now 26, became by contemporary accounts, one of the wealthiest women in Virginia.

A year after her husband's death, while visiting a neighbor's plantation, Martha met the tall, handsome Colonel George Washington. Although Martha was not Washington's first love (he had once proposed to a young woman in Yonkers, New York, and had a life-long affection for his one-time neighbor, Sally Fairfax), they had a natural affinity for each other. The young widow needed someone to manage her vast estates and act as a father for her children. George Washington had an excellent reputation, but little money. Since, in those days, a wife's income and property became her husband's to own and to manage, the match was a good solution for each of them. Despite this practical arrangement, it would be wrong to conclude that their marriage was without romance. There is no doubt that through their long life together, the couple loved and cherished each other, and although the Washingtons never had any children of their own, Washington treated young Martha (also called "Patsy"), and her son Jackey, as his own children and was known to spoil them.

Martha Washington was a loyal wife, and although she was used to carrying on without him when in 1775 Washington was appointed Commander-in-Chief of the colonial army, she spent time with him at his headquarters whenever she could. And she prepared food, recruited nurses and personally provided nursing attention to the troops, established knitting and sewing groups, and tried to keep up the morale of not only her husband, but also his sometimes bedraggled and beleaguered army.

Martha and George planned to "grow old together in solitude and tranquillity…the first and dearest wish of my heart." General Washington resigned his commission on Christmas Eve, 1783 and the next years at Mount Vernon were happy ones. They entertained friends so frequently that Washington wrote to his mother that his house often seemed like a hotel. Many of their visitors were political figures, including two future Presidents, James Madison and James Monroe. Martha Washington never participated in their discussions of what she described as "man talk."

She always enjoyed her role as mother, wife and housekeeper, and liked to make the atmosphere pleasant in all the houses she lived in. Among her writings and letters that still exist, there is a recipe for a room freshener, written in her own poor spelling: (Like many upper-class women of her time, including the educated Abigail Adams, Martha wrote phonetically, with consequent often imaginative spelling, punctuation and capitalization):

> *Take two or three quarts of roses buds or ye leaves of damask roses and put them in a pot with bay salt, 3 or 4 grayns of musk and as much of ambergreece, 20 or 30 drops of oyle of rodium, a little benjamin & Storeax, beat together in a cheyney pot or any other yt is handsome and keep it allways covered, but when you have a mind to have yr roome sweet you must take of ye cover.[1]*

In May 1787, Washington agreed to head the Virginia delegation to the Constitutional Convention in Philadelphia. Martha Washington told her mother-in-law, "George was always a good boy—he always does his duty." Two years later, when he was elected President of the new Republic, his wife was not pleased: their happy retirement had been short-lived. In New York, the United States capital at that time, she knew she would have to act as hostess, but wasn't quite sure what those duties would entail, since nobody had held the post before. In addition, the Washingtons would be expected to pay for all their expenses, including entertainment, on a salary of $25,000 a year. Although they had land and slaves, they had many debts and few liquid assets. (This was not a problem unique to the Washingtons; Jefferson, on paper, was considered a very wealthy man, but property, livestock and slaves were not easily converted to cash to pay Presidential bills. The John Adams family was in an even worse financial position during their Presidential years).

There were other problems. At 58, Martha was no longer a young woman, and had never worried much about being fashionable. Now she would be in a high-profile position and expected to *set* style. Her one fashion foible, if you will, was elegant shoes (a weakness of other First Ladies through the years), but her gowns, adequate for the Virginia plantation, had to be re-designed to reflect more current modes. And she was too thrifty to order designer originals from Paris, or even enlist American dressmakers.

As for terminology, she would continue to call her husband "General," but there was no appropriate title for *her* role in the new government. John Adams was very involved in what the new leader's title should be. He considered such choices as "His Majesty," "Excellence," "His Most Benign Highness," "High Mightiness," "Elective Majesty," and "Elective Highness." Another faction, which ultimately won, wanted nothing more than "President of the United States of America." Adams thought that heads of companies and cricket clubs were called "President," and spoke for forty impassioned minutes in favor of "His Highness," finally concluding by asking, "What will the common people of foreign countries—what will the sailors and soldiers say, 'George Washington, President of the United States?' They will despise him *to all eternity*."[2] Fortunately, his royal choice was over-ruled.

Martha Washington was also worried about comparisons to Abigail Adams (wife of Vice-President John Adams), who was known as an educated and intelligent woman. Martha was so uncomfortable about her poor spelling that she either dictated letters for others to write, or George Washington himself would write them for her to copy. She wrote to her friend Mercy Warren, author of the first history of the American Revolution and a friend of Abigail Adams, "I sometimes think the arrangement is not quite as it ought to have been, that I, who had much rather be at home, should occupy a place with which a great many younger and gayer women would be extremely pleased."[3]

When Martha, accompanied by her maid and two grandchildren, arrived in New York a month after the inauguration, she was greeted by a cheering crowd. Unfortunately, no one recorded her exact words of thanks, and "Lady Washington" (which seemed to be her new title) never again made a public statement. The first Executive Mansion, on Cherry Street in downtown Manhattan, was smaller than Mount Vernon, ill-kept, unfashionably located, overcrowded, and not very impressive.

Still, Martha, with her talent for organizing, began to plan her first reception, which became the most elegant of any the Washingtons gave during his two terms in office. "Lady Washington" wore a white dress trimmed in silver, but her costume was overshadowed by the elaborate regalia of her more sophisticated guests, who wore satin, velvet, brocade, and lace, had elaborate hairdos and accessories, and glowed with fabulous jewelry. Nonetheless, at 9:00, Martha announced, "The General retires at nine o'clock, and I usually precede him. Good night."[4]

That was the start of ridiculing Martha's entertaining skills, and the beginning of what she called her "lost days." It would be wrong to believe that only the contemporary, headline-seeking press could be so cruel to celebrities, and especially First Families, because Martha was widely criticized for her lack of social graces. When she and the President went to the theater, which both enjoyed, they were rebuked for their encouragement of such foolish and disreputable entertainment. The Washingtons—and every other First Family since then—were definitely fair game for the media.

Despite the criticism, Martha Washington, always a good housekeeper and helpmeet, carried out her duties of running the Presidential house. Her great-granddaughter, Mary Custis Lee, recorded that during her inspection tours of the dairy, the cellar, the living rooms or the kitchen, she wore a "white dimity dress...(that) was spotless and served for a morning dress the whole week." Martha was economical and hated to throw things out. Some of her "at home" dresses were made from fabric woven from old stockings or discarded chair upholstery.

However, she was unhappy and hurt by the gossip and very homesick for Virginia. In October, 1789, she wrote her niece Fanny (who was house-sitting at Mount Vernon), "I live a very dull life here...I never goe to any publick place...I think I am more like a state prisoner than anything else...and as I cannot doe as I like I am obstinate and stay at home a great deal."[5]

On December 1, 1790, the capital was relocated to Philadelphia, and the Washingtons moved into a house owned by their friends, Mr. and Mrs. Robert Morris. Although the quarters were still tight, at least Martha was surrounded by old friends, and she gradually became more accustomed to being "Lady Washington," with all its responsibilities *and* honors.

An unexpected bonus was her new friendship with the more sophisticated, better-educated and widely traveled Abigail Adams, whom she had formerly feared. The two women, with their behind-the-scenes influence, helped to smooth the working relationship between the President and his second-in-command, John Adams. In March, 1797 the Washingtons happily returned to Mount Vernon, eager to retire once again "under our vine and fig tree." Martha Washington wrote to Lucy Knox (wife of General Henry Knox, the first Secretary of War), "The twilight is gathering around our lives. I am again fairly settled down to the pleasant duties of an old-fashioned Virginia housekeeper, steady as a clock, busy as a bee, and cheerful as a cricket."[6]

ABIGAIL SMITH ADAMS

While Martha Washington was growing up in her rather sheltered and moneyed environment of Virginia, Abigail Smith Adams, born on November 11, 1744, to Parson and Mrs. William Smith, had quite a different childhood. Abigail's parents were educated, respected and definitely middle-class in terms of assets. While Martha learned domestic arts, Abigail learned Latin, philosophy, literature, and history, attributes considered "unfeminine" at the time. She had also read Shakespeare, Moliere, the poets, Locke, the *Spectator*, and most of the "classics," and John Adams thought she was the best educated woman he had ever met.

Francis Russell, in his book *Adams: An American Dynasty*, describes Abigail as a "sharp-eyed, sharp-tongued sprightly (woman with) a robust mind, witty, engaging, at times impish."[1] Paintings show that she was not a beauty, and unmarried at eighteen (in those days) she was on the way to being a spinster. However, her family was not so eager to see her married that they would agree to an "inferior match." Abigail Smith, after all, was a Quincy, and related to one of New England's leading families. In fact, while George Washington, although short on assets, was considered a good catch, John Adams was studying to be a lawyer—a position about as respected as that of an ambulance-chasing attorney today. John ranked fourteenth in his Harvard class, not because of academic standing, but based on his mother's social position as a Boylston.[2]

Aside from parental reservations, their courtship was somewhat rocky, or perhaps one could say, "spirited," since John Adams was as smart, stubborn and proud as his wife-to-be. At one point, when Adams was quarantined for six weeks after a small pox inoculation, Abigail wrote him that his treatment had not made him more sociable and she listed his faults. He wrote back with his own fault-list, including the fact that she never learned to play cards, a "noble and elegant Diversion," or "learn to sing," that she hung her head "like a Bulrush," and had a bad habit of "sitting with the Leggs across (which ruins the figure and the Air; this injures the Health.)" He also noted that she had a habit of "Walking with the Toes bending inward...commonly called Parrot-toed." Undaunted and spunky as ever, she thanked him for his "Catalogue, but must confess I was so hardened as to read over most of my Faults with as much pleasure as any other person could have read their perfections." She listed her defenses for each of his "Faults," and then concluded, "You know I think that a gentleman has no business to concern himself about the Leggs of a Lady...The sixth and last (Parrot-toes) can be cured only by a Dancing School."[3] (Even with their high level of education and extensive reading, both Abigail and John had some quaint spelling and grammar customs, many of which were edited from their letters and papers by grandson Charles Francis Adams fifty years after they died.)

Despite her parents' opposition and the couple's mutual fault list, John and Abigail were married, and in 1768, in a curious historical coincidence, they, too, moved into a house called the "White House," in Brattle Square, Boston. These first years of marriage were very busy for the young family. Within a year or so, they moved back to Braintree (later renamed Quincy), and John Adams became very involved in Commonwealth of Massachusetts and "national" politics. (Along with his rebellious cousin, James Adams, John was one of the plotters of the Boston Tea Party and unquestionably, his wife knew about the scheme.)

While Adams dedicatedly followed his political interests, Abigail ran the farm and the family. In the first seven years of marriage she had five children, and a sixth, stillborn child, in 1777; another child died in infancy. Abigail supervised the children's education and shepherded them through illnesses and problems. Of the four children who survived, Abigail (called "Nabby") was unhappily married and died of cancer; Charles, the second son, became an alcoholic, was heavily in debt, and died of cirrhosis of the liver at age thirty; the youngest son led a moderate, unspectacular life as a judge; and the eldest son, John Quincy Adams, undoubtedly the favorite, took a page from his father's book and became the sixth President of the United States.

Reportedly, John Adams was not an easy man to live with during the brief periods when he was at home. He was a hypochondriac and a food faddist, and was convinced he would diet at a young age. (He lived to be 91). Abigail actually was in more delicate health than her husband all during her life, suffering from migraines, insomnia, colds and fevers, perhaps a result of all those years when she not only raised the children on her own, but also managed the farm, and dealt with her loneliness.

Abigail and John Adams were apart for long periods when John made only infrequent trips back to Quincy. During those years, when he lived in Philadelphia and worked with the Constitutional Congress, and later, when he served as Minister to England, Abigail wrote hundreds of letters as many as three a day. She was not a woman to sit quietly in a corner, tending to her knitting. She was always giving advice, and sometimes it exasperated her husband. At one point during the drafting of the Constitution he wrote to her: "I think you shine as a stateswoman of late, as well as a farmeress. Pray, where do you get your maxims of state? They are very apropos." He also asked his farmeress, "Pray, how does your asparagus peform?"

Before the Declaration of Independence was drafted, she wrote, "What course you can or will take is all wrapped in the bosom of futurity. Uncertainty and expectation leave the mind great scope. Did ever any kingdom or state regain its liberty, when once it was invaded, without bloodshed? I cannot think of it without horror."[4]

When Colonial Independence seemed to be the chosen path, she wrote, "The reins of government have been so long slackened that I fear the people will not quietly submit to those restraints which are necessary for the peace and security of the community. How shall we be governed so as to retain our liberties?" Regarding the drafting of the Constitution, here is one of her strongest comments:

> *I desire you would remember the ladies and be more generous and favorable to them than your ancestors. Do not put such unlimited power into the hands of the husbands. Remember, all men would be tyrants if they could. If particular care and attention is not paid to the ladies, we are determined to foment a rebellion and will not hold ourselves bound by any laws in which we have no voice or representation.*[5]

John Adams responded to her impassioned plea for feminist rights rather humorously:

> *Your letter was the first intimation that another tribe (other than the Negro slaves), were grown discontented...Depend on it, we know better than to repeal our masculine systems...We have only the name of masters, and rather than give up this, which would*

completely subject us to the despotism of the petticoat, I hope General Washington and all our brave heroes would fight.

Abigail did not give up *her* fight so easily, and she had the last word on this issue:

You insist upon retaining absolute power over wives. But you must remember that arbitrary power is like most other things which are very hard…and, notwithstanding all your wise laws and maxims, we have it in our power, not only to free ourselves, but to subdue our masters. and without violence, throw both your natural and legal authority at our feet. [6]

The feminists who followed Abigail Adams 200 years later couldn't have said it better.

Yet, Abigail was neither a strident nor a cold woman. She deeply loved John and missed him all those years they were apart. Their letters to each other—over a thousand survived—were, in fact, love letters, and she expressed her affection and devotion in her own prose, as well as with poetry, her own and others. She also wrote about her loneliness: "Who shall give me back time? Who shall compensate to me those years I cannot recall? How dearly have I paid for a titled husband? Should I wish you less wise, that I might enjoy more happiness? I cannot find that in my heart. [7]

Although she described their marriage of 54 years as a passionate "love feast," she also wrote, "I cannot sometimes refrain from considering the honors with which he is invested as badges of my unhappiness." John Adams also missed her desperately. He wrote her from France, "I must go to you or you must come to me…I cannot live without you."

In 1784, after the peace treaty with England had been negotiated by John Jay and Benjamin Franklin, Abigail joined her husband and son in London; she was now forty and had never been more than forty miles away from home. For the next sixteen years, Abigail, raised in rural Massachusetts, lived in London, Paris, New York, Philadelphia, and finally in the new capital, Washington. But she never liked any of these cities, or any of the grand houses (and some not so grand houses) as much as she liked Quincy. In London, it was the country "girl," Abigail, who found and rented a mansion in Grosvenor Square, the very first American Embassy in London. (John Adams was always too busy with affairs of state to tend to such tasks). Her heart remained in Quincy, however, and she wrote her friend Mercy Warren, "I long, my dear madam, to return to my native land. My little cottage, encompassed with my friends, has more charms for me than the drawing room of St. James, where studied civility and disguised coldness cover malignant hearts.[8]

In 1788, Adams resigned as Minister to Great Britain, and Abigail planned to return to her new home in Quincy; she wrote detailed letters about the painting and wallpapering and which furniture was to go where. The couple had every hope of retiring there.

However, in 1789, nine months after his return to the United States, John Adams was elected as the first Vice President. Instead of retiring to her Quincy home, now Abigail was the mistress of a house in Richmond Hill, in New York, and although she admired the scenery and depicted it enthusiastically in many letters, she hated the New York ambiance and bitterly complained about being unable to find good help. In eighteen months she had seven cooks and wrote there was "not a virtuous woman amongst them all; the most of them drunkards." Another concern was money to keep up her household, since she and John had far fewer resources than Martha and George.

Still, she gamely carried on, and when Adams became President, ironically, Abigail Adams took her social cues from Martha Washington, who had always felt that Abigail was much more worldly than she was. Abigail wasn't present for her husband's inauguration because the mansion in Philadelphia had been trashed by the servants, and most of the rooms weren't fit to sleep in. One humorous note: a 110-pound cartwheel-shaped cheese had arrived as a gift from Rhode Island, and Abigail speculated about whether or not the President could survive on this food when his money ran out. Although she was a farmwoman, when she joined her husband in Philadelphia, Abigail wanted to dress well and wore gowns of elegant fabrics, rich laces and vivid colors. (Muslin was the popular material for winter dresses, but Abigail disliked this coarse fabric and chose silk instead, establishing the popularity of that more luxurious fabric). She also liked fashionable high-heeled shoes, and would arrange her hair elaborately with curls, ribbons, bows and feathers.

Despite her stylish efforts, the Adams' receptions were very stiff and formal; undoubtedly, Abigail's passion was politics, not parties. She tried to emulate Martha Washington's behavior as the President's hostess, but, although they were friends, temperamentally and emotionally, the two First Ladies were very different. For one thing, Martha Washington never interfered in government affairs. Abigail Adams, on the other hand, was very outspoken and shared her husband's political responsibilities to the point that she was often sarcastically referred to as "Her Majesty." Some critics even said she made John Adams's decisions for him.

Abigail attended meetings of the House of Representatives (although she was never admitted to the Senate chambers) to hear debates, and she expressed her opinions so openly that one political figure, Albert Gallatin, called her "Mrs. President not of the United States, but of a faction" (the Federalist party). The President (and his family) were criticized and Abigail, as always, defended her husband in her letters.

> *I feel perhaps too keenly the abuse of party. Washington endured it; but he had the support of the people...and a combination of circumstances which no other man can look for...What is the expected lot of a successor? He must be armed as Washington with integrity, with firmness, with intrepidity. These must be his shield and his wall of brass; and religion too, or he never will be able to stand sure and steadfast.* [9]

Adams needed defending because he was often feisty, outspoken, and would not compromise his ideals, even when it meant stepping on powerful toes, such as those of Thomas Jefferson. As one biographer, Page Smith said, "Abigail insured his sanity." Jefferson, the tall, elegant squire of Monticello, the chief drafter of the Declaration, has always been history's favorite son, with John Adams, tainted by his difficult temperament, often second-rated in terms of his accomplishments. That traditional attitude was largely reversed by two scholarly and well received books published in 2001 which revealed that while Jefferson's contributions always showed "grace and eloquence," it was the hard-driving Adams who delivered the goods...and the votes. David McCullough, Pulitzer Prize-winning biographer of Harry S. Truman, initially planned a joint biography of old pals/bitter enemies Adams and Jefferson. Instead his research led to a 751-page tome, *John Adams*, which clearly makes Adams the prime player, not Jefferson. At the same time, Joseph J. Ellis, wrote *Founding Brothers*, after writing separate books about both Adams and Jefferson, and concluded that of the two statesmen, Adams had for centuries been underestimated, and Jefferson's achievements overblown.

One of John Adams's most pressing problems during his administration was the threat of war with France, a situation he inherited from Washington. Abigail encouraged her husband's stand of dispatching new envoys to France to calm the troubled waters: "We should hold the sword in one hand and the olive branch in the other...Pray am I not a good politician?" [10]

Perhaps she was a better politician than her husband, because John Adams was defeated by Thomas Jefferson and it was then that Abigail spent the last few months of her husband's lame duck presidency as the first mistress of the White House. They were shocked that after eight years had been spent on construction, only a handful of rooms could be inhabited. The main stairway wasn't finished, there was no plumbing, no wood for the fires, and the walls were damp. The Presidential Palace was far short of palatial. Never one to mince words, Abigail wrote that the mirrors in the few livable rooms were "dwarfs," and there wasn't a "twentieth part enough lamps to light" the Mansion. She complained about having to dry laundry in the "audience room" and her clothes and household possessions either hadn't arrived or were "more than half missing." As for the neighborhood,, she considered Georgetown the "very dirtiest hole I ever saw for a place of any trade or respectability."

In addition, when John Adams left the White House, it was not under happy terms. He deeply disapproved of Jefferson's election (the former fast friends were now dedicated adversaries), and would not join in the inaugural proceedings. Still, Adams hoped the White House would stand as a hallmark for the presidency, and wrote in a letter to his wife, "I pray heaven to bestow the best of blessings on this house, and on all that shall hereafter inhabit it. May none but honest and wise men ever rule under this roof."[11]

Abigail Adams returned to Quincy, took over the management of her new "mansion," and continued to write letters in defense of her husband. In 1801, when her son, John Quincy, came home after his ambassadorship to Berlin with wife Louisa Catherine and their son George Washington Adams (Abigail's seventh grandchild), she welcomed them and played the role of matriarch.

In 1816, John Quincy was appointed Secretary of State in James Monroe's cabinet, a post that in the brief history of the United States was often a springboard to the presidency. Abigail must have been very proud. Unfortunately, after suffering a stroke in 1818, she died at the age of seventy—three years before her son became President. John Adams lived for eight more years and died on July 4, 1826, on the 50th anniversary of our nation's independence, within a few hours of the death of his former old friend, Thomas Jefferson.

Marianne Means, in her book, *The Woman in the White House*, reports that Harry Truman said Abigail Adams "would have made a better President than her husband." Means describes Abigail as "self-taught, outspoken, incredibly brilliant, chafed all her life under the arbitrary limitations put upon her by her femaleness. She was the wife of a President and the mother of one, but she could not even vote."[12]

MARTHA "PATSY" JEFFERSON RANDOLPH

Ideally, Thomas Jefferson, one of the founders of the nation and instrumental in establishing Washington as the Capital and the White House as the official "President's House" should have lived there with his wife and his children. However, his wife, Martha Wayles Jefferson, never served as First Lady and died in 1782, after ten brief years of marriage, well before Jefferson was elected as our nation's third President.

According to contemporary accounts, the petite Martha had a lovely complexion; she was a graceful rider and spirited dancer; and she sang and played the spinet and harpsichord. (Jefferson played the violin while they sang duets together). In addition to her talents and her love, Martha also brought to Jefferson's estate a handsome dowry. When her father died, she inherited 11,000 acres and 135 slaves. As the recipient of good fortune similar to George Washington's, Jefferson not only managed his wife's inheritance, but joined it to his own estate, a windfall he described as "about equal to my own patrimony, and consequently doubled the ease of our circumstances."

The Jeffersons had six children, five girls and one boy, but only two girls survived their mother and reached maturity: Martha (called "Patsy") and Mary ("Polly").

There is a story, perhaps apocryphal, that the manager of the Jefferson plantation heard Martha ask for a deathbed promise that Jefferson would never marry again, that his children would never have a stepmother. Jefferson never did remarry, a choice very unusual for the time, when wives often died young after repeated childbearing. Patsy and Polly were raised by Philadelphia relatives, the Eppes family, until May, 1784, when Jefferson, then 41, was named minister plenipotentiary to replace Benjamin Franklin in Paris. He took Patsy with him, and in Paris chose a Catholic convent school for her education, even though the family was not Catholic.

Three years later, he sent for Polly, and although she wrote letters expressing her wish to stay with her aunt, Jefferson insisted and Polly arrived in Europe in July, 1787, accompanied by a pretty teenage slave named Sally Hemings. The little girl was met in England by Abigail Adams, who wrote Jefferson about Polly's safe arrival and suggested it might be a good idea for Jefferson to come to London to escort Polly to Paris.

Jefferson was too busy in Paris to come to London personally, but according to some accounts, a London visit would have been pleasant because he was very interested in a woman named Maria Louisa Catherine Cecilia Cosway, who was living in London. Maria Louisa, unfortunately for Jefferson, or perhaps fortunately, if you consider his legendary vow never to marry again, was already married. The two enjoyed each other's company immensely, and they exchanged many letters until Jefferson's death. But after his return to the United States, he never saw her again.

All his life, scandals and innuendoes circulated about Jefferson and his love life, some involving Maria, but most of them relating to his slave, Sally. *In The Women in Their Lives*, Frank Donovan dismisses these rumors:

> *Franklin was accused of having a child by his serving wench Barbara and throwing her out in the cold. Adams was accused of sending his Secretary of War to England in a frigate to bring back four beautiful British women as mistresses—two for Adams and two for himself...Jefferson was a prime target for similar scurrilous innuendo.* [1]

While there was no firm evidence that Jefferson had an affair with Maria...for two hundred years the rumors persisted about Sally. In the last five years, however, facts have emerged which are so convincing that even the Thomas Jefferson Foundation has published a paper verifying them. Perhaps the most important breakthrough was the November 5, 1998 article in *Nature* providing DNA evidence that Jefferson could have fathered at least one of Sally's sons. After that report was published the Thomas Jefferson Foundation commissioned a two-year long study of dozens of papers, books, articles, oral history and other sources and concluded that "the weight of evidence...indicated a high probability that

Thomas Jefferson was the father of Eston Hemings, and that he was most likely the father of all six of Sally Hemings' children listed in Monticello records. Among other aspects of the thirty-eight-year relationship "generally accepted" by the foundation:

- *Thomas Jefferson was at Monticello at the likely conception times of Sally Hemings' six known children. (There are no records suggesting she was anywhere else)*

- *Sally's children were all light-skinned, and three of them lived as members of white society as adults. According to family reports, some of her children strongly resembled Jefferson.*

- *Jefferson freed Sally's children, allowing two to leave Monticello in 1822, and freeing two others in his will. (He did not give freedom to the rest of his slaves)[2]*

There is another irony to the story: Sally was one of several children born to John Wayles, Jefferson's father-in-law, and one of his slaves, Elizabeth Hemings. This makes Sally the half-sister of Jefferson's wife, Martha, and the aunt of Patsy who ruled Monticello as hostess and also presided as First Lady at the White House after Jefferson became our third President in 1801.

Patsy was well-suited to the job, given her convent-bred manners, European education, fluency in several languages, and her ease in the company of cultured and sophisticated men and women. Patsy had married her second cousin, Thomas Mann Randolph, whom she had met in Europe (Polly also married a cousin, John Wayles Eppes, her childhood companion), and by the time her father became President she was also a busy young wife and mother. Over the years Patsy had twelve children (eleven reached adulthood), many of whom she educated herself at home, with a willing assist from Jefferson. In addition to the responsibilities of parenting so many children, Patsy also ran her home, managed the many slaves on her father's estate, and then cared for her sister's children after Polly died.

In 1802, both daughters were with Jefferson at the White House and Dolley Madison, the wife of Secretary of State James Madison, took the girls under her wing, helped them select gowns, turbans, shawls, and other items of clothing she deemed appropriate for their positions as daughters of the President. There were occasions, however, when Patsy and Polly were occupied with their own households and Jefferson called on Dolley to serve as official hostess. In 1805, at the beginning of his second term, Patsy was able to leave her Virginia home and stay at the White House for the entire winter season. During that stay, her eighth child was born, a son, James Madison Randolph, the first child born in the White House.

Except for the times when his daughters were in residence, Thomas Jefferson lived in the Mansion alone, and aside from his official appointments, one can imagine that he must have been lonely. Nonetheless, the always elegant Jefferson hoped to make the White House a sophisticated and refined environment, an oasis in the under-construction chaos of the new Capital city. He brought with him furniture and accessories he had collected during his diplomatic sojourn abroad and personal possessions from Monticello. He had a French steward and a French chef, and imported wines from France, Spain, Italy, and Portugal. (In 1804, his bill for Madeira, claret, sauterne and champagne amounted to $3,000, a vast sum for that time.)

It was not to show off his fine tastes, but more to the point, to establish the White House as a refined representation of the new government, a place where foreign ministers as well as members of Congress could conduct business and discuss important international and national events and ideas. In addition to American cuisine (notably southern specialties), he served European delicacies: pasta from Italy, waffles from Holland, anchovies from Spain and Portugal, ice cream served in warm pastry shells.[3]

Patsy lived at Monticello during her father's last years and he left the estate to her. However, when he died he was almost bankrupt; Patsy sold off the furniture, paintings, and china at auction, and finally sold the house itself to a pharmacist who planned to raise silkworms on the estate. At sixty, Patsy left Monticello, widowed, impoverished and dependent on her children for a place to stay. She wrote in her diary: "There is a time in human suffering when succeeding sufferings are but like snow falling on an iceberg."

DOLLEY PAYNE TODD MADISON

D olley Madison grew up living simply as a Quaker, and died at age 82 as an elegant, sophisticated ex-President's wife, world famous in her own time and still regarded today as one of the most successful and gracious First Ladies. Although Dolley was not "to the manor born," she had a natural flair as a hostess, and by the time she reached the White House as the fourth President's wife in 1809, she also had more experience than her predecessors, having served as part-time unofficial hostess for Jefferson. Dolley's parties—and she gave so many parties she surely would rival any other First Lady for the record—were "sensational, extravagant, and overcrowded." For example, at the New Year's Day reception in 1814

Gentlemen in lace and women in flowers, feathers, gloves and teetering headdresses waltzed in the great audience room, nibbled ice cream, drank Madeira, and tried to worm their way close enough for a word or two with their elegant host and hostess. The First Lady, beaming and bobbing, was wearing a new gown from France, soft pink satin trimmed in ermine. She had on a new turban, fashionably done in white satin and velvet, topped with ostrich plumes. By her side, bowing to the guests, stood the diminutive Madison—a good three inches shorter than his wife, several pounds lighter, seventeen years older, formal, reserved, and enveloped in an air of abstraction.[1]

In 1814, the country was at war with England—and the English were winning most of the battles—but Dolley believed that her parties were good for the nation's morale, and she carried on business as usual, even though it was difficult for her to replenish her wardrobe with luxurious frocks from France. She liked to set off her gowns with matching accessories and owned a dozen pairs of gold, silver or beaded slippers. Her style and her habits were widely copied. Since she took snuff, for example, it became fashionable for other women; if she wore emeralds, they became the vogue; after she bought a macaw for a pet, it became *de rigeur* to own a macaw.

When the Madisons moved into the White House in March 1809, there was still confusion about what the wife of the President should be called, and Dolley was sometimes addressed as "Her Majesty" or "Lady Presidentess." Dolley's first party became a tradition: she was the first President's wife to hold a gala inaugural ball. Mrs. Margaret Bayard Smith, who was married to an important publisher and later wrote *The First Forty Years of Washington Society*, described Dolley at the ball:

> *She looked like a queen. She had on a pale buff-colored velvet, made plain, with a very long train, but not the least trimming, and beautiful pearl necklace, earrings, and bracelets. Her headdress was a turban of the same colored velvet and white satin (from Paris) with two superb plumes, the bird-of-paradise feathers. It would be absolutely impossible for anyone to behave with more perfect propriety than she did...It seems to me that such manners would disarm envy itself, and conciliate even enemies.[2]*

Perhaps Mrs. Smith was referring to those who gossiped about the Madisons. James Madison was not a popular President, particularly because of his wavering position on England. He had wanted to remain neutral in the battle between the French and the British (the Napoleonic Wars), which would enable the United States to continue important trade with both countries. However, responding to the spirit of "new" nationalism, along with British violations of America's neutrality by seizing ships and goods, Madison was finally forced into a declaration of war against England in 1812, a move seconded by Congress. The War of 1812, known then as "Mr. Madison's War," was a disaster, with few triumphs for the Americans.

Not only was Madison criticized by the press for his reluctant stand on the war, but also personal insinuations about both Madisons became a subject for press coverage. The difference in their ages and the fact that they had not had children led to rumors, which then found their way to print. One anonymous pamphlet included a chapter *"L'Amour et la fumée ne peuvent se cacher"*—Love and smoke can't hide themselves—with implications about the alleged sexual activities of the famous wife of an equally famous, but allegedly impotent husband.

Despite gossip, invitations to Dolley's parties were in demand because she treated her guests so graciously. She doubled the number of White House servants from 14 to 30, a figure which has remained more or less constant since then, and for large parties she hired additional help (for 35 cents each) so there would be one waiter for each guest. She redecorated the White House (at a cost of $11,000), and bought new china and silver. One of her innovations was to invite guests to sing-alongs around the grand piano.

At her soirées or levées as they were known then, she made sure that the conversation was entertaining, and always avoided—and steered her guests away from—the war or political problems. She remembered faces and names (the President did not). Dolley often spearheaded a lively discussion by carrying a popular book with her, quoting sections that would generate responses. (Of all the portraits in the Smithsonian Institute, hers is the only one depicting a First Lady carrying a book, a distinction she would have enjoyed.) She also always carried an elaborately decorated little snuffbox...but this touch isn't included in the portrait.

A party scheduled for August 23, 1814, had to be canceled, however. The British were about to attack Washington, and the President left the city to supervise its defense with troops stationed in nearby Maryland. He ordered a hundred men to protect his wife, but most of these joined other military divisions or conveniently headed for more congenial cities. Dolley spent this crucial day on matters which were definitely non-entertaining. She packed the national seal, the original draft of the Constitution, the Declaration of Independence, and important national papers in one trunk. Other packages and boxes held her silver, her wardrobe, and favorite yellow velvet and satin curtains and tablecloths.

The one person left to defend her and the White House was Jean Pierre Sioussant, her steward, who offered to fire a cannon to deter the British from entering the house. Dolley rejected this idea, gave Sioussant her pet parrot to take to a safer house (the macaw survived), and remarkably, with all of Washington fleeing past her windows, sat down to write a letter to her sister, Lucy. Her note has become an important part of our historical heritage, recording the only time in our history a President's family has been forced to escape from an invasion of the capital. In addition, Dolley's calm under such traumatic circumstances more than balances the image of her as a frivolous party-giver. She wrote,

Dear Sister: My husband left me yesterday morning...and inquired anxiously whether I had courage, or firmness to remain in the President's house until his return...He desires I should be ready at a moment's warning to enter my carriage and leave the city...I am determined not to go myself until I see Mr. Madison safe...My friends and acquaintances are all gone...3

The following day, August 24, there was still no sign of the President and his entourage. That afternoon she once again wrote to Lucy. (Today it is hard to imagine how these letters were ever delivered in the midst of such chaos). "Mr. Madison comes not. May God protect us! Two messengers, covered with dust, come to bid me fly," but her letter was interrupted by a friend, Charles Carroll, who, she noted, was in a "very bad humor with me." Nonetheless, before she left she took time to remove the Stuart portrait of George Washington from its frame, which today remains the only surviving furnishing from the original White House. She also finished her letter: "And now dear sister, I must leave this house, or the retreating army will make me a prisoner in it...When I shall again write to you, or where I shall be tomorrow, I cannot tell!"

Shortly after the brave Dolley Madison, in her carriage laden with important state possessions, and accompanied only by her black maid, Sukey, left Washington for an army camp in Georgetown, the British arrived. Their leader, Admiral Cockburn, directed his soldiers to burn the government buildings and ransack the White House for souvenirs before piling all the furniture in one room and setting it on fire. Nothing remained of the Mansion but the walls. Later Cockburn displayed *his* souvenir, a chair cushion, and announced it would help him "remember Mrs. Madison's seat.4

After the pillage of the White House, President Madison considered moving the capital back to Philadelphia, but his wife believed Washington should remain the seat of the government, as planned by the Founding Fathers. She persuaded Madison to rebuild not only the Mansion, but also, the government buildings. The Madisons leased several houses for the rest of Madison's term while the White House was being rebuilt, but Dolley Madison, known as the residence's most famous hostess, never again lived in "The President's House." During the rest of her long life, however, she often returned to the White House as a guest of other Presidents.

Although cramped quarters cramped her style, Dolley carried on as a gracious hostess. Washington Irving described her as a "fine, portly, buxom dame who has a smile and a pleasant word for everybody," even though he viewed President Madison as "poor Jemmy—he is but a withered little apple-John."

When Andrew Jackson, a hero of the War of 1812, visited Washington in 1816, Dolley Madison gave him a lavish reception, which her critics labeled as a "barbarous grandeur," and an "Egyptian display."

(There were) so many guests they could barely jam into her house, and she spread a wastefully lavish table. She placed Negro servants holding lighted candles or torches in front of each window. Her reasoning was that these eerie human candles would provide more light for her dark drawing room by which the guests could see her hero.[5]

At her final reception as the President's wife, just before James Monroe was inaugurated, Dolley wore a gown of rose-colored satin, with a long velvet train, a wide gold belt, gold necklace and bracelets, and an ostrich feather trimmed turban *plus* a gold crown. She was less than svelte, and certainly, less than a young matron, but the incoming British ambassador declared that Dolley Madison looked "every inch a queen."

Even though she was raised as a Quaker, Dolley was never a "shrinking violet." She was one of nine children born to John and Mary Coles Payne; while some historians record her name as Dorothy or Dorothea, the Church registry lists "Dolley." She was born on May 20, 1768, but Dolley Madison, not unlike other women through the centuries, including First Lady Nancy Reagan, shaved a year here, and a year there, for a total of five years by the time she wrote a friend in 1839: "Being anxious to disavow the affectation of curtailing some precious years I will give you a true copy of the notice of me in our family Bible. Dolley Payne, born May 20, 1773."

Dolley spent her earliest years on a farm in Virginia, where she learned to read and write, faithfully attended prayer meetings, wore the traditional drab Quaker costume, and learned that dancing and other gaieties were "sinful." She was a healthy, robust, big-boned, broad-shouldered young woman, with an impish smile and a personality to match. When Virginia passed a law in 1782 that allowed farmers to free their slaves, Dolley's father immediately complied, and since the family could not afford to pay worker's wages, they moved to Philadelphia, where Payne established a business making laundry starch. When the business failed, Payne's debts led to his public disgrace, and he became a recluse for three years until his death at 52. To support the family, Dolley's mother took in boarders, but neither this lowly situation, nor her father's disgrace deflated young Dolley. At 21, she married a friend she had met at a Quaker meeting, a 26-year-old lawyer, John Todd.

Life was fine for the young couple; the Continental Congress was meeting in Philadelphia and there was work for able lawyers. Two sons were born within three years, but unfortunately, a yellow fever epidemic killed her husband and their younger son, William. Fortunately, Todd left her some money, so she and her surviving son, Payne, were able to manage. When she marketed or ran errands, she liked to walk past the Indian Queen, a fine hotel where many of the representatives to the Congress stayed. Bachelor James Madison noticed her, and asked Aaron Burr, a boarder at her mother's house, to introduce them. Word about the courtship reached Dolley's distant cousin, Martha Washington, and after tea at the President's House, Martha Washington gave her approval to the marriage.

Dolley seemed to have some doubts about the liaison and stalled all summer before giving the 43-year-old Madison her decision. Even on her wedding day she wrote to a friend (and put the wrong date on the letter), explaining she had given her hand "to the man...I most admire," also noting that her son, Payne, would now have a "generous and tender protector." She first signed the note "Dolley Payne Todd," and ended with a postscript, "Evening—Dolley Madison! Alass! Alass!6

Her marriage to Madison cost Dolley her membership in the Quaker community, since she married a "person not in membership with us, before a hireling priest." The Madisons remained in Philadelphia for several years, and while he conducted his "public business," she began to enjoy a new social life. Her clothes were now fashionable, of rich materials and bright colors. In 1797, they retired to Madison's plantation, Montpelier, and then in 1801, seven years after they were married, Jefferson named James Madison his Secretary of State and took advantage of an unplanned bonus: Dolley not only helped his daughters adjust to life in Washington, but she was a willing and brilliantly successful hostess.

Madison was devoted to Dolley and very proud of her popularity. He gave her jewelry and indulged her, and she, in turn, was very solicitous of him, worrying about his health and position. Contrary to her doubts on her wedding day, they were very happily married. She was 49 and Madison 66 when he left the Presidency in 1817. They lived at Montpelier for the next 18 years until his death. He continued to spoil her by creating special flower gardens and encouraging lavish house parties. But Dolley was not just a social butterfly. She served as her husband's secretary, organized his papers, and helped him supervise the University of Virginia, a job he had inherited from Thomas Jefferson.

After Madison's death in 1835, Dolley moved back to Washington and regained her status as the Capital's leading hostess.

President Van Buren relied on Dolley for social advice; she was so helpful she introduced a relative, Angelica Singleton, to Van Buren's son Abraham and, after their marriage, then helped Angelica serve as White House hostess. President Tyler's daughter-in-law, overwhelmed by White House duties, reserved a seat in her carriage for Dolley for official social calls, and President Polk, who made only three social calls during his first year in office, paid one of them to Dolley. The former First Lady was there when Samuel F.B. Morse opened the telegraph line from Washington to Baltimore, and after the message "What hath God wrought?" was received from Baltimore, Morse asked Dolley to dictate a return message. "Message from Mrs. Madison. She sends her love to Mrs. Wethered."

Dolley also served on a committee with Louisa Adams and Betsey Hamilton to raise funds for the Washington Monument. She played whist with former President John Quincy Adams, and Congress voted her a lifetime seat on the floor of the House of Representatives. In her last days, she had very little money, but was such a favorite in Washington that Congress purchased the remainder of her husband's papers for $25,000, and set up the payment of the award so that her ne'er-do-well son, Payne, wouldn't be able to get his hands on any of it. (Payne took advantage of Dolley, and led an aimless, unsettled life, usually communicating with his mother only when he needed money. He was jailed for not paying his bills and died in a rundown hotel in 1852, at age 61).

The last White House reception Dolley attended was given by President and Mrs. Polk in February, 1849. Even at 82, Dolley Madison presented a dashing, elegant figure: her white satin gown revealed still-beautiful arms and shoulders and she wore one of her trademark fringed turbans. Dolley Madison died on July 12, 1849. Among her mourners were the current President, Zachary Taylor, a number of former Presidents, and many members of Congress. Newspaper reports indicate her funeral was as elaborate as any President's.

ELIZABETH
KORTRIGHT MONROE

When Elizabeth and James Monroe moved into the White House in 1817, a Washington journalist wrote, "Mrs. Monroe is an elegant, accomplished woman. She possesses a charming mind and dignity of manners which peculiarly fit her for elevated position." But although Elizabeth Monroe, known as "Eliza," would play gracious hostess to the crowds of people who came to the public receptions or "drawing rooms," it soon became obvious that she did not enjoy her position as First Lady. She rarely issued special invitations, and did not enjoy mingling with the rest of Washington society.

In fact, most history books use the same word to describe Mrs. Monroe (*and* her two daughters): snobbish. Another word frequently used is *dominating*. She and her daughters dominated James Monroe to such a degree that eventually his career as fifth President of the United States was affected.

Perhaps the haughty attitude began with her background. Eliza Kortright was born to a wealthy New York family and had a pampered childhood. (She always considered New York much more elegant and chic than Washington). Portraits and contemporary accounts reveal Eliza as a beautiful woman, tall and graceful with classic features and dark curly hair, which she accented with ribbons. While her husband served abroad as a diplomat in France, she became polished and sophisticated: she was proud of the fact that her eldest daughter, also named Elizabeth, was a schoolmate of Empress Josephine's daughter, Hortense de Beauharnais (the future Queen of Holland and Mother of Napoleon III.)

Unfortunately, the Monroes' stay in Paris was cut short. France was in the throes of the bloody French Revolution and aristocrats, regardless of their former contributions, were imprisoned and executed. Lafayette—so loved by Americans for his dedicated support during the American Revolution—was imprisoned in Austria, and Madame Lafayette was scheduled to be guillotined. Eliza and James Monroe succeeded in obtaining Madame Lafayette's release, and ultimately, George Washington and Bonaparte were able to free Lafayette. As a result of his actions, Monroe was recalled from France by President Jefferson, and ironically, Eliza was snubbed by American as well as French political wives because of her role in the rescue.

More than a decade later, President Madison appointed James Monroe to the post of Secretary of State *and*, simultaneously, Secretary of War during the War of 1812. At that point, Eliza regained some of the status the couple had lost when Monroe's Paris assignment was aborted, and although she was seen at social events, evidently she wasn't very friendly. One observer of the scene, Mrs. Seaton, who clearly favored Dolley Madison, wrote, "Mrs. Monroe paints very much, and has, besides, an appearance of youth which would induce a stranger to suppose her age to be thirty." (Mrs. Seaton also wrote, "Mrs. Madison is said to rouge, but it is not evident to my eyes, and I do not think it true.")[1]

Secretary of State Monroe, in typical progression for those days, became President and an eager Washington public looked forward to the traditional New Year's Day, 1818, reception, not only for an audience with the President and his family, but also to see the rebuilt White House. Everything was new and clean and shining, and contemporary accounts tell us that although James Monroe looked grave and dour, Eliza Monroe looked—and acted—queenly and elegant.

Because the British had sacked and burned everything in the Mansion during the War of 1812, when James Monroe was elected, there were literally *no* furnishings. The Monroes sold their own antique French furniture, paintings and domestic pieces to the government for $9,000, but even with their former possessions in place were only able to furnish two bedrooms, the State dining room, and several receiving rooms. It was necessary to decorate the rest of the White House, and Eliza placed this task in the hands of a French firm from Le Havre, Russell and La Farge, who soon made it clear that furnishing the "President's Palace" would not be a simple (or inexpensive) project. They recommended that all the furniture be custom made, and that mahogany was not suitable, even in "private gentlemen's houses," so gilded wood should be used instead. In addition, although the handmade Aubusson and other rugs would take longer to manufacture than expected, these were, of course, necessary.

The cost was high, but the results were aristocratic and impressive. Everything was in the French style, with French clocks, draperies, ornaments and even table settings. The Monroes brought a new style to the White House, unlike the tenure of Jefferson and Madison when, although the furnishings were elegant and the food was internationally inspired, the entertaining was rather informal.

Eliza Monroe did not feel she was obliged, as Dolley Madison had, to call on anybody who called on her. In fact, she would neither make calls...nor return them. Although her well-educated and sophisticated daughters were also not enthusiastic about the Washington social scene, much less their duties as the President's children, eventually, the older daughter, Eliza Hay, took over most of her mother's social responsibilities. The senior Eliza often used as her excuse (with a cue from Mrs. John Quincy Adams, the wife of the Secretary of State), that her health was very "delicate." Eliza Hay, unfortunately, was very rigid: Based on her French education, she insisted that she would not call on diplomats' wives unless they called on her *first*. When this did not occur, Eliza convinced her father to remain aloof toward foreign diplomats, which did not accomplish much for James Monroe's international image.

The situation became so awkward that John Quincy Adams was forced to get into the middle of this muddle, labeling Monroe's daughter as an "obstinate little firebrand," who constantly interrupted him with her "senseless war of etiquette visiting." Monroe's fuss with international relationships became a crisis in 1818 when the French minister planned a ball to celebrate the evacuation of France by the troops of Germany, England, Austria and Russia. Monroe learned that President Washington had never visited a foreign minister, so he declined the invitation to the ball and asked his daughter to go instead. Eliza agreed only under certain conditions. She insisted on appearing as a private person, would not change her stand about diplomatic wives, and refused to allow any publicity. According to John Quincy Adams's diary, this "mortified" the French Minister and certainly did not foster diplomatic relationships with France.

By the fall of 1819, most of the Monroe receptions had become men-only affairs, as the Washington ladies boycotted snobby Mrs. Monroe and her daughter. Mrs. Seaton wrote about one event, "Only five females attended, three of whom were foreigners." And the only women sure to come to Mrs. Monroe's Tuesday receptions were her sisters.

If you look at a picture of the "obstinate little firebrand," Eliza Hay looks very innocent and sweet; in fact, her dark curls and wide eyes remind me of the actress Valerie Bertinelli. Eliza Hay missed an opportunity to clear up some of these social gaffes. In 1820, the other Monroe daughter, 16-year-old Maria Hester, was engaged to marry Samuel L. Gouverneur, her cousin and one of Monroe's deputies. The forthcoming marriage would be the first wedding of a daughter in the White House, a very coveted invitation. However, Eliza Hay arranged the wedding in the "New York style," and invited only relatives and close friends. She informed the embassies that not only were they not to be invited, but furthermore, they should send no gifts, another affront to international diplomacy.

One visitor to the White House, writer James Fenimore Cooper, thought the conversation at one reception dull and commonplace, and felt the entire evening, in his words, had "rather a cold than a formal air."[2]

Obviously, the Monroe family was not very hospitable, even to old friends. When the aging Marquis de Lafayette, after a thirty-day trip from France, and a tour of the East, came to visit the Monroes on New Year's Day, 1825, a stiff reception was held in his honor at the White House. But the real party took place afterwards at Williamson's Hotel where Congress feted Lafayette with a dinner for 200 guests.

The final reception at the Monroe White House was given shortly after the crucial Presidential election in which Henry Clay ruined Andrew Jackson's chances by handing over his votes to John Quincy Adams. At the reception in his honor, it was clear Adams had a new enemy. Andrew Jackson, who arrived with a handsome woman on his right arm, said to the President-elect, "I give you my left hand, for my right, as you see, is devoted to the fair." This was a portent of years to come as the bitter political feud between the two continued.

As for James Monroe and his family, after they left the White House, Eliza and her daughters spent so much money that the former President was very heavily in debt by the time he died, six years later, in 1831, in New York City. Eliza had died some months earlier, at their home in Virginia, on September 30, 1830.

LOUISA JOHNSON ADAMS

John Quincy Adams did not enter the White House with the wide popular support given the five Presidents (including his father) who preceded him. Andrew Jackson had actually won more popular votes as well as electoral votes, but failed to win a clear majority. When the election was then thrown into the House of Representatives, Henry Clay, also a candidate, gave his support to John Quincy Adams, and Adams became President. Adams consequently not only had Andrew Jackson as an enemy, but many members of Congress as well. He was forced to work long, hard hours to keep these factions at bay. At night, he spent time with visitors and favor-seekers, time writing his son, George Washington Adams (who, like many Presidential sons, was floundering), time with his other children, but he never quite found enough time for his wife, Louisa.

Although Adams entered the White House by a "side door," Louisa would probably have preferred not to enter at all. Once there, she found the White House vast, cold, and shabby, without the comforts of "any private mechanic's family." Louisa's negative attitude was perhaps understandable. From their marriage in 1797 until her husband became President in 1825, the family had lived in temporary homes in Berlin, St. Petersburg, and Paris, as well as Quincy, Boston, and Washington. During those twenty-eight years, not only had Louisa had many miscarriages and given birth to four children, but she also suffered from "delicate health" as well as her husband's sometimes exasperating career moves.

Louisa and John met in 1795 when Adams, as U.S. minister to the Netherlands, stationed at the Hague, traveled to London to assist John Jay in negotiations for a treaty with England to resolve existing conflicts between England and the United States. (These conflicts ultimately led to the War of 1812). John and Louisa, one of seven daughters of the American consul, Joshua Johnson, spent a good deal of time together at the Johnson house. By the time John returned to Holland, he and Louisa were engaged. Perhaps for John the alliance was more a case of head over heart; he wrote his mother that he thought it was time to marry and start a family. Abigail Adams had reservations about his engagement, citing the ten-year age difference (He was 28; Louisa, just 18) and the fact that Louisa had never been to the United States and was not used to American ways.

Perhaps John had reservations of his own, because he dragged his heels about setting a definite date; he said affairs in Holland were so unsettled their engagement could last from *one to seven* years. By 1796, Louisa was getting restless and wrote John about her despair. He, in turn, criticized her lack of self-control. But when he was named minister to Portugal that year, he suggested she prepare for a quick departure. She eagerly bought her trousseau and wedding gown, only to discover that John had no definite date in mind. Humiliated, Louisa expressed her feelings in a letter, and he coldly replied

> *You say 'I should be sorry to put it in your power or in that of the world to say I wished to force myself upon any man or into any family...I see the suspicion of your heart (but) my bosom is protected by the clear and unhesitating consciousness that the suspicion is without any foundation...My dignity, my Station, or my family, have no sort of concern with any subject of debate between you and me.*[1]

Possibly, the fact that John was a very good "catch" allowed Louisa to put up with this verbal abuse; maybe she was deeply in love with him. In any case, she backed down and held on, and in March 1797, when his Portuguese appointment became official, he wrote to Louisa, "Our difficulties are ended." She wrote back, full of enthusiasm (and probably, relief), "The more I know you the more I admire, esteem and love you."

Father Johnson—one can imagine his exasperation—offered to send a ship to pick up the recalcitrant suitor, but Adams made his own way to London, and then didn't see his fiancée until a day after his arrival. When he asked her to name a wedding date, she mentioned a day the following week. This was the start of a marriage filled with misunderstandings and manipulations, which sometimes backfired on John Quincy Adams.

John and Louisa were finally married in 1797, and after a brief honeymoon, Adams was sent, not to Portugal, but upon his father's decision (John Adams had now become our second President), to Berlin. The lonely, homesick bride attended few receptions, causing rumors to spread among the Germans and diplomatic corps that she was ugly and ill and her husband was ashamed of her. Several months later, her health improved and so did her reputation; when she was presented to Queen Louise, she was judged young and pretty and attained instant popularity. Louisa enjoyed her status as the wife of an important diplomat and daughter-in-law of the American President. She liked being called "Your Excellency" or "Princess Royal." However, John's modest salary prevented them from entertaining as lavishly as other diplomats—a problem that plagued them most in their married life.

The Berlin mission ended in 1801 when John Adams' bid for re-election was defeated by Jefferson. The couple remained in Europe a few months until Louisa gave birth to George Washington Adams in April. Unfortunately, the midwife's incompetence in delivering the baby caused Louisa to lose the use of her left leg for some time, and this delayed their return home, a rough trip that took fifty-eight days. Obliged to live with John's family in Quincy for several months until their Boston house was ready, English-bred Louisa experienced instant culture shock when introduced to New England ways.

To make matters worse, she was also thrust into close living quarters with a very strong family, led by a disapproving mother-in-law. The beleaguered Louisa wrote, "Had I stepped into Noah's Ark, I do not think I could have been astonished." She found many aspects of New England life foreign and rough. "I was literally and without knowing it a *fine* lady." Abigail wasn't pleased with the "fine lady," but the "Old Gentleman," John Adams, became fond of his daughter-in-law and protected her for the rest of his life.[2]

When they finally moved to Boston, Louisa was too inexperienced to run the household, and her husband, in a typically one-sided decision, dismissed her personal maid, informed her she would take complete charge of baby George, and criticized her lack of skill in managing the household. (Remember, his mother had run her house and farm for years by herself while John Adams was in Europe or Philadelphia.) John was also frustrated about his stalemated career. In 1804, however, he was elected to the Senate, a happy event that coincided with the birth of his second son, John.

Louisa found unrefined, unfinished Washington a far cry from the capitals of Europe. In addition, during Senate recesses, she wanted to stay in Washington with *her* young family; he wanted to be in Quincy with *his* family. During the next years the family traveled back and forth, tried separate vacations, and often left the two boys and the new baby, Charles, in Quincy with their grandparents.

In 1809, President Madison named Adams Secretary of War, stationed in St. Petersburg, Russia. Adams didn't discuss this with Louisa; she was informed that she and baby Charles would accompany him while the two older boys stayed with their grandparents. The trip to St. Petersburg took *eighty days*. There they lived in a five-room suite so dismal Louisa described it as "a stone hole entered by a stone passage," where she battled rats trying to steal her baby's bread. Despite miserable accommodations and meager funds, they became friendly with Czar Alexander. In 1811, they were overjoyed when Louisa gave birth to a daughter, who her husband named, against her wishes, Louisa Catherine, in honor of the czarina.

Adams was then sent to Ghent to negotiate the treaty ending the War of 1812, and then went on to Paris, while Napoleon was re-emerging as "l'Empereur." Louisa, once again pregnant, made a slow and hazardous trip alone from St. Petersburg to Paris with Charles and the baby girl. Adams was now regarded as one of the country's most able diplomats, and, when James Monroe was elected the country's fifth President in 1816, he chose Adams as his Secretary of State. The Adams family finally returned home after eight years abroad. Neither John nor Louisa would ever visit Europe again.

After serving as Monroe's Secretary of State for eight years, John Quincy Adams then won the Presidential nomination and election for himself, marking the second time an Adams family would occupy the White House. (175 years later, this father-son feat would be duplicated when George W. Bush (#43) followed in the footsteps of his father, George Herbert Walker Bush (#41.) John, however, was too overworked to enjoy his stay in the Mansion, and Louisa was exhausted by years of traveling, ill health, and emotional crises. She dressed well and entertained elegantly, but their parties were dull and dispirited. And even though the Adams White House included three of John and Louisa's children as well as the three orphaned children of her sister, instead of adding to Louisa's joy, the young people only exacerbated her problems. A major row developed when her niece Mary and son John decided to marry, and the family was torn with dissension. (Both Charlie and George refused to attend their brother's wedding.) In 1828, Mary gave birth to a daughter, the second child born in the White House.

Louisa became increasingly depressed and reclusive, a state not helped by the erratic adventures of son George, who committed suicide in 1829. Her poor health, and John Quincy's disappointment when he was defeated for a second term, led him to skip the inaugural ceremonies (as he father had) and move the family to a rented house, enabling his successor, Andrew Jackson, to hold a triumphant reception at the White House.

In 1830, John Quincy Adams returned to government service and spent the last eighteen years of his life as a congressman. In 1847, he and Louisa celebrated their fiftieth wedding anniversary, and according to her grandson, Henry Adams, she seemed "singularly peaceful, a vision of silver gray...an exotic, like her Sevres china; an object of deference to every one, and of great affection to her son Charles; but hardly more Bostonian than she had been fifty years before, on her wedding day, in the shadow of the Tower of London."[3]

PRIVATE
LIVES

Anna Symmes Harrison
1775-1864

Lucy Webb Hayes
1831-1889

Caroline Scott Harrison
1832-1892

Elizabeth Virginia "Bess"
Wallace Truman
1885-1982

S ome First Ladies regarded their jobs as no-frills missions and conducted their lives in the White House in the same way they might have lived "back home." Anna Symmes Harrison, wife of the ninth President, William Henry Harrison, was reportedly a "stolid matron" with little interest in her husband's career. Then again, as a woman with ten children and forty-nine grandchildren, she might have been otherwise occupied. Caroline, the wife of Anna Harrison's grandson, President Benjamin Harrison (#23), was also chiefly concerned with the comfort of her husband, children and grandchildren. Although she was a popular First Lady, Caroline Harrison also worked hard for local charities and became the first President General of the Daughters of the American Revolution (DAR). Many of the White House events during her stay were specifically parties and "entertainments" for family members.

Lucy Webb Hayes, married to President Rutherford Birchard Hayes (#19), was also energetic and intelligent, but she disliked the party scene and banned all alcoholic beverages from the White House, which earned her the sobriquet of "Lemonade Lucy."

Bess Truman (President Truman was #33) was not quite so strait-laced, and held a special place in the hearts of her "public," but she made sure that the Trumans' private lives remained just that: *private*. She managed to balance her official duties as First Lady with what to her were far more important responsibilities as Harry Truman's wife and her daughter Margaret's mother.

ANNA SYMMES HARRISON

Anna Symmes Harrison did not approve of her husband's election as the ninth President of the United States. She felt that at age 68, William Henry Harrison was too exhausted from his years as a general and the many battles he had fought and deserved rest and a peaceful retirement. She, herself, was in ill health and could not attend her husband's inaugural ceremonies in 1841. Instead, she sent her daughter-in-law, Jane Findlay Harrison, to serve as hostess, while she remained at home in North Bend, Ohio, trying to recover her strength for the move to Washington.

Born in 1775, Anna Harrison had lived a long and busy life. The daughter of a frontier judge, she eloped with dashing Captain Harrison in 1795. The family lived in Vincennes, Indiana, and like Abigail Adams before her, and other Presidential wives to come, she was largely responsible for bringing up her children—in this case *ten* of them—on the family farm. Although not formally educated, Anna had been taught religion, history and economy by her grandmother. Since there weren't any schools near Vincennes, Anna tutored not only her own children, but also founded a school where she taught neighboring children.

She was very religious, and a generous and hospitable neighbor. Every Sunday after church, the *entire congregation* returned to the Harrison house for dinner—every item on the menu had been produced on the farm. Remember, for most of these years, Anna was a "single parent" while General Harrison was off fighting his wars.

Anna Harrison never had an opportunity to carry out her role as First Lady. By late March, President Harrison was bedridden with a very severe cold that turned into pneumonia. Exactly one month after he had assumed office, he died, and reportedly, his last words—perhaps in reference to the many patronage appeals made in his short term of office—were "I cannot bear this; don't trouble me." William Henry Harrison's death marked the first time a President lay in state in the East Room. Sadly, this was a precursor of many state funerals. The new President, John Tyler, arranged many of the details, and the newspapers reported, somewhat cynically, that the funeral had been "better arranged than the Inauguration."[1]

Anna recovered her strength sufficiently to live until her eight-ninth year, but not long enough to see one of her forty-nine grandchildren, Benjamin Harrison, become the twenty-third President of the United States.

LUCY WEBB HAYES

When Rutherford Birchard Hayes and his wife, Lucy, left Ohio for the inaugural ceremonies in March 1877, they didn't know whether Hayes had, in fact, been elected nineteenth President. Hayes had lost the popular vote, but was ahead in the Electoral College vote. By the time they reached Harrisburg, Pennsylvania, they learned, to their relief, that he had actually won. Hayes became the first President to take the oath of office in the White House, in the Red Room, dominated by a lifesize portrait of Ulysses S. Grant and his family. Grant, the outgoing President, and his wife were also there in person, and after the swearing in, the President and 200 guests sat down to a twenty course meal with six wine glasses at each setting.

This was to remain one of the few occasions during Hayes' administration when wine—or any other alcoholic beverage—would be served at the White House. The new abstinence was blamed on Lucy Hayes, who was promptly dubbed "Lemonade Lucy" by cynical socialites and the gossipy Washington press corps. This nickname was not at odds with Lucy's image. Her somber official portrait (which incidentally, was donated to the White House collection by a women's temperance organization), reveals a rather stern-faced woman, with deep set eyes, hair parted exactly in the middle and severely pulled back in a bun, hands clasped firmly in front of her. She is depicted wearing a high-necked dress, relieved by just the slightest bit of lace at the neck. Despite the public ridicule, Lucy was a caring woman, a doctor's daughter cited for her devotion to wounded soldiers during the Civil War.

She was also devoted to her seven sons and more concerned with her family's welfare than her official duties. She viewed the White House as a private home, as the *residence* of the Hayes family. In 1878, Austine Snead, a journalist who wrote under the *nom de plume* of "Miss Grundy," toured the family quarters and wrote, "There are only eight bedrooms, a library and a bathroom in this part of the house...The prettiest of the bedrooms...is the one used by the President and Mrs. Hayes." Grundy described the fireplace and even the Presidential bed. "At its foot is a marble-top table...and books lie nearby, showing that the luxury of reading in bed is sometimes enjoyed by one or the other of the occupants of the apartment."[1]

Although Lucy was a serious and intellectual woman—a graduate of Weslyan Women's College of Cincinnati, and the first college-educated First Lady—she loved to plan parties for her children, and these were the best events held at the White House during the Hayes's four-year stay. One sixteen-year-old guest at a birthday party was so impressed she said she wanted to marry a President of the United States so that she could live in the mansion. Her name was Helen Herron and her wish was to be fulfilled when she later became the wife of President William Howard Taft.

During their stay in the White House, the President and Mrs. Hayes celebrated their twenty-fifth anniversary, with another gala family event, *not* an official reception. For this special occasion, Lucy Hayes eschewed her more somber gowns and wore her wedding dress of white silk. Another happy family celebration was the wedding of the President's niece, Emily Platt, to General Russell Hastings, on June 19, 1878, and the White House was decorated with 15,000 flowers.

Although Lucy Hayes preferred family parties, she dutifully appeared at official receptions, which were very sedate. At ten o'clock promptly, the Marine Corps Band would play "Home Sweet Home" as a signal for dismissing the guests. Reportedly, the party that led to the "Lemonade Lucy" nickname occurred not long after the 1877 Inauguration, when a drunken incident marred a reception held for two Russian Grand Dukes and the decision was made to banish liquor from all future receptions. From that point on Lucy Hayes was called the hostess of a "cold-water regime," in which "water flowed like wine." Although his wife was blamed for this dictum, in 1881, after leaving office, Rutherford B. Hayes set the record straight:

When I became President I was fully convinced that whatever might be the case in other countries and with other people, in our climate and with the excitable nervous temperament of our people, the habitual use of intoxicating drinks was not safe...It seemed to me that to exclude liquors from the White House would be wise and useful as an example...The suggestion was particularly agreeable to Mrs. Hayes. She had been a total abstinence woman from childhood. We had never used liquors in our own home and it was determined to continue (this)...[2]

In November 1881, the President and Mrs. Hayes gave a dinner for incoming President James Garfield and his wife, demonstrating one of the friendliest changes of power thus far. The Garfields and the Hayes's were good friends, and the event was marked, as newspaper accounts cited, "by more than usual cordiality."

CAROLINE SCOTT HARRISON

Caroline Scott and Benjamin Harrison had been sweethearts while he attended Miami University in Ohio and she was enrolled at the Oxford Female Institute. After their marriage they spent many years in Washington while he served in the Senate. She knew the city and Washington society well, and easily moved into her new role when Harrison became the twenty-third President.

Although Caroline was a cordial, competent and popular First Lady, her major interest was her family's well being. Three generations lived in the Harrison White House: The President and his wife, a daughter-in-law, a widowed daughter (Mary Harrison McKee, and her children), and Caroline's niece, Mary Dimmick. Many activities planned were events and parties especially for the grandchildren. In fact, during the Harrison years, the first Christmas tree was set up in the President's House.

It was traditional for new First Ladies to do some renovating based on congressional appropriations. While Caroline Harrison viewed the White House as an historical mansion and was dedicated to preserving and restoring it, she was concerned about the comfort of all First Families. In an 1889 interview, she said,

We are here for four years: I do not look beyond that, as many things may occur in that time, but I am very anxious to see the family of the President provided for properly…I hope to be able to get the present building put into good condition. Very few people

understand...(that) there are only five sleeping apartments and there is no feeling of privacy.[1]

Caroline was not the first First Lady—nor the last—to complain about cramped living quarters in the White House. She made major changes: the engine room was rebuilt; as many as five layers of decayed floor boards were removed and new floors laid; the kitchens were remodeled; the infamous White House rats were exterminated. Most significant: electricity was installed by the Edison Electric Company. Irwin "Ike" Hoover served as a consultant, and remained for forty-two years as Chief Usher from Grover Cleveland's administration until Franklin Delano Roosevelt's. In his memoirs, *Forty-two Years in the White House*, he remembered the "old open fireplaces once used for broiling the chickens and baking the hoecakes...(and) to the rear there yet remained the old winevault, the meathouse, and the smokehouse."[2]

After four months, the wiring was completed, but the First Family distrusted the "magic lights," and continued to use the gaslights. The servants, too, were afraid of getting electric shocks. Often Ike would turn on the lights, only to find them still burning the next morning because no one had the courage to turn them off.

The First Lady also discovered that the official china service needed to be replaced. She had whatever she could repaired, and decided to use some of her allocated budget for new china. Caroline designed a pattern with forty-four stars in a blue border, in the style of china used by President Lincoln. The special shade of blue was a secret of the famous Limoges company so the china was ordered from France and each piece of the six dozen place settings was marked "Harrison, 1892."

Under Caroline's direction, bedrooms were repainted and repapered; in the state rooms, woodwork was repainted ivory, and some windows were embellished with blue stained glass. One treasure she unearthed in the Mansion's warehouse: an ornate desk, made from wood of the British ship "Resolute," presented by Queen Victoria to President Hayes. Harrison used it as his desk and years later it was the desk chosen by John F. Kennedy, and then, in 1992, by William Jefferson Clinton.

In 1891, Caroline Harrison caught a cold (called "la grippe," similar to what we know as the "flu") which developed into tuberculosis. She never regained her strength and by 1892 was unable to attend official functions...although her family and grandchildren did. One report noted that

Baby McKee, wearing a white flannel suit with blue stockings...stood within reaching distance of the file of Cabinet

*officers...(the) President was as easy-going as anyone. He danced
Baby McKee in the air, and came out into the corridor, and
personally invited some of the loiterers to come in and have some
luncheon. It was a general jollification.*[3]

During 1891 and 1892, Caroline's daughter, Mary Harrison
McKee served as the White House manager and official hostess. She
was young and beautiful and some veteran White House watchers
compared her to earlier charmers, Dolley Madison and Frances
Cleveland.

By the summer of 1892, the First Lady's health deteriorated and
on October 24th she died in the same room where President Garfield
had lingered so long. The sad air of mourning after her death was
offset by Mary McKee's young children who had always brightened
Benjamin Harrison's days in the White House.

Postscript: Caroline Harrison's young widowed niece, Mary
Dimmick, was never an official hostess, but lived in the White
House for two years until her aunt died. In 1893, she moved to New
York City, and in 1896, married the former President. (They had
one child, Elizabeth, who became a lawyer and an active member of
social and political life in New York City).

ELIZABETH VIRGINIA "BESS" WALLACE TRUMAN

B ess Truman, First Lady of the thirty-third President, was thrust
into that role with the sudden death of President Franklin
Delano Roosevelt, when Vice President Truman succeeded
him. She never planned it, never dreamed it; she carried out her
responsibilities diligently and effectively, but her stint as First Lady
was not the favorite time of her life. Bess believed the best assets a
President's wife could have were good health and a well-developed
sense of humor; she didn't think a woman would ever be elected
President, and her greatest hope was to retire in Independence,
Missouri.

Bess Wallace and Harry Truman were childhood sweethearts.
They met at Sunday School and Truman described her at age six as
"a beautiful little girl with golden curls. I was smitten with her and
still am." Bess, christened Elizabeth Virginia, grew up to be
willowy, popular and athletic, known as the only girl in
Independence who could whistle through her teeth. She came from
a leading family—her father had been mayor—and lived in the
biggest house in town. In contrast, Truman was the son of a mule
trader and farmer, and her family looked down on his, even after he
became President. Bess had many boyfriends, but waited for Harry.
(All during his World War I army service, Harry wrote to Bess every
day.) Overcoming these parental obstacles, the not-so-young
couple married twenty-nine years after their first meeting, when she
was 34 and he was 35. After their marriage, he worked in a men's
clothing store and began to move up in Democratic party

politics...from county court judge, aide to political boss Tom Pendergast, and then, triumphantly, to U.S. Senator.

When the Trumans arrived in Washington, they had very little money; they rented an inexpensive apartment, bought budget furniture and saved money to rent a piano. Bess cooked and cleaned and was assisted every night by Harry, who dried the dishes. Bess also worked at her husband's office, handling his bookkeeping and other official matters. Harry put his wife on his staff payroll, and years later, when Republicans complained, Truman said, "She earns every cent of it. I never make a speech without going over it with her, and I never make any decision unless she is in on it."[1]

The morning after Harry S. Truman was nominated as Vice President, Bess Truman gave her first—and last—press conference. She admitted she was not really enthusiastic about Harry serving in that post (undoubtedly an understatement), but she gave a few personal details about the Trumans' lifestyle. She described her husband as "the type of person who could be satisfied to eat beefsteak and fried potatoes every night." Truman referred to her as "The Boss," even in public, and when he made speeches, if Bess and daughter Margaret were in the audience, he would not only introduce "The Boss," but would point to his daughter as "The boss that bosses the boss." (This was an affectionate and not uncommon nickname sixty years ago when most women did not have careers and their home was the place where they were actually in charge.)

Bess Truman was a very spunky lady, perhaps as feisty as her husband. Once she was shopping in a Kansas City department store and overheard one shopper say to another: "That's Mrs. Truman," and her friend replied, with some disdain, "She's wearing seersucker!" Although Bess was too much the lady to confront them directly (her husband most certainly would have), she later groused to Harry, "I wonder if they thought a Vice-Presidential candidate's wife should be dressed in royal purple?"[2]

The Trumans never anticipated becoming the First Family, and it was with a great deal of shock that Truman met with Eleanor Roosevelt on April 12, 1945, to take the oath of office. When Truman asked Mrs. Roosevelt, "Is there anything I can do for you?" she asked, in reply, what could she do for *him*. It was undeniably a catastrophic time for a new President to take control.

During Truman's first three months in the White House, the European war ended, the atomic bomb had been dropped in Japan, bringing about the end of the war in the Pacific, and the United Nations was founded. In fact, Truman's first order as President was to emphasize the fact that the United Nations conference in San Francisco two weeks after FDR's death would go on as planned, and he named Eleanor Roosevelt as a delegate.

The Truman family was called "The Three Musketeers," but they were really "Four Musketeers," because Bess Truman's mother, Mrs. D.W. Wallace, was also a member of the household. As First Lady, Bess tried to stay out of the limelight, and so she was perceived as drab and dull, especially following on the heels of Superlady Roosevelt. Initially, Bess was so successful at avoiding publicity that nine months after Truman became President, she was able to shop for Christmas presents in Washington department stores without being recognized.

Another early pleasure she experienced as First Lady was driving her Chrysler—she vehemently disliked limousines. It was a sad day when she admitted driving her car "caused too much commotion." Since then, First Ladies haven't been able to move freely without security guards and chauffeurs, and recent First Ladies have regretted the restriction of this basic freedom—the ability to drive your own car and go where you want to go, when you want to go.

Margaret Truman, at 21, a popular college senior, also felt these constraints on her private life. Not only did she have Secret Service agents accompanying her on dates, but her *mother* also waited up until she returned home. (However, Margaret enjoyed some White House perks: she could screen movies whenever she wanted to, and she sat through her favorite, "The Scarlet Pimpernel," starring Stewart Granger, sixteen times!).

Bess Truman not only mothered her daughter, she also mothered others. If reporters had colds, she gave them aspirins; if a male staff member was missing a button, she would sew it on; and she worried about secretaries, ushers, aides, and tried to make sure they were comfortable in their jobs.

According to veteran White House seamstress/maid Lillian Parks, in her book *My Thirty Years in the White House*, Bess "was neither too sentimental, nor too harsh" in her treatment of the White House staff. "She didn't keep looking over our shoulders, as Mrs. Eisenhower did; and she didn't ignore the work that was done, as Mrs. Roosevelt did." Bess Truman showed consideration for the staff and if it was too hot, or she noticed that servants had been working too long, she would tell them to take a rest. She always sent the maids home on Sunday, because, as she said, "I can turn down beds perfectly well by myself." Her one idiosyncrasy regarding housekeeping seemed to be fresh soap. Parks recalled that a new bar of soap had to be put in each bathroom every morning.[3]

Bess had no intention of changing her ways and her habits at the age of 60, when she became First Lady. Her sense of propriety dictated that no one would be admitted to her bedroom until she was properly dressed; she received visitors in her sitting room. But she was wild about baseball—her girlhood passion—and would listen to the Washington Senators' games on the radio in her sitting room. She also was passionate about her bridge game, and enthusiastic about the Spanish class she organized for a few friends, which met regularly at the White House.

She took over the bookkeeping for the Mansion, checked the food bill, cut out breakfast for sleep-out employees and ran the White House as if it were a business. She answered her own mail, in longhand, and in response to requests for souvenirs, she bought a box of ordinary buttons and sent these to people who asked for "something from the White House," a distinct difference from Eleanor Roosevelt's charming, but impractical practice of giving away sterling silver teaspoons.[4]

Although Bess tried to keep out of the limelight, when she did act as hostess she was charming and efficient. She never forgot a name or face, and at dinner parties, if the President was ignoring a guest, she would send a note via the steward that he should pay attention to him or her.

Bess Truman also reassembled the Lincoln Room.

> *The poor Lincoln bed had wandered all through the White House in the previous administrations. Some Presidents had brought it to their bedrooms and slept in it. The second Mrs. Wilson had brought it to her room. In the Roosevelt administration, everyone had fought to sleep in it, but Colonel Louis Howe (FDR's top advisor) had it installed in his Green Bedroom. Then, of course, the Green Room was changed to a pastel pink for the ladies...Mrs. Truman worked diligently to restore the Lincoln Room, in which the great man had signed the Emancipation Proclamation, with all the Lincoln furniture, which had been spread all over the house.*[5]

In addition to Lincoln's bed, Bess Truman reinstated his old dresser and tables, and found several Lincoln chairs in the White House storerooms to complete the restoration.

Bess did not seek publicity for any of her White House efforts. In fact, as J.B. West, Chief Usher at the White House, wrote, "In public, Mrs. Truman never said a word. She stayed as far in the background as Mrs. Roosevelt had projected her own personality into the foreground."[6] Bess was fierce about protecting her private life and her private responsibilities. Behind the scenes, however, the White House staff was aware that she blue-penciled her husband's speeches, and undoubtedly counseled him about political decisions.

In other areas she played a more traditional role. She was very critical of her husband's "cuss words," and was constantly chiding Truman for his "damns" and "hells." She also was the family's wardrobe watchdog, making sure her husband reserved his red slacks and bright flowered shirts for his trips to Key West, Florida. And if Margaret chose something Bess didn't approve of, that item, along with Harry's offensive additions to his wardrobe, would be packed up and given away to members of the White House staff or charity.

The President was equally protective of his wife and daughter. One famous flap occurred when the Daughters of the American Revolution refused to allow black singer Hazel Scott to sing in Constitution Hall and Bess shortly afterwards attended a DAR tea. Scott's husband, Congressman Adam Clayton Powell, referred to Bess as "the *Last* Lady of the Land." Although Bess was confused by the furor and explained she wasn't endorsing the DAR's actions, but she didn't think it was proper to break a promised engagement, President Truman was so angry at Powell's criticism that he banned him from White House receptions. Years after he left the presidency, when Marianne Means interviewed Truman for her book, he said, "If you don't say nice things about the Madam, I will spank you."[7]

Another over-publicized example of Truman's protective attitude involved his daughter. After a concert, *Washington Post* critic Paul Hume wrote that Margaret sang flat and didn't have professional finish. The angry President wrote a letter to Hume about his "lousy review" and warned that if they ever met, Hume would "need a new nose and plenty of beefsteak."

During the 1948 election campaign, the polls confidently predicted Truman's defeat by his Republican opponent, New York governor, Thomas Dewey. When election eve arrived, the only confident Truman was Harry, who went to bed early. Bess and Margaret stayed up all night listening to returns, and the Chicago *Tribune* printed its premature, historic edition headlined "Dewey Defeats Truman." Later, commentators attributed part of Truman's upset to his family's popularity: the Boss, and the Boss of Bosses, who had enthusiastically appeared at whistle-stops during his campaign.

Unfortunately, after the 1948 election, President Truman's popularity declined greatly, and many members of Congress were eager to find fault with the feisty mid-westerner. His plan to spend $10,000 building a small balcony where he and Bess could take their meals in good weather was quickly attacked as "Truman's Folly." Even as the President and Congress battled over the funds, the subject became moot as graver architectural problems surfaced. One day, the First Lady was entertaining guests and heard a tinkling of glass. She looked up and saw the crystal chandelier moving and clinking back and forth. Not long afterwards, one leg of Margaret's piano nearly went through the floor into the Red Room below.

Congress finally called for a full-fledged inspection. Among other things, the inspection team found that the White House was a fire hazard; the electrical system was dangerously overloaded; inadequate, weak clay footings supported 180,000 pounds of interior walls; many beams were badly split, and walls were cracked on the inside; floors sagged and sloped; old lead pipes, originally installed in 1840, were side by side with other pipes and all these pipes seriously undermined the Mansion's structure. A newly established Renovation Commission rejected the idea of razing the White House, and instead recommended for historical reasons that the walls be preserved and underpinned with piers, a new steel frame be erected inside the old walls, and that a new two-story basement be created to house essential facilities (heating, air conditioning, etc.). Further, every historic piece of molding, paneling or flooring was to be carefully marked so that it could be re-installed in the refurbished White House. Before the house literally came down around their heads, the Truman family moved into nearby Blair House.

Almost $6 million dollars was spent on the White House reconstruction. When it was finished in 1951, Bess Truman chose fabrics and colors for her family rooms, but left the rest of the decorating choices to the Commission on Renovation and B. Altman Company, since she was only going to live there another few months and felt it unfair to impose her ideas on the next First Family. Consequently, the White House looked very much like furniture display rooms in a department store. In addition, the furniture budget had been limited to $150,000, which had to be spread among some *sixty-six rooms.*[8]

In 1952, Truman declined to run for re-election, much to his wife's relief. She was now 67 (he was 68), disliked public scrutiny of her figure, clothes and hair, and wanted to go home, where she was Bess to everyone and not the First Lady.

First Lady or not, Bess Truman was such a lady that she burned most of her husband's letters to her, and although Harry Truman said she shouldn't do it, she replied, "Why not? I've read them several times." When he reminded her to "think of history, " she answered, "I have."[9]

The Trumans retired to their home in Independence, Missouri, where the former President worked on his memoirs, and Bess enjoyed being Bess again on her home turf. Harry S. Truman died in 1972, and Bess Truman lived another decade. As Margaret Truman recalled when her mother died in October 1982, "At ninety-seven, she had become the oldest First Lady in American history. I remembered teasing her when Mrs. Wilson died at eighty-nine. I wondered if there was something in the air of the Big White Jail that contributed to longevity, little knowing I was talking to the coming champion. I thought of the staggering sweep of history that Mother's life encompassed. Born when Chester Arthur was in the White House, she had seen the nation through five wars and eighteen Presidents." Three former First Ladies sat in the front pew at Bess Truman's funeral service—Nancy Reagan, Betty Ford, and Rosalynn Carter. In her book *First Ladies*, Margaret Truman wrote that it was the presence of these three who "personified the amazing variety of talents and personalities who had held this unique un-elected office" that inspired her to tell their stories.[10]

PRIVATE
PAIN

Margaret Smith Taylor
1788-1853

Abigail Powers Fillmore
1798-1853

Elizabeth Taylor Bliss (Not Pictured)
1824-1909

Jane Means Appleton Pierce
1806-1863

Mary Todd Lincoln
1818-1882

Eliza McCardle Johnson
1810-1876

Lucretia Rudolph Garfield
1832-1918

Ida Saxton McKinley
1847-1907

Grace Goodhue Coolidge
1879-1957

M any of the nation's First Ladies had to deal with personal tragedies and problems before, during or after their years in the White House. Some coped with grief over losing a child or beloved relative; others had emotional or physical illnesses that today might be treated and cured. Still, most of the Presidents' wives—whatever their personal tragedy or grief—were able to work long and hard at their unpaid jobs. Eight, however, although they lived in the White House, didn't find the strength or the will to carry out all their responsibilities.

Margaret Smith Taylor, wife of Zachary Taylor (#12), spent most of her brief White House stay "shivering by the fire." She relied on her daughter, Elizabeth, to manage the Mansion and serve as official hostess. Jane Appleton Pierce, wife of Franklin Pierce (#14) disdained politics, disliked Washington, and hated Pierce's "dissipated life." After their three sons died, she wore black and spent time writing letters to one of her dead boys.

Mary Todd Lincoln (#16) also mourned dead sons, which, coupled with ongoing mental problems, marred her time as First Lady.

Other Presidential wives who were incapacitated by physical or emotional illness included Abigail Fillmore (#13), Eliza Johnson (#17), Lucretia Garfield (#20), Ida McKinley (#25), and Grace Coolidge (#30).

MARGARET SMITH TAYLOR
AND
ELIZABETH TAYLOR BLISS

Margaret Taylor had not wanted to be First Lady or live in Washington, and had opposed her husband's run for the Presidency. In fact, she thought Zachary Taylor's election was a "plot to deprive me of my husband's society and to shorten his life by unnecessary care and responsibility." Margaret had no social ambition and sidestepped her own responsibilities as First Lady.[1]

While she remained in seclusion in an upstairs bedroom, her daughter Elizabeth Taylor Bliss, 22, who was married to President Taylor's secretary, Colonel William Bliss, took over running the household and official duties. Mrs. Bliss, or "Miss Betty," as she was known, was a graceful, accomplished young woman who "did the honors of the establishment with the artlessness of a rustic belle and the grace of a duchess."[2]

Once again, the Washington gossips had a field day with the reclusive Mrs. Taylor's reputation, accusing her of staying out of sight because she smoked a pipe. (How different these slights were from the open acceptance of Dolley Madison's snuff-taking.) Margaret Taylor, however, born and bred a Maryland aristocrat, didn't dignify the charges by responding to them.

Zachary Taylor and Margaret Smith met when she was fourteen, and he spent a night at the Smith farm on his way from Maryland to Washington on horseback. Taylor had been injured and Margaret cleansed and dressed his foot. Six years later, after his graduation from West Point, he returned to marry her. For twenty-four years, while he advanced in military rank, Margaret steadfastly followed him from camp to camp, usually living in rough barracks. The couple had five daughters and a son, and she would send her children to live with relatives to ensure that they would be properly educated. One daughter married Jefferson Davis, the future President of the Confederacy—and Zachary Taylor never forgave her for this mutiny. (She died shortly after the marriage, but in later years Zachary Taylor befriended his son-in-law and regarded him as a gallant soldier.)[3]

In 1849, Zachary Taylor, now a popular hero of the Mexican War and known as "Old Rough and Ready," was elected the twelfth American President, a position he had not sought and didn't particularly want. His wife was also against the move—possibly because she knew her soldier husband was not really experienced enough for the role, and also, more importantly, because after all those years spent in Army camps, she desperately wanted to settle down in their own permanent home.

Zachary Taylor's term was cut short after sixteen months when he became ill after July Fourth ceremonies at the Washington Monument, and perhaps as a result of a mistaken diagnosis of cholera, or the effects of heat stroke, he died five days later. As Margaret Taylor remained cloistered in her room upstairs, preparations for the funeral on the ground floor continued. She could hear hammering as the bier was constructed and mourning draperies were hung, and then, finally, the somber music of the state funeral.

Margaret lived only two years after her husband's death, burdened with the memories of her few, tragic months in the White House.

ABIGAIL POWERS FILLMORE

A bigail Powers Fillmore, the wife of the thirteenth President, Millard Fillmore, had been in ill health for years and was looking forward to returning to her home after her husband's term. It was said she received her death warrant while standing on the cold marble terrace of the Capitol, listening to the Inaugural Address of Franklin Pierce, her husband's successor. She died three weeks later.

Abigail Powers was the daughter of a Baptist minister in upstate New York. After he died, Abigail's mother took in boarders and Abigail taught school—two of the few occupations open to respectable women in those days.

One of Abigail's students was Millard Fillmore, who was two years younger than she. Although he had planned to be a weaver, an occupation he had apprenticed for with his father, Abigail urged him to aim higher. Ultimately, he taught school, studied law, clerked in a Buffalo New York law from and then stated his own law practice. The couple married in 1826. Fillmore took his wife's advice and aimed really high—serving three terms in the New York state legislature and another two terms in the United States Congress until he was elected Vice President.[1] When Zachary Taylor died, Fillmore became President.

The tall, fair-haired, fair-skinned Abigail was Fillmore's "right hand" during all this upward mobility. She had an aristocratic bearing and the soul of a writer. Like her First Lady namesake, Abigail Adams, she and Millard Fillmore exchanged many letters over the years, even though they were never more than 150 miles apart.

Unfortunately, Abigail Fillmore was another First Lady who did not enjoy good health during her stay in the "President's House." She found it difficult—or perhaps not pleasing—to enter into the social routines of the White House, and instead relegated many of her duties to her daughter, eighteen-year-old Mary Abigail. Despite his wife's withdrawal, Millard Fillmore personally tried to offset some of the disadvantages of the cold and still rather crude White House. He replaced the open basement fireplace in which food had been prepared with a new "small hotel size" stove, and taught the cook how to use it.

Aside from her poor health, Abigail was probably the most intellectual First Lady who had served in the White House until then. When she came to Washington and found no books in the Mansion, not even a Bible or dictionary, she set about securing a Congressional appropriation for books, and her one major contribution as First Lady was establishing the first library in the White House. The thousands of books she bought included all the classics, plus the works of such contemporary authors as Thackeray and Dickens.[2] In March, 1853, when the Fillmores attended the Inauguration of the new President, Franklin Pierce, among the guests at the reception were William Makepeace Thackeray and Washington Irving, who had made the first of his visits to the White House forty years earlier, during Dolley Madison's years as First Lady.

JANE MEANS
APPLETON PIERCE

When Jane Appleton Pierce became First Lady in 1853, she was the third woman in a row (following Margaret Taylor and Abigail Fillmore) who would rather have been someplace else, doing something else. She hated politics, disliked social life in general and Franklin Pierce's dissipated life in particular. She was pretty, cultured, educated and shy; she preferred New England to Washington and most of all, she grieved for her three boys, who had died before Pierce became the nation's fourteenth President.

Jane was the daughter of the reverend Jesse Appleton, President of Bowdoin College in Maine. Proving the theory that "opposites attract," quiet Jane married outgoing army-man Franklin Pierce in 1834. Pierce went on to become a hero of the Mexican War (like Zachary Taylor), a state legislator, a congressman and a senator.

While Franklin Pierce enjoyed his military and political success, Jane Pierce enjoyed motherhood—until the deaths of her three sons. Two died of childhood illnesses, but the youngest son, Benjamin, was killed in a freak railroad accident while traveling with his parents from Andover to Lawrence, Massachusetts, only two months before his father's inauguration. The Pierces were not injured, but Jane never recovered mentally. Benjamin's death shattered what was left of her health, and clearly, her heart wasn't in her new role as First Lady, which she had never sought in the first place.

She was too ill to attend the Inauguration, and taking a cue from several predecessors, chose a stand-in, her aunt, Abby Kent Means, from Amherst, Massachusetts. Later, Mrs. Means acted as hostess for official events while Jane Pierce, dressed in black, stayed upstairs, usually spending her days writing letters to her dead son, Benjamin. Occasionally Jane would venture out for a ride in her carriage. Understandably, social life during Pierce's term in the White House was anything but sparkling.

Two years after Pierce's election, the First Lady did appear at the important New Year's Day reception. It was a somber affair, with no refreshments—no punch, no eggnog—but even so, the public wanted to meet her and shake her hand. She was making an effort and kind commentators appreciated that effort. Mrs. Robert E. Lee wrote in a letter:

> *I have known many (first) ladies, none more truly excellent than the afflicted wife of President Pierce. Her health was a bar to any great effort on her part to meet the expectations of the public in her high position, but she was a refined, extremely religious, and well-educated lady.* [1]

For the last two years of Pierce's term, Jane attended state dinners (very stuffy events, by all accounts), but she seemed to be, as one guest said, "the very picture of melancholy." Jane Pierce died five years later, and after her death, Pierce abandoned his lifelong battle against alcoholism—the dissipated life she so hated—and became a very heavy drinker.

Happily, this melancholy picture of the White House would change with the administration of the next President, bachelor James Buchanan, whose beautiful, young, sophisticated niece would restore some of the social graces—and good times—to the White House, in the tradition of Dolley Madison.

MARY TODD LINCOLN

When Mary Todd became engaged to Abraham Lincoln, they seemed mismatched. She was a member of one of the most influential and prosperous pioneer families of Kentucky and Illinois and had been properly and "carefully" educated in Lexington. Lincoln, in contrast, was a rough-hewn, self-educated, clumsy, gangly, *poor*, 31-year-old bachelor. But aside from an evident attraction for each other, they both were interested in politics.

When Mary was 21, she visited her sister in Springfield, Illinois. The pretty southern belle met many eligible men who were involved in the political scene, including Lincoln's arch-rival, Stephen Douglas. But "Honest Abe" was her choice and despite her parents' opposition, they were married in 1842. The conflict with her family was to cause friction in the marriage, which escalated during the Civil War when several relatives were killed fighting for the South.

Not only did Stephen Douglas lose Mary; he lost his crucial final debates with Lincoln. Just as charismatic John F. Kennedy's compelling debates with the more established but stiff Richard M. Nixon propelled Kennedy into the national spotlight (and a close election win) one hundred years later, Lincoln's victory over Douglas had a similar result. When Lincoln learned he had been nominated on the third ballot in May, 1860, he said, "There's a little woman down at our house would like to hear this. I'll go down and tell her."

Mary was thrilled at the prospect of living in the White House, but she was nervous, too. Although regarded as sophisticated and witty in Springfield, she was afraid the Washington "nobility" would look upon her as a country girl and criticize her husband. There had already been gossip that Abe Lincoln, who at 52 was about to be inaugurated as the sixteenth President, was gauche, ungainly, and inexperienced, and he had received threats telling him to resign.

A few days before the Inauguration, a Washington journalist commented: "The ladies are dying to see how Mrs. Lincoln fills the place of Miss Lane (Buchanan's popular niece/hostess); how the new divinity of the office seekers fills the place of "Old Buck"; how Madame is dressed, how she looks, how she will do."

For the Inauguration Ball, Madame did her best—which sometimes was too much. Mary was not a beauty; portraits show her well dressed but overwhelmed by her clothes. She looks shy, diffident, rather like a doll dressed up for an occasion…too many frills, too many flowers, too many ruffles, as if the clothes were taking the place of her own personality. Her expression is often a little sad and she seems somewhat ill-at-ease.

Lincoln's first Inauguration and ball on March 8, 1861, was called a "Monster Levée," a "Monster Gathering." The ball, originally limited to two hours, continued for *two* more, and was described by a terribly enthusiastic writer as

> *A jam, it was a rush, it was a cram, it was a crush, it was an* omnium gatherum *of all sorts of people, an 'irrepressible conflict', a suffocating pressure, an overwhelming manifestation of private interest and public curiosity in the new dynasty without precedent for comparison in the history of this government.*[1]

During her first year in the White House, Mary utilized the usual redecorating allowance for First Ladies, and added handmade rugs, velvet wallpaper and draperies, lace curtains, silk and brocade upholstery, new china and luxurious accessories. However, she spent $7,000 over her budget, and appealed for more money. The President was outraged and railed about where a rug costing $2,500 could be placed in the White House.

By now the Washington busy-birds were clucking about Mary's social gaffes and the fact that she had married such a poor catch, and she had heard rumors that she was regarded as vulgar and silly. Perhaps this pressure led to her excesses in clothes and entertaining; she told her black dressmaker and confidante, Elizabeth Keckley, "I must dress in costly materials. The people scrutinize every article that I wear with critical curiosity."[2] It wasn't long before Mary's shopping sprees became public knowledge. Like a modern-day shopaholic, Mary couldn't resist buying "things," even though wearing her purchases might require two lifetimes. In four months alone she purchased three hundred pairs of gloves; she spent another $500 on *one* lace shawl, and $5,000 for three evening gowns.

Not only was Mary criticized for extravagance but her patriotic leanings were also attacked. One brother, three half-brothers, and three brothers-in-law served in the confederate army and people wondered whether her sympathies were with the North...or the South. Some even suspected she was a confederate spy!

All the criticism and all the rumors exacerbated emotional and physical problems Mary had had for years. She suffered from devastating headaches, which sometimes forced her to take to her bed for two or three days at a time, and she also had a dreadful temper. (According to one perhaps apocryphal story, before Lincoln became President she had once gotten so angry with him that she chased him with a butcher knife.) The death of their son, Edward, some years earlier at age four often caused her to become over-protective of their three surviving sons. And then sometimes she would completely neglect them.

The Lincolns obviously adored each other, but on occasion, the President had to play a very strong role with his wife, who was given to tantrums and hysterical screaming. He called her his "child-wife," and once told a guest. "My wife is as handsome as when she was a girl, and I, a poor nobody then fell in love with her, and what is more, I have never fallen out."[3]

Mary seemed to swing in manic extremes from gracious, charming hostess to angry, depressed virago...and the mood swings became more frequent, and less easily hidden. One White House aide records, "The Hell-cat is getting more Hell-cattical day by day." Other officials regarded her as eccentric and observed, "Mrs. Lincoln is—Mrs. Lincoln...She is not easy to get along with."[4]

When she was not in a depressed mood, she tried to soothe and comfort Lincoln, bringing him special treats, inviting old friends over, reciting poetry or passages from the Bible.

The First Lady also tried to give the President advice, which infuriated his advisors. She complained so much about cabinet members that Lincoln told her, "Mother, if I listened to you, I should soon be without a Cabinet...I give you credit for sagacity, but you are disposed to magnify trifles." Mary relentlessly continued to write letters with her recommendations for appointments. She had breached that important nineteenth century rule that a "woman's place is in the home,"[5] and brought on herself the opprobrium that confronted Abigail Adams and other First Ladies through history, including Nancy Reagan and Hillary Clinton.

The President responded calmly to such criticism. "I myself manage all important matters. In little things I have got along through life by letting my wife run her end of the machine pretty much in her own way." At the same time, Mary made other grievous political mistakes: she accepted costly gifts (assuming they were her due, and not realizing such acceptance compromised her husband), until he finally shut down this practice.

In spite of all this furor, the Lincolns continued to give receptions at the White House, including one for General Tom Thumb and his wife Lavinia, who were what we would call today—in our politically correct way—"vertically challenged," but were then called midgets, prime exhibits of P.T. Barnham's circus. This was a popular reception, but other gatherings were not so well regarded. One that was particularly criticized was a party in 1862 which was supposed to be limited to 500, but was attended by a thousand guests. Not only was Mary castigated for her extravagance, and for having the bad taste to give such a gala during the war, but two of her sons were ill upstairs, and she was denigrated as non-motherly and non-loving.

When the guests left, the Lincolns learned that Willie's "cold" was really typhoid fever, and the couple took turns nursing him, until, on February 20, eleven-year-old Willie Lincoln died. The President put up a gallant front, but Mary Lincoln was devastated and could not attend the funeral in the East Room, nor did she rally to console or take care of their youngest son, ten-year-old Thomas "Tad," who also had typhoid. The White House remained in mourning mode and for months afterward she would not have flowers in the mansion, nor would she allow the Marine Band to play at receptions.[6]

Ordinarily, women would have sympathized with her, but remember that the war was on, and many of *their* sons were, unfortunately, not much more than cannon fodder. Her grief was characterized as "excessive and ostentatious." One bitter mother wrote a widely-printed letter pointing out that at least Mary had seen her son die; that *she* didn't have to send him out to be killed.

With Willie's death, Mary fell into a state of depression from which she never quite emerged. Lincoln was so desperate to bring her out of her black hole that one day, according to Mrs. Keckley, he took Mary to the window, pointed to a nearby asylum, and said, "Mother, do you see that large white building on the hill yonder? Try and control your grief, or it will drive you mad, and we will have to send you there."[7]

On January 1, 1863, for the first time since Willie's death, Mary joined in the traditional New Year's Day celebration in the East Room. It was on this day that Abraham Lincoln, after shaking thousands of hands, used his hand once more for a loftier purpose: to sign the Emancipation Proclamation.

By the Inaugural ceremonies of 1865, both Abe and Mary were showing the strains of the war, so evident in photographs and portraits. The journalist Jane Grey Swisshelm observed that Lincoln was "working like a man pumping for life on a sinking vessel." Mary was sinking, too, even as she wore beautiful gowns, and tried to maintain the old, elegant order.

She told Elizabeth Keckley that clothing purchases during the 1865 campaign had cost $27,000, and if her husband were defeated, "I do not know what would become of us all." She was safe for the moment after Lincoln's re-election, and at the Inaugural Ball she wore a $2,000 white silk and lace gown with an elaborate headdress and fan. Despite her gala attire, the mood was not festive. The President told Harriet Beecher Stowe, author of *Uncle Tom's Cabin*, prophetically, "I shall never live to see peace; this war is killing me." It is said that Mary also had a sense of dread, and had purchased over $1,000 worth of mourning apparel.[8]

On April 14, a month after the Inauguration, after visiting General Grant in Virginia, Abraham Lincoln returned to Washington in time for a theater party at Ford's Theatre where Miss Laura Keene was starring in the light comedy, "Our American Cousin." John Wilkes Booth, a well-known actor and Confederate sympathizer, who had long planned the assassination, shot at the President, who was sitting in a rocking chair in his box. Some members of the audience thought the shot was part of the action on stage. It was Mary Lincoln's screams that alerted the audience to the real-life drama taking place. The agile Booth leaped to the stage, and although he injured an ankle, he was able to escape by a back door.

The President was carried to a house across the street, where he would die. At the White House, while the devastated Mary remained upstairs, cared for by Elizabeth Keckley, downstairs, the arrangements for Abraham Lincoln's funeral were underway. They included a catafalque on which Lincoln's body would rest in state, guarded by soldiers; the chandeliers and windows in the East Room were draped in black and all mirrors were masked with white. These same funeral plans were repeated a century later when President John F. Kennedy was also assassinated. Unlike Jacqueline Kennedy, however, Mary Lincoln would not leave her bed. During the funeral services and while the funeral train carried the President back to Springfield for burial, Mary stayed in her room and saw no one but Tad and Mrs. Keckley. She remained in bed for five weeks, and these weren't five calm weeks: she shrieked, she moaned, she wept, she tossed, and neither Tad nor Elizabeth could comfort her.

In the public rooms of the White House there was confusion, as thousands of tourists took advantage of the chaos, roaming the Mansion in search of souvenirs. Not only did they stomp on the exquisite rugs Mary had bought, but with scissors and knives they collected pieces of rugs, strips of wallpaper, bits of lace curtains, whatever they could put their hands on.

While the White House was fast becoming a shambles, the private financial affairs of the Lincolns were in a similar state. Lincoln left an estate of about $100,000, which in 1865 should have meant a comfortable existence for his widow. But she had run up all those bills on credit, and immediately after Lincoln's death, the creditors pounced, and the public was not sympathetic to Mary's plight.

Mary Lincoln had never quite captured the hearts of Americans, especially those who lived in Washington. Even though her letters indicate that she was always faithful to her husband's beliefs and to the Union, she had never been trusted. Abraham Lincoln, like other Presidents, including Jimmy Carter, and Ronald Reagan, defended his wife and regretted the "stabs given Mary." On the day Lincoln gave his Gettysburg Address, Mary was thrown from her carriage and hit her head on a rock. Later, it was proven that the seat had been tampered with, perhaps in an attempt on the President's life. In any case, shortly after Lincoln died, their son Robert told his Aunt Emilie, "I think Mother has never quite recovered from the effects of her fall." Aside from all these stresses, psychological hindsight seems to indicate that Mary suffered from bi-polar disorder (which used to be called "manic depression") or another form of mental illness which today most likely could have been treated with medication and/or therapy. However, there were no "shrinks" practicing then, and people and families, even Presidents, coped as well as they could.

Ten years after Lincoln's assassination, and several years after Tad died, Mary was committed to an asylum, upon the decision of Robert and physicians who judged her "insane." She never forgave Robert and refused to live with him after her release. Mary Todd Lincoln died in 1882, a victim of paralysis, and was buried next to Abraham Lincoln in Springfield, Illinois.

ELIZA MCCARDLE JOHNSON

Eliza McCardle Johnson, the wife of the seventeenth President, Andrew Johnson, was described as a "woman of refinement" who devoted herself to Johnson's interest and education. She had spent years raising five children (including two alcoholic sons), and helping her husband with his career. By the time Johnson became Lincoln's Vice President, she was in her 50's, tired, worn out, and in poor health; she desired nothing more than to remain at home in Greeneville, Tennessee.

Eliza had been a schoolteacher and one of her students was Johnson, at that time an apprentice tailor whom she taught to read and write at night, as he worked. In fact, it wasn't until Johnson had been elected to Congress that he was able to write with any ease. While Johnson, the only southern Senator to remain loyal to the Union, served in Washington, Eliza stayed in Greeneville. By 1862, however, it was clear she would be safer in the Capital, and after a harrowing first try, which was aborted by threats of capture, she was finally able to join her husband.

During her residence in Washington as a Senator's wife, Eliza appeared in society as infrequently as possible, perhaps because of a combination of poor health and her reluctance to become involved in the Washington scene. In 1865, after Lincoln's assassination, she suddenly became First Lady, a role she neither wanted nor was able to carry out because of her illness, her retiring personality, and undoubtedly, the circumstances under which Johnson became President.[1]

To begin with, there was the dreadful fact of the assassination itself, during such a terrible time for the country. Then, while Mary Lincoln had remained upstairs in seclusion, souvenir-hunting soldiers and tourists had wandered through the White House, leaving the "President's House" in an almost unlivable state. More than two months went by before the Johnsons (the President and his wife, two daughters, three sons and five grandchildren) were able to move in. As a semi-invalid, Eliza retired to a small bedroom, gathered her favorite books and her knitting, and named her daughter, Martha Patterson, as hostess in her place. The dutiful Martha described her family as "just plain people from the mountains of Tennessee, placed in this position by a great tragedy and we have no desire to put on airs."[2]

Martha was not really so plain. Educated at Georgetown, she had spent many years in Washington, often as a guest at President Polk's White House. She plunged into her duties and her initial inspection turned up bugs in the furniture, tobacco juice stains on upholstery and drapery, ripped and peeling wallpaper and rugs, and dirt and grime everywhere. Shortly after the Johnsons moved in, Congress appropriated $30,000 for refurbishing. Martha efficiently supervised the purchase of expensive new furnishings, but she was also very thrifty and kept cows on the White House lawn to provide milk for family and staff. A newspaper reporter wrote that Martha would rise at dawn, "don a calico dress and spotless apron, then descend to skim the milk and attend the dairy before breakfast."[3]

Martha's widowed sister, Mary Stover, assisted as hostess during receptions, and the sisters presented an attractive image. One observer reported: "Mrs. Patterson was attired in black velvet, low neck and short sleeves, with illusion bodice, hair ornamented with flowers and back curls. Mrs. Stover wore a rich black silk trimmed with lace, with hair tastefully arranged and back curls."[4]

A less attractive image was presented by President Johnson, who soon became the first President of the United States to face impeachment. Johnson had been named Vice President because of his steadfast loyalty, but he was not really prepared to be President. Immediately after he took the oath of office he was besieged by lobbyists and patronage seekers. Johnson saw so many of them that he neglected other duties, drove himself into a state of exhaustion, and engendered a great deal of criticism. His battles with the Radical Republican Party were divisive to a country trying to recuperate from the war. Congress passed the Tenure of Office Act, which prevented the President from firing a cabinet member without congressional approval. Johnson defied the act and dismissed Secretary of War Edwin Stanton, who refused to resign and with Senate backing, barricaded himself in his office. On March 13,

1868, Congress brought impeachment charges against President Johnson for breaking the Tenure of Office Act. But two months later, he was acquitted, and the family spent the rest of his term in a happier ambiance.

Even so, Eliza only attended one White House reception, a party for her grandchildren and friends. She once remarked to a member of the White House staff, Colonel W.H. Crook, "I don't like the public life at all. I often wish the time would come when we could return to where I feel we best belong."[5]

LUCRETIA RUDOLPH GARFIELD

James Abram Garfield, the twentieth President, had one of the shortest terms: 199 days from March 4, 1881, until his death on September 19, 1881. His wife's term as First Lady was even shorter. Two months after the Inauguration, she caught malaria and left the White House to recuperate in Elberon, New Jersey, where the Garfields had a summer home.

Lucretia was a farmer's daughter who met Garfield when she was a student and he was a professor of Latin and Greek at Hiram College in Ohio. Garfield, who incidentally was the first left-handed President and the last born in a log cabin, was from a religious New England family, and he and his wife became devout members of the Disciples of Christ, opposed to war and slavery. They were married in 1858, shortly after he became President of Hiram College; in the next dozen years, the couple had seven children. James and Lucretia Garfield shared a great interest in classical literature, and Garfield taught his wife Latin. (He was such a good teacher that twenty years later she was able to teach the language to her own sons.)

Lucretia was more at home in the mansion she had designed at Hiram, but she made an effort to be a gracious First Lady in the President's mansion. At the Inauguration, she wore a gown of mauve satin, trimmed with point lace, but no jewelry. In keeping with the family's religious belief (an echo of Lemonade Lucy's attitude), no liquor was served at the ball. A contemporary reporter,

E.V. Smalley, notes that Mrs. Garfield tried to separate her public life from her private, family life.

> *Her reading of books and magazines, her oversight of the education of the children and her care of her household and all its inmates...No one who has a home and appreciates its ties and duties will find fault with her...The new mistress of the White House shows the quiet dignity and grace and the adaptability to the requirements of a social circle suddenly expanded to a hundred fold which all her friends knew she would display. And the 'little mother' mingles as much or as little as she pleases in this circle.[1]*

Although her family responsibilities came first, Lucretia Garfield was officially "at home" twice a week to receive guests from the diplomatic corps, military wives, and Congressmen and their wives, until she became ill in May. President Garfield remained at her side often long into the night. In mid-June, she left Washington to recuperate at the New Jersey shore.

In his first months in office, Garfield was besieged by campaign workers, politicians and office-seekers, looking for jobs or appointments. He tried to be impartial, but his every decision was criticized and he was accused of showing favoritism and reneging on patronage agreements. To his secretary he said, "These people would take my very brain, flesh and blood if they could. They are totally without mercy."[2]

President Garfield had planned to address the graduation class at his alma mater, Williams College, and enroll his two older sons. On July 2, 1881, about 9:20 a.m., he and aides arrived at the Baltimore and Potomac terminal and as he walked across the waiting room, a short, thin man dressed in black fired two shots at Garfield, one hitting him in the back and the other just missing his arm. The President collapsed and was moved to a nearby office while a policeman stopped the gunman. The assassin identified himself as Charles Guiteau, a "Stalwart of the Stalwarts," a band of Radical Republicans who opposed Reconstruction and Garfield's election. The group also viewed Garfield's appointments as "double dealing and dishonest."

The President wasn't expected to survive and Vice President Chester Arthur was prepared to assume office. Lucretia Garfield immediately returned from Elberon, watched over her husband and prepared his favorite foods to build up his strength. Doctors decided it was impossible to remove the bullet lodged behind Garfield's pancreas. But the President surprised everyone: within a few days he recovered sufficiently to tell stories about his youth. Even his children were allowed to visit him.

For eighty days, all through the summer, visitors came and went, and reports of the President's health were the nation's major concern. In August, doctors decided to try Alexander Graham Bell's new device for locating the exact position of the bullet so that it could be removed. The experiment failed because Garfield was resting on a mattress with metal springs, which distorted the results of Bell's apparatus. The President wanted to leave Washington and recuperate at Elberon, and on September 6, 1881, his wish was fulfilled when he was carried to a special train, which took him to New Jersey. During all these months, Vice President Arthur was in limbo, and the government was at a standstill while Garfield lingered. The President continued to rally until September 19, 1881,when he died from an apparent heart attack. Ironically, Chester Arthur, a favorite of the Stalwarts, became the twenty-first President.

After James Garfield died, friends raised a fund of $250,000 to support Lucretia Garfield and her family.

IDA SAXTON MCKINLEY

Ida Saxton McKinley, like many other First Ladies, as born to a wealthy family—her father was the leading banker in Canton, Ohio. She was sent to boarding schools and afterwards, traveled in Europe. When she returned, her father gave her a job as cashier in his bank. Ida taught Sunday school and was a popular and prominent addition to Canton's social life. William McKinley's father, on the other hand was an iron molder, and his mother, a farmer's daughter, but they wanted their nine children to be well educated.

To their credit, Ida's parents did not look down on McKinley, and gave the newlyweds a fine house for a wedding present. Their faith in McKinley was well placed as he became teacher, lawyer, major in the Union Army, Congressman for fourteen years, Governor of Ohio, and ultimately, twenty-fifth President. What seemed like the best of all possible worlds for Ida turned sour four years after their marriage when their two daughters died in infancy. For the rest of her life the grief-stricken mother had frequent nervous attacks which eventually became episodes of epilepsy.

Nonetheless, Ida set off for the inauguration ceremonies with an elaborate $10,000 wardrobe to suit any occasion. Her shaky health did not enable her to enjoy either her clothes or her role as First Lady. Ida often ate her meals alone in an upstairs sitting room, and she would occasionally entertain nieces and other family members at small, informal gatherings. Her most ambitious White House reception was a reunion held for 160 high school friends. She appeared at official receptions such as the New Year's Day parties in

1900 and 1901, but had no real part in how they were arranged or decorated or even which meals were served. At the infrequent White House dinners she attended, Ida was always seated at the President's right, so that should she have an epileptic attack, he would be able to help her. In fact, the McKinleys were never separated for more than a few hours at a time.

Official photographs depict McKinley as a portly, straight-shouldered, jowlish, and stern-looking man. His feet are firmly planted and there is nothing casual about his stance or mien. But appearances notwithstanding, he was kind and caring. Chief Usher Ike Hoover wrote of McKinley: "It was his one idea in life to make those around him feel he was their friend."

Portraits of Ida McKinley, in contrast, show a woman who seems overpowered by her voluminous gown, with hands tightly clenched on her lap, mouth firmly set, and a perky, but somehow incongruous, feather in her curled hair. But her big eyes are so sad, and her mouth so set, it is apparent that even with this finery, she was not having a fine time as First Lady.

Ida's semi-invalid state, combined with the lack of children in the White House made for a somber setting. In addition, the President was under heavy criticism from political rivals, especially over his stance on Spain's war against Cuba and the Philippines. McKinley did not want to intervene in what he considered a private fight, but Congress was against him. He was forced to declare war when the battleship "Maine" was blown up in the harbor of Havana, on February 16, 1898, with many American lives lost. Assistant Secretary of the Navy (and future President) Theodore Roosevelt organized his famous "Rough Riders," and their courageous and successful battles turned the tide of the Spanish-American War. When the smoke cleared and the war was over, the United States became responsible for Puerto Rico and several other Caribbean islands, and the Philippines became a U.S. "colony," governed by a judge from Ohio who later become President William Howard Taft.

On September 6, 1901, McKinley was scheduled to address the Pan American Exposition in Buffalo, New York. Mrs. McKinley accompanied him, resting at the home of friends while he gave his speech. Before the address, McKinley greeted people in the audience. One young man, whose right hand was bandaged, used his left to shake hands with the President, and then fired two shots point blank from the gun hidden in his bandage. The assassin's name was Leon Czolgosz, a follower of Communist founder Karl Marx. The President's last words to his secretary showed loving concern for his wife. "My wife—be careful, Cortelyou, how you tell her! Oh, be careful!"

President McKinley lingered for a week before he died. Theodore Roosevelt, who had become Vice President, traveled to Buffalo, and with McKinley's cabinet as witnesses, became the twenty-sixth President of the United States.

Her husband's assassination did not help Ida McKinley's precarious mental and physical state. The couple had had a loving marriage, and as a friend of Ida's once wrote, "To her he is far more than a perfect man. He is divine." Ida McKinley was cared for by her nieces and other family members until her death a few years later in 1907.[1]

GRACE GOODHUE COOLIDGE

When Calvin Coolidge became the thirtieth U.S. President after Harding's death, the stock market was booming, the Jazz Age was in full swing, and the nation was enjoying prosperity, postwar optimism, and high spirits.

The Coolidges entered the White House on the wave of this positive attitude—his Vice Presidential campaign slogan had been "Keep Cool with Coolidge"—and after the confused Wilson administration and the Harding scandals, Americans welcomed a good, "All-American Couple." Which the Coolidge's were, in many ways. Their two young sons were handsome and bright, Grace Goodhue Coolidge was well-educated and attractive, and her outgoing personality made up for Coolidge's tendency to undercommunicate. In fact, the new President was known as "Silent Cal." Coolidge was so taciturn that one wag, learning that Grace used to teach at a school for the deaf, said, "Having taught the deaf to hear she may now inspire the dumb to speak."

The youthful-looking First Lady wore a stylish short bob; her strong, square-shaped face was softened by a lovely, regal smile. The President was very proud of his wife and loved to buy her presents, although some gifts were not to her conservative, understated taste. He bought her elaborate frocks, trimmed with beads or fringe or heavy embroidery, and he liked to see her in huge hats bedecked with flowers.

Grace pursued her new duties energetically and enthusiastically. One of her first redecorating efforts concerned the famous, peripatetic Lincoln bed. Mrs. Coolidge decided it would be *her* bed, and moved it into her room. According to Lillian Parks, whose mother, Maggie Rogers, was a White House maid during the Coolidges' time, Grace had a doll collection, which she kept on the Lincoln bed. Every night when the bed was turned down, Maggie moved the dolls and then set them up in place again the next day. Grace was clearly fond of that huge Lincoln bed: before she left the White House she crocheted a special bedspread for it, completing one square per month.[1]

During official receptions, the First Lady countered her husband's reserved attitude by being friendly and solicitous. In receiving lines, President Coolidge, eager to conclude what to him was an odious task, would prod the guest a little past him in order to move the line along. Grace Coolidge would counteract this by smiling and adding a friendly word or two. One woman, teasing the President, told him she made a bet that she could make him speak more than two words. "You lose," he replied. But that was in keeping with his theory. "If you don't say anything, you won't be called on to repeat it." Alice Roosevelt, the vivacious and outspoken daughter of Theodore Roosevelt, was not amused. "Calvin Coolidge," she said, "was weaned on a pickle."

Cool public demeanor aside, Coolidge was warm and affectionate toward his wife and wanted to spare her the details of running the White House, even though his own management of the Mansion was so economical—some said "stingy"—that the beleaguered chef quit. (Perhaps Coolidge's thriftiness was inherited from his father, Colonel John Coolidge, who refused to install a telephone because of the expense. When President Harding died, Vice President Coolidge was vacationing at his father's Vermont farm, and the news that he was now President was brought to him by car. His father, a notary public, administered the oath of office in the middle of the night. According to news reports, afterward, both Coolidges went back to sleep.)[2]

Grace's happy days at the White House ended in July, 1924, when Calvin, Jr., 16, after a game of tennis, limped into the mansion with a blister on his foot. The sore became infected; he developed a fever, and became steadily weaker. Doctors could do little for him, since his illness predated antibiotics and tetanus shots. When he died a few days later, the President mourned openly, but Grace Coolidge's grief was quieter and longer lasting, and the rest of her time in the White House was shadowed by this loss. Although she continued her duties and responsibilities, the spark was gone...she was a woman going through the motions.

In 1927, the Coolidges, like other First Families, left the White House while repairs were under way, and moved into the nearby

Patterson mansion, where one of the guests they entertained in 1927 was Charles Lindbergh, after his solo flight to Paris.

Not only was the White House roof replaced, it was *raised*, and now the "President's Palace" had eighteen new rooms for guests and servants' quarters on the top floor. Grace, like Jacqueline Kennedy and other First Ladies before and after her, thought the Mansion should be furnished in the period in which it had been designed—the early nineteenth century. At her suggestion, congress authorized acceptance of donations of "rare old pieces," and although she did not receive as many articles as she had hoped, several rooms were authentically refinished before she left.

In August, 1927, Coolidge announced "I do not choose to run," rejecting a bid for re-election in 1928. Evidently the Republican Party took him at his word, and whether Coolidge meant it or not, he was *not* nominated: Herbert Hoover was.

The Coolidges retired to their home in Northampton, Massachusetts, where Calvin Coolidge, the only President born on the Fourth of July (1872), died in 1933. Coolidge had said, "The business of America is business," but by the time he died, the stock market had crashed and the business of most Americans had become their efforts to survive the worst depression in history.

THE ELEGANT
ENTERTAINERS

Letitia Christian Tyler
1790-1842

Julia Gardiner Tyler
1820-1889

Julia Dent Grant
1826-1902

Rose Elizabeth Cleveland

Frances Folsom Cleveland
1864-1947

Edith Carow Roosevelt
1861-1948

Lou Henry Hoover
1874-1944

Mamie Doud Eisenhower
1896-1979

All the Presidents' wives were expected to serve as official hostesses in the Executive Mansion. Most First Ladies tried their best; some refused to try at all; and some excelled in the fine art of entertaining. Perhaps these last took their cues from Dolley Madison, or simply had a natural talent for planning gala receptions and events. The legendary hostesses included Julia Gardiner Tyler, second wife of John Tyler (#10); Harriet Lane, the niece of bachelor James Buchanan (#15), profiled in Part V; and Frances Folsom Cleveland, the young wife and former ward of Grover Cleveland (#24).

Lou Henry Hoover was also well-educated and gave splendid fetes, as did Jacqueline Bouvier Kennedy, whose dazzling receptions included artists, writers, and intellectuals, the same mix favored by Nancy Reagan and Hillary Clinton. Three military wives can also be counted as very successful White House hostesses: Julia Dent Grant, wife of Ulysses S. Grant (#18); Edith Carow Roosevelt, Theodore Roosevelt's First Lady (#26); and the extremely popular Mamie Eisenhower, wife of President Dwight David Eisenhower (#34).

Eleanor Roosevelt, rather paradoxically, was a great party-giver, too, but her major accomplishments were in another area, as were those of Jacqueline Kennedy, Lady Bird Johnson, Nancy Reagan, Hillary Clinton, and our current First Lady, Laura Bush, whose profiles appear in subsequent chapters.

LETITIA CHRISTIAN TYLER
AND
JULIA GARDINER TYLER

L etitia Christian Tyler was an invalid when her husband became
the tenth President, following William Henry Harrison's death
after only 31 days in office. Letitia Tyler had had a stroke a few
years before, and although brought up in ways, which would have
suited her role as a First Lady, she wasn't well enough to practice
these skills. Her three daughters and daughter-in-law would visit
her in the family rooms in the White House, where she remained in
seclusion, reading her Bible and knitting. She made only one
entrance in the Mansion's public rooms, in January, 1842, when her
daughter Elizabeth was married in the East Room. Several months
later, Letitia died.

During her illness, Tyler told his daughters and daughter-in-
law, "My daughters, you are now occupying a position of deep
importance. I desire you to bear in mind three things: show no
favoritism, accept no gifts, receive no seekers after office."[1]

The young women also received expert advice about hostessing
duties from the ever-vigilant Dolley Madison, now well past
seventy. Early on, John Tyler's official hostess was his
daughter-in-law, Priscilla Cooper Tyler, whom Dolley advised to
return *all* calls. Later Priscilla wrote to her sister, "Three days in the
week I am to spend three hours a day driving from one street to
another in this city of magnificent distances."[2]

In 1843, one of the visitors to Washington was a very
sophisticated and chic young woman, Julia Gardiner, 23, who had
toured Paris, London, and Rome. The gray-eyed, olive-skinned
brunette possessed wonderful grace and posture, and a distinguished
background. Her father, David Gardiner, was a former New York

111

State senator, one of the Gardiners who still own New York's Gardiner's Island. Letitia had been dead almost a year, and John Tyler at 53, was still another White House widower. He asked Julia to marry him, but the thirty-year age gap gave her pause, and at first she declined.

However, in spring, 1844, while the First Family and guests were cruising on the steamer "Princeton," one of the big guns on board, ironically called a "Peacemaker," exploded, killing eight men, including two cabinet members and Julia's father. (The ubiquitous Dolley was also aboard). All eight men were given a state funeral in the East Room of the White House, and President Tyler spent a great deal of time trying to assuage Julia Gardiner's grief. Within three months she agreed to become Mrs. Tyler, and a few months later they were married in a private ceremony in New York City marking the first time a President of the United States had been married while in office.

You can imagine the fun the Washington press had with this May-September wedding. Former President John Quincy Adams, now a crotchety 77, wrote that the couple was the "laughing-stock of Washington," while in Virginia, the children of Letitia and John Tyler—seven daughters and sons, some of them older than Julia—tried to remain discreetly cool.

After their marriage only eight months remained of Tyler's term, but Julia used those months to transform the White House into a royal court, with twelve "maids of honour" attending her at official receptions, where she wore the royal purple in long-trained gowns set off by headdresses of bugle beads that came close to looking like a crown. Her guests were announced before they entered, in a procedure not unlike that practiced at England's royal court. Julia enjoyed her brief reign as First Lady, and especially liked being addressed as "Mrs. Presidentess."

Credit must be give to Julia as the First Lady who introduced the Marine Band's custom of playing "Hail to the Chief" when the President appears. She enjoyed her husband's merits, especially his "musical voice," his "inspired eloquence," and his "manners and poise." Julia was also responsible for some changes in Tyler; she taught him to dance the quadrille, the polka and the waltz, a dance he objected to as "vulgar" only a few years earlier.

The party came to an end after James K. Polk won the election. On March 8, 1845, at the inaugural ceremonies in the Blue Room, the young, glamorous First Lady described her husband's farewell speech as a "burst of beautiful and poetic eloquence."[3] After they left the White House, Julia and John Tyler ultimately had seven children, the last born when the former President was 70. When her husband died, the still young widow had to ask Congress for a pension; it was granted and she spent the rest of her life in Georgetown.

JULIA DENT GRANT

Julia Dent, born in St. Louis, Missouri, was another "gently bred" belle. At eleven she was sent to Miss Moreau's boarding school, and after "finishing" her education she returned home and fortuitously met one of her brother's West Point classmates, Lieutenant Ulysses S. Grant. (Grant's real name was Hiram Ulysses, but he was always called Ulysses. A teacher, assuming his middle name was Simpson, his mother's maiden name, appended an S., never corrected by Grant.)

Julia and Grant became engaged in the spring of 1844, but the Mexican War deferred their marriage until August, 1848. They had five children (one died in infancy), and she, like other army wives who became First Ladies, accompanied him to various posts until 1852 when she returned to St. Louis because her health wasn't strong enough to follow Grant to California. In 1854, Grant resigned from the army and joined his family in St. Louis; when the Civil War broke out, he rejoined the army, and, after many important and successful battles and the subsequent Union victory, became the nation's hero.

In 1868, he was elected eighteenth President to great popular acclaim and succeeded the hapless Andrew Johnson. When the Grants moved into the White House, two children, Jesse and Nellie, were still living at home. An older son was at West Point; the other at Harvard. Another White House resident was Julia's father, "Colonel" Frederick Dent, a traditional (and opinionated) "Southern Gentleman." A frequent visitor was the President's

113

father, Jesse, who resided at a nearby hotel rather than stay at the White House with "that tribe of Dents."[1] The two fathers were not fond of each other, representing as they did, opposing political positions.

Upon her husband's election, Julia had two major goals she hoped to achieve. The first was to have an operation to correct her crossed eyes, which she felt would improve her appearance and consequently enhance her husband's image. Grant's exact reply is not recorded, but in effect he told Julia he had fallen in love and married her with her eyes as they were and they were going to stay that way. There was no operation, and in many photographs and portraits, Julia posed either in full or semi-profile. Her second goal was to convince the new President that they should continue to live in their Washington house and use the White House only for official entertaining. (At that time there were only six bedrooms on the second floor; the remaining rooms were used as offices.) This idea was also dismissed, but after an inspection showed that the White House was once more falling apart, Julia supervised extensive renovations, not only to make the family more comfortable but to rebuild and redecorate many of the public rooms.

While plans for the renovation were reviewed, the Grants entertained on a grander "official" scale than their predecessors, the Johnsons, had. Julia initiated once-weekly two-hour public receptions and held morning receptions in the Blue Room. For formal dinners, the Grants' guests ranged from diplomats and aristocrats to *nouveaux riches* profiteers and rough as well as polished politicians. The Washington press corps gushed over the social activity and dozens of society writers (all female) waxed effusively about details of the Grant White House, from flowers and food to dresses and entertainment. Receptions were "gala," "brilliant," or "elegant;" lengthy paragraphs described Julia's dresses of "Lyons silk velvet, with high bodice, trimmed with black lace and satin," or "pink grenadine, with flounced over-skirt, hair ornaments of fresh flowers and diamond necklace."[2]

At dinner parties, French wine flowed freely; usually there were six wineglasses at each place setting. (President Grant, who had conquered a drinking problem, turned his glass upside down when waiters served the wine. Although he abstained from alcoholic beverages, he continued to smoke 20 cigars a day. He also continued to enjoy his favorite snack: a cucumber soaked in vinegar.)

During the Grant Administration, the average State dinner cost about $700; special dinners cost twice that. A dinner for Prince Arthur, Queen Victoria's third son, cost $1,500, not including wine and other beverages, and consisted of *twenty-nine courses*.[3]

By 1871, official inspection of the White House, almost 60 years after the construction that followed the fire of 1814, showed that wood used in floors and on the roof had decayed, the basement was "damp and unhealthy," ceilings were cracked (one had caved in the year before, but no one was injured), and there were no closets or clothes-presses "which are now considered indispensable." According to the Commissioner of Public Buildings and Grounds, "It hardly seems possible to state anything in favor of the house as a residence."

Based on investigations of what needed to be replaced, refurbished, built or bought, hundreds of thousands of dollars were earmarked for renovations. Even from the vantage point of more than 100 years, when such costs have multiplied many times over, these expenditures are still rather shocking. Consider $28,000 for the care of the White House grounds; $692,000 for lighting the Capitol and the White House (although in later years, these costs were separated); fuel for the House, $40,000; $14,000 for a stable, and $1,500 for a road from the stable to the White House; removing water pipes to the White House, $5,500; piping Potomac water into the mansion, $4,420, and another $3,000 to pipe water into the office portion. The cost for completing iron fencing of the White House grounds was $27,000; painting the fence required another $1,000. Included in this laundry list of renovating costs is another item for "Repairs, refitting, etc., President's summer residence (in Long Branch, New Jersey), $3,000."

With the completion of renovations in 1873, the basic simplicity of the White House was replaced by ornate over-embellishment. Huge cut glass chandeliers, gilded wallpaper, white and gold woodwork, and black and gold ebony furniture typified the new "Pure Greek" atmosphere—not really Greek at all. Years Later, Jacqueline Kennedy, who abhorred the gaudy décor of this and later redecorating, worked hard to recreate the mansion as originally conceived in the early 1800's by architect James Hoban, Thomas Jefferson and other consultants.

During President Grant's second term, the refurbished White House served as the setting for one of the major social events of his administration: the wedding of daughter Nellie, who became the first bride to be married in the White House since John Tyler's daughter, two decades earlier. To say that Nellie was not of an intellectual bent would be an understatement. For example, after *one day* at a New England boarding school she sent a "get me out of here" wire home. From that point on, the pretty young woman's life revolved around parties and beaux instead of French verbs and English novels. Her parents indulged her in a Grand Tour abroad, and on the way home she met and became engaged to Algernon

Sartoris, a nephew of the celebrated actress Fanny Kemble. Against the President's advice, a wedding was scheduled shortly before her nineteenth birthday in May, 1874. A contemporary journalist described the flowers, receiving line, and of course, Nellie's gown:

> *The bride wore a white satin dress, elaborately trimmed with point lace and a tulle veil, and her hair was adorned with orange blossoms. There was nothing particularly noticeable in the dress of the groom, which was, of course, in the latest style, with the conventional white necktie.* [4]

Unfortunately, Grant's two terms were marred by scandals, which obscured positive developments under his aegis, and he lost his bid for a third term. But the White House had regained its glamorous glow during the Grant family's eight years, and when they left they still commanded favorable publicity and attention.

The popular ex-President embarked on a round-the-world trip and Julia accompanied him. She wrote, speaking in the third person, "Having learned a lesson from her predecessor, Penelope, she accompanied her Ulysses in his wanderings around the world." When the Grants returned, he incurred a debt of $16 million dollars in a disastrous Wall Street venture. Although he recouped some money with his best selling *Memoirs*, after his death Julia Grant appealed to Congress for financial assistance. A bill was passed giving her a pension of $5,000 a year for life.

ROSE ELIZABETH CLEVELAND
AND
FRANCES FOLSOM CLEVELAND

Grover Cleveland was the only President to be elected for two *non-consecutive terms*, which made him the twenty-second, as well as the twenty-fourth President. He claimed other Presidential "firsts" as well: Although he wasn't the first bachelor President, he was the first—*and only one*—to get married in the White House. His wife was the youngest First Lady. And his was the first President's child born in the White House. Clearly, these "firsts" belong to his wife, Frances Folsom, as well.

But when Cleveland was elected, Frances was still a student at Wells College, and Cleveland depended on his obliging sister Rose Elizabeth, known as Libby, to act as his official hostess. Libby was well-educated and comfortable around sophisticated intellectuals. One story has it that she alleviated the boredom of long receiving lines by conjugating Greek verbs in her head while she stood smiling and shaking hands. As some other White House hostesses had, she too, took her cues from Lucy Hayes and vetoed wine at parties which somewhat irritated her brother.

Libby served as surrogate First Lady until the second year of Cleveland's first term, when he asked Frances Folsom to marry him, and his sister happily left to pursue her own career as a teacher, lawyer, political speaker and writer. Frances was the 23-year-old daughter of Cleveland's friend and law partner Oscar Folsom of Buffalo. From the time her father died when Frances (Frank, as Cleveland called her) was twelve, Cleveland had acted as an informal guardian, supervised her education, and arranged a trip to Europe.

Frances was young and beautiful and her engagement to the middle-aged, corpulent (260 pounds) President caused a good deal of talk.

The wedding took place in the White House the evening of June 2, 1886, amid banks of roses, pansies, begonias, orchids, palms, ferns and potted plants. At 7:00 p.m. the couple was honored with a twenty-one gun salute, along with the simultaneous ringing of church bells all over the capital. Then, the Marine Band led by John Philip Sousa played the traditional Mendelssohn wedding march. One writer was astonished by the bride's ivory satin wedding gown and fifteen-foot-long train: "The train was a marvel of graceful arrangement, and it was marvelous how she handled it in a small well-filled room, for it was nearly as long as the room itself..."[1]

The Clevelands did not have a tranquil honeymoon. They were hounded by journalists (some equipped with binoculars) who wanted first hand news of the couple's stay at a Maryland resort. Cleveland was so outraged he wrote a letter censuring this type of journalism, which was printed in New York newspapers.

The engaging, pretty Francis was news, however—what she wore, how she entertained, what she said were all grist for the media mill. Some of her public receptions, attended by as many as five or six thousand people, became so crushed as people held up the receiving line to talk to her, that White House guards were called in to move the crowd along. The First Lady scheduled two public receptions a week, one on Saturday afternoon so working women would have a chance to meet her.

The bride's popularity notwithstanding, Cleveland was defeated in 1888 by Benjamin Harrison, grandson of William Henry Harrison, the ninth President. Cleveland looked forward to a change of pace and leisure time with his wife, but Frances liked the White House life, and as she left on March 4, 1889, she told an older servant, "Now Jerry...take good care of all the furniture and ornaments in the house, for I want to find everything just as it is now when we come back again...just four years from today."[2]

And, as we know, the Clevelands *did* return in 1893, and Benjamin Harrison was polite enough to stay for the Inauguration.

After the four-year hiatus, Frances was enthusiastically welcomed back to the Mansion—the staff and her public adored her and heralded her charm and her beauty.

During the second term the social highlights included visits from many foreign celebrities and receptions for ministers from dozens of countries, including Italy, France, England, and China, capped by a final 1897 New Year's Day reception for ministers from Turkey, Haiti, Central America, Korea, Japan and China. During the public part of the reception, over seven thousand visitors shook hands with the President and his wife.

Frances Cleveland restored the practice of serving wine at White House receptions and dinners, and in fact, six wineglasses were at each place setting, but only one glass stood at her place and that held a glass of water. (President Cleveland's weight indicates he enjoyed the multi-course, gourmet dinners, but his very favorite meal was corned beef and cabbage.)

Aside from the many dinner parties and receptions, the Clevelands spent less time at the White House during this second term than any other family before—and probably since—then. They would retire to the house they had rented on Woodley Lane in Georgetown and drive to the White House where they spent a few hours. During summers they vacationed in New England.

On reason the Clevelands were away so much was the President's hatred of journalists who invaded his privacy. Another, far more important reason was that in an economically troubled time—the Panic of 1893—Cleveland was diagnosed as having cancer of the mouth and it was feared that if word of his illness leaked it would further upset the country's wavering economic situation.

The decision was made to keep his illness a secret, and the recommended operation—to remove his entire left upper jaw—was performed in 1893 under such secrecy that most of his friends didn't know about it. (The details weren't made public until 1917). Surgery was performed on a yacht , which set sail from New York Harbor; although a long period of recuperation was required, President Cleveland was fitted with an artificial jaw made of rubber and was able to carry on all his official duties.

The Clevelands were also distressed at the excessive attention paid their daughter, Ruth, who had been born between Presidential terms, in New York. The young mother wanted to be able to take Ruth outdoors in her baby carriage but this soon became impossible. Crowds gathered to see the baby, and one day, strangers picked up Ruth and passed her around while a nursemaid stood by, unable to control them. The birth of Esther, the first President's child born in the White House, compounded the problem. Instead of the earlier "open door policy," the White House gates were closed and locked, and in response, the hungry press put forth the word that the Clevelands didn't want the public to see the baby because she was malformed, half-witted and deaf-mute, none of which were true.

On their last night in the White House, the Clevelands entertained incoming President William McKinley—who came alone, since his wife was suffering from an attack of epilepsy—and the mood was somber. The Clevelands and the President-elect talked about what everyone else in Washington and most of the country was concerned about: the ominous shadow of war with Spain, which under President McKinley's watch became a terrible reality known as the Spanish-American War.

After the Clevelands left the White House, they retired to Princeton, New Jersey, where the ex-President became involved in activities at Princeton University, and Frances had three more children and enjoyed life as a suburban mother. The parties she gave in Princeton were much smaller, of course, but she was known as a gracious and charming hostess for the rest of her life.

EDITH CAROW ROOSEVELT

Edith Kermit Carow Roosevelt, wife of the twenty-sixth President, Theodore Roosevelt, led an extraordinarily busy and hectic life during her eight years as First Lady. Her husband, the "Rough Rider," sportsman, big game hunter, raconteur, was not about to sit by the fire, quietly enjoying a good book. And neither were their six children, ranging in age from 17-year-old Alice, Edith's stepdaughter, to the baby, Quentin.

When the Roosevelts were not entertaining officially, they were entertaining informally, and when they weren't entertaining, they were riding horses, playing sports (fencing, medicine ball, lawn tennis, billiards), planning games, and enjoying life in a very vigorous way. The younger children considered the Executive Mansion a great setting for fun—and they roller-skated in the upstairs corridor, practiced walking on stilts in the high ceilinged rooms, had water fights, and used the elegant furniture to play leap-frog. Their many pets included dogs, cats, a black bear, a kangaroo rat, and a pony called Algonquin.

Edith Roosevelt engaged in most of the physical activity, but sometimes she retreated to a quiet room, because the six kids *and* President Roosevelt were too much even for her patient soul. Edith was youthful, charming, bright-eyed; a dignified woman, with an affable smile and the bearing to carry off large hats and cumbersome, but fashionable clothing. Her inaugural gown is one of the most beautiful in the Smithsonian collection.

Edith ran an efficient, organized household, while instilling in her children a sense of responsibility as well as the capacity to enjoy life and have fun. Archie Butt, an aide to Roosevelt, described her as serving "eight years in the White House without making a mistake." Edith was Roosevelt's second wife. He had previously been married to his college sweetheart, Alice Lee, who died when daughter Alice was born. Edith Carow had been Roosevelt's childhood friend, and although their marriage might not be described as "passionate," it was for the most part, happy. (At one point, there were rumors that Roosevelt was having an affair with a Washington woman-about-town. Edith sent Archie Butt to impart a very strong message to the woman, which he did, and the affair, whether rumored or actual, was squelched).

The close family life of the Roosevelts extended to their dining habits. When the Roosevelts weren't entertaining officially, dinner for all family members was served every evening at seven-thirty in the State Dining Room, and according to Butt, the First Lady would become angry if the conversation stressed prize fights, or sports, and she would scold the children if they ate with their elbows on the table. Breakfast for the family was served at eight-thirty and luncheon at half-past one: the children and their governesses joined their mother and father, even though the President often had government guests for lunch.

The first major social event for the Roosevelts occurred at the New Year's Day reception in 1901, when the President and First Lady shook hands with 8,100 callers. A few days later, on January 3, the White House was the scene of another important reception, as Alice made her debut, which was covered by the press as a national event and garnered nationwide publicity. Actually, the party itself was a little dull because there was only fruit punch to drink, but still, the affair launched Alice's public life and her enduring and spectacular career as a social leader.

Alice wasn't a princess, but she was treated like one. Whatever she did, wore, or said, was recorded by the ever-hungry media. Her favorite shade of blue became known as "Alice blue," and inspired a waltz about "Alice Blue Gown." Unquestionably, Alice had a great time as a White House deb. In one official photograph, you'll see a spunky looking, cute rather than pretty, slim-waisted young woman with dark curly hair and enough aplomb to carry off a large, flower-bedecked hat. Her hands are firmly planted on the arms of a high-backed chair, and Alice looks as if she's thinking, "Here I am, World. Ready, get set, GO!" And go she did.

She was the pet of princes, a delight when she smashed a bottle of champagne on a ship's prow, a rebel, but always a loving and devoted daughter. It is not surprising that she has been the subject of many books, and most recently of *Teddy and Alice*, a Broadway show in which her escapades and social successes were heralded. Edith always encouraged her stepdaughter's independence, and Alice, aided and abetted by the indulgent T.R., and later an equally indulgent husband, became a legendary celebrity. During her long life she was quoted, feted, respected and even feared. She had a sharp tongue and sharp wit, and in later years, she had few qualms about using both.

Alice settled down a bit, though, when she decided to marry a young bachelor, Representative Nicholas Longworth of Ohio, whom she met on a junket to the Orient in 1905. When they returned, their engagement was officially announced and gifts from all over the world poured into the White House, including some freakish presents of snakes, mousetraps, a barrel of popcorn, as well as brooms, feather dusters, and washing machines, which were not exactly necessities for this new bride.

Alice—the twelfth White House bride—and Nick were married on February 17, 1906, and it was probably the most elaborate White House wedding until then. At noon, the bride, escorted by her father, walked down the aisle in the East Room to music played by the Marine Band. She carried a bouquet of orchids; her gown was of white satin and point lace with a six-yard-long train of silver brocade, even longer than Frances Folsom Cleveland's. White House aides admitted 800 guests through three separate entrances to avoid a traffic jam. There were *two* bridal receptions, one in the dining room for the bridal party and friends; the other in the State Dining Room. Edith Roosevelt masterminded the wedding which in spite of the complicated details, ran smoothly.

Edith was an adept, gracious and imaginative hostess, whether she was planning such family galas (which became "semi-official" parties) or formal state receptions. She launched a new program for the traditional weekly receptions. Every Friday evening during the Season, the First Lady scheduled a concert or a "Musicale." A limited number of guests were invited to dinner before the concert, and then, at ten o'clock, another 200 to 500 additional guests would arrive for the musical performance. The President's wife would receive these guests *alone*, while Roosevelt entertained the dinner guests.

The ornate piano used for these concerts was presented to the White House in 1903 and commanded attention even when no one was playing it, as described in Esther Singleton's 1907 book, *The Story of the White House*:

The entire instrument is overlaid with gold of varying tones of green and yellow. The body is supported by three eagles with outspread wings and talons that firmly grasp the base. The body of the piano is adorned with scrolls of acanthus framing shields bearing the arms of the thirteen states. Musical instruments ornament the music rack and the inside of the cover is painted with a picture of the nine muses in a semi-circle before the young republic.[1]

State dinners for such royal foreign visitors as Prince Henry of Prussia, brother of the Emperor of Germany, included ten wines (and sherry), and nine courses, plus café. In addition to all the requisite wineglasses at each place setting, at President Roosevelt's place there was always a gold goblet given to him by the San Francisco Chamber of Commerce in 1904. The goblet was about 12 inches high, shaped like a champagne glass and perfectly plain. But then, why embellish solid gold?

The First Lady carried out her busy family and official schedule in the middle of renovations that went far beyond normal appropriations made for each new administration. During Roosevelt's term, $65,000 was approved

For a building to accommodate offices of the President, to be located in the grounds of the Executive Mansion...(and) removal of greenhouses. In addition, $475,500 for repairs and refurbishing the Executive Mansion...including all necessary alterations, repairs, cabinetwork, decoration of rooms, covered ways and approaches, grading, paving, porte-cochère, gates and electric wiring and light fixtures for house and grounds.[2]

After the Roosevelts left the White House in 1909, the former President remained involved in national politics and ran, unsuccessfully, for President in 1912 as the Progressive Party candidate. After his defeat, he and Edith traveled extensively and he lectured all over the world; they retired to their estate, Sagamore Hill, in New York State where T.R. died in 1919. Edith continued to travel and work with several Long Island charities; she outlived her husband by almost three decades, dying in 1948, at age 87.

LOU HENRY HOOVER

Lou Henry Hoover and her husband, the thirty-first President, Herbert Clark Hoover, entered the White House in 1929 at the tail end of the economic and social high times following World War I. A very happy and outgoing couple, they left Washington downhearted and defeated four years later, as the country floundered in the worst depression in its history.

The Hoovers met while both were attending Stanford University in California. Herbert Hoover was an orphan born in Iowa and sent to live with an uncle in California. He was the first student at Stanford to actually live on campus and earned a degree as a Mining Engineer. Lou Henry, California born, was a kindred spirit, interested in geology and mineralogy. After their marriage in 1899, the Hoovers traveled widely and lived in China, England, Australia, New Zealand, Burma, and Russia. They collected fifteenth and sixteenth century books on science, engineering, metallurgy, mathematics and alchemy. In 1905, they acquired a copy of Georgius Agricola's *De Re Metallica*, which had been published in Latin in 1556, and spent five years translating the work into English. Lou and Herbert Hoover had two sons, one of whom had circled the world three times by age four.

During World War I, Herbert Hoover coordinated worldwide efforts to provide food for war victims, a program that propelled him into national prominence, led to his appointment as Secretary of Commerce, and ultimately, in 1928, to his first bid for elective office as the Republican Party candidate. He was successful, beating Democrat Al Smith, the first Catholic to seek the presidency.

Lou Hoover was not overwhelmed by her new duties as First Lady. She was tall, statuesque and poised, with strong eyebrows, handsome gray hair, and a warm smile. The private and public functions of the White House taxed neither her energies nor her capabilities. On Inauguration Day, March 4, 1929, she welcomed 1,800 luncheon guests at the White House, and another 1,500 guests for tea, including the governors of all the states and their staffs.

The Hoovers entertained a great deal and would schedule many last minute or impromptu events. At one party 500 visitors showed up instead of the 200 who had been expected, and members of the White House staff bought out nearby food shops in order to "stretch" the food which had been prepared for a smaller crowd.[1]

The very organized First Lady employed three secretaries to attend to her guest lists and often the secretaries would spend days addressing three or four thousand invitations to just one affair. While her staff was working, Lou Hoover attended to other details. One of the first changes the scholarly President's wife made in the White House was to have bookcases built along the long upstairs corridor, which had always been bare and cold. Another important goal was to restore the Monroe bedroom. After studying the old records, she searched the White House warehouse for furniture that was once used by President James Monroe and his wife, and reinstated his suite as authentically as possible.

Emphasis on White House redecoration and social events ended, however, when the stock market crashed in the fall of 1929, not only devastating the country, but also effectively ruining President Hoover's political career. As he said, he had been "overtaken by the economic hurricane." Hoover's name became a sad joke: "Hoovervilles," were shantytowns inhabited by people who had lost their homes and jobs; "Hoover blankets" were newspapers the homeless and/or heatless wrapped around their bodies to keep warm.

Although the Republicans nominated Hoover and his vice President, Charles Curtis, they were defeated overwhelmingly by the Democratic candidates, Franklin Delano Roosevelt and John N. Garner, who carried 42 states and won 472 electoral votes. Hoover's campaign had promised "A Chicken in Every Pot." Roosevelt's campaign pledged "A New Deal."

After the Hoovers left the White House, Herbert Hoover continued his humanitarian efforts to provide food to starving people all over the world, and years later, during the Truman and Eisenhower administrations, the former President chaired committees on government reorganization. Lou Hoover in her retirement pursued her own academic interests and continued her longtime support of the Girl Scouts.

MAMIE DOUD EISENHOWER

Mamie Doud Eisenhower loved the color pink. She wore pink clothes and pink nail polish, painted her rooms pink, used pink tablecloths and pink bed linens. America loved Mamie and her propensity for pink—a pink carnation was even named for her. When she and Dwight David ("Ike") Eisenhower, the thirty-fourth President, moved into the White House, the country was enchanted with this glamorous, "suburban matron."

Mamie, however, was not "suburban," and would have disliked being described as "matronly." She was born Mary Geneva Doud in 1896; her family had always called her "Mamie," or "Baby." From her childhood as the pampered daughter of a prosperous Denver businessman, through most of her marriage to a top Army General, she lived in houses with butlers, maids and servants. As a child, she loved playing the piano, but books bored her. When she met young Dwight Eisenhower, she thought he was "the spiffiest-looking man I ever talked to in all my born life...big, blond and masterful." Mamie and Ike were married in the Doud home on July 1, 1916, when she was 19. Even then she showed her passion for pink: her white dress had a pale pink satin sash, and she carried pink rosebuds.

Although Mamie couldn't follow Ike to Europe during World War II, in twenty years they lived in thirty temporary homes. For eight years, the White House became a "real home," but both President Eisenhower and Mamie dreamed of retiring to their beloved farm at Gettysburg, Pennsylvania.

Just as Ulysses S. Grant, the hero of the Civil War was elected President by popular acclaim, so too was Eisenhower in 1952, when he defeated Adlai Stevenson, who was nominated as the Democratic candidate after President Truman declined to run. Eisenhower's campaign slogan was "I like Ike." Neither of the Eisenhowers had been at all political before then and Mamie never even voted until her husband became a Presidential candidate. As a matter of fact, it wasn't until January 7, 1952, that Eisenhower formally declared himself a Republican. He admitted at that time, "I could have been a conservative Democrat."

Although Mamie Eisenhower wasn't much interested in politics, she had no reservations about her husband's running for President. As she said to one reporter, "What American woman wouldn't want her husband to be President?"

Until the time that Eisenhower was nominated, the Denver deb, who had been a career soldier's wife for decades, had never appeared on stage or addressed a public audience. Hours before that momentous appearance at the nominating convention, Mamie Eisenhower was lying in her Chicago hotel room, incapacitated by a violent headache. She rose to the occasion, however, and faced 15,000 delegates in the convention hall. Later she said, "I determined to do what Ike and everyone who believed in him expected of me."

After Ike was elected, Mamie slipped comfortably into the role of First Lady. "Ike runs the country, and I turn the pork chops," she liked to say. She became involved in the running of the White House and periodically checked such minor details as the number of light bulbs purchased or the amount of food bought for both official and family meals. She held staff meetings in bed, usually wearing a ruffled, pink bedjacket and a pink hair ribbon. In fact, she used her bed as an office, signing letters, paying bills, and writing notes, and did not use the small office where Eleanor Roosevelt and Bess Truman had worked. (That little room became President Eisenhower's studio where he would paint in the afternoon or on weekends.)

Mamie may not have considered herself a "suburban matron," but she acted like one, carefully plowing through newspapers every morning, checking for food bargains, coupons, and specials on household items. Then she would call the manager of the store or department to place an order. According to Chief Usher West, she advised her staff: "When you go into a store, go straight to the top. Don't fool around with some clerk."[1]

Another long-time White House staff member, Lillian Parks, recalls that while Eleanor Roosevelt always reminded staff and visitors that "This house belongs to all the people," Mamie often acted as if the house belonged to *her* and the President. "She would constantly refer to 'my rug,' 'my drapery,' and 'my elevator'...and she didn't want reporters to walk on 'my rug'." Parks remembers that Mamie had a "thing" about footprints on rugs. Before she went out, the rug was brushed and before she came back, *her own footprints* were brushed off.[2]

Another difference between Mamie Eisenhower and her predecessors, Eleanor Roosevelt and Bess Truman, was that Mamie loved clothes, especially pink clothes. And she kept them for years. Her wardrobe grew and grew and grew until, as Parks reports, by the time she left the White House two entire bedrooms held her evening gowns alone.

Mamie always wanted to look and act youthful, and didn't want her grandchildren to call her "Grandma." Instead, they called her "Mimi." She watched her diet and enjoyed visits to Elizabeth Arden's "Maine Chance" beauty spa for rejuvenating treatments. But she was hampered in carrying out her duties by a heart murmur and an inner ear illness, Ménière's Disease, which affected her sense of balance. (Observers and reporters wrongly speculated that drugs or alcohol abuse made her tipsy). She also suffered from violent headaches and asthma attacks. Consequently, Mamie was never a very physically active First Lady. She didn't exercise, she didn't enjoy being outdoors and didn't participate in sports. In fact, her attitude was: Why walk if you can ride?

Health problems did not prevent Mamie from enjoying her role as White House hostess. She planned parties with pink food, pink tablecloths, and pink candles. Parks writes that "Whatever wasn't peppermint-pink was mint-green." Her favorite shade of pink became known as "Mamie Pink" and the press called the White House, "The Pink Palace."[3]

Among the many guests entertained by the Eisenhowers were England's Queen Elizabeth and Prince Phillip, and Russia's Nikita Krushchev and his wife, Nina. While there were problems satisfying the Queen's maids (who had *their own maids*), the problem with the Krushchev entourage was that the men refused to wear formal dress for the gala state dinner, since such attire was considered inappropriate in the egalitarian Soviet Union. Almost thirty years later, President and Mrs. Reagan experienced the same resistance when Mikhail Gorbachev wore a business suit at the formal reception in his honor.

Aside from the many official functions, Mamie Eisenhower loved to celebrate seasonal holidays and orchestrated elaborate decorations for Halloween, Christmas, Thanksgiving, Easter, and especially, St. Patrick's Day—she was unquestionably sentimental. Mamie wore charm bracelets and her favorite recreation was to play canasta or scrabble with "the girls." She—and President Eisenhower—preferred steak, French fries, and fried chicken to "fancy food"; she loved pop tunes, romance novels, and mystery stories, and was a devoted TV soap opera fan. In the evening Mamie preferred watching musicals on film to ballet or even the theater.

Her own health problems were relegated to second place when her beloved Ike had *his* health crises, and he had quite a few after his return from Europe and his election as President. Mamie was always there, sleeping near his bed in hospitals when he suffered from a heart attack, an attack of ileitis, and even a stroke during his first term as President. Everybody liked Ike, however, and despite his illnesses, he was re-elected with an overwhelming popular vote in 1956.

The Eisenhowers were historically, and demonstrably, a very affectionate couple. In fact, until Ronald Reagan, no other President kissed his wife during the inauguration ceremonies. And instead of riding back to the White House with the Vice President to view the parade—a custom followed by many Presidents—Eisenhower rode with his wife...which started a new and prevailing trend, upheld until the Clintons.

Mamie Eisenhower's one major contribution to the white House, aside from painting everything in sight pink—which her successor, Jacqueline Kennedy soon reversed—was to create the "China Room" which displayed samples of china used by every administration.

Mamie had her quirks, as we all do, but she was devoted to her husband and their surviving son, John (another baby, Doud Dwight died in infancy). Once she said, "I had a career. His name was Ike."[4] Sometimes she was overprotective of Ike, as she was when Richard Nixon was running as Vice President in 1952 and faced criticism, which Ike could have quelled. At that time, however, Eisenhower was ill, and Mamie told Nixon's wife Pat that her husband shouldn't put added pressure on Eisenhower. On the other hand, she could be fiercely loyal, which she demonstrated when President Nixon was embroiled in the Watergate scandal years later, and she sent Pat Nixon many loving and encouraging notes, reiterating her support.

Chief Usher West said of Mamie Eisenhower: "Underneath that buoyant spirit, there was a spine of steel, forged by years of military discipline...she understood the hierarchy of a large establishment (and) the division of responsibilities...Regal, sentimental Mamie Eisenhower was the last First Lady born in the nineteenth century. She was the first to leave the White House in the Space Age.[5]

In 1960 the Eisenhowers retired to Gettysburg; Ike died there in 1969, after his seventh heart attack. Mamie Eisenhower continued to live at Gettysburg until her death in 1979.

THE SUPPORTIVE STAND-INS

Emily Donelson
1807-1836

Angelica Singleton Van Buren
1816-1877

Sarah Yorke Jackson (Not Pictured)
1805-1887

Harriet Lane
1830-1903

Mary Arthur McElroy
1842-1917

Thomas Jefferson, the first widower-President, was extremely fortunate to have Dolley Madison serve as his hostess, and as noted, her style of entertaining became a standard for many other women in the White House. Dolley also acted as a tutor, friend and protector of the third President's daughter, Martha Randolph, whose devotion to her father extended well beyond her years as White House hostess.

Jefferson was the first of several Presidents who were unmarried when they were elected. Those who remained single throughout their terms, including the widowers Andrew Jackson, Martin Van Buren and Chester Arthur, relied on relatives and friends for hostessing duties.

The one and only President who remained a bachelor all his life was James Buchanan, yet his hostess, niece Harriet Lane, was one of the most sparkling and gracious women ever to preside at White House receptions.

Through the years, there were other stand-ins, too, especially for those First Ladies who have been profiled in Part III, whose unhappy private lives prevented them from enjoying their time in the White House or fulfilling their responsibilities as Presidential helpmates. These included the wives of Zachary Taylor (#12), Franklin Pierce (#14), and Andrew Johnson (#17).

EMILY DONELSON
AND
SARAH JACKSON
(for Andrew Jackson)

The election fight between John Quincy Adams and Andrew Jackson was one of the most acrimonious in our nation's history. Not only were there bitter political blasts, but Adams's supporters also threw verbal mud at Jackson's robust, homespun, pipe-smoking wife, Rachel, spreading rumors that the two had been living together before marriage. One pro-Adams pamphlet asked, "Ought a convicted adulteress and her paramour husband be placed in the highest offices of this free and Christian land?" "Old Hickory," so strong on the battlefield, was cut to the quick by attacks against his wife, but he said, "I never war against females and it is only the base and cowardly that do."[1]

Jackson won the election, but tragically, shortly before he was about to be inaugurated as seventh President, his beloved wife died. Rachel Donelson was the bright-eyed, black-haired, sweet-faced daughter of Colonel John Donelson who settled in Nashville, Tennessee. Shortly after Rachel, 17, married Lewis Robards, her father died and the Donelson family lost everything. Robards turned out to be lazy and shiftless and was not interested or not able to help the family out of the mess. In fact, he soon announced he was divorcing Rachel.

As many impoverished women did in those days, Rachel's mother took in boarders, one of whom was Andrew Jackson. Rachel and Jackson fell in love, and when they received news that Robards had filed for his divorce, they were married. Two years later the errant former husband put out the word that only *now* had the divorce been granted. In other words, Jackson and his Rachel had been "living in sin." They immediately remarried, but this "gap" caused the gossip almost forty years later.

Jackson, of course, became a hero during the War of 1812 at the Battle of New Orleans, which led to his political prominence, subsequent nomination, and election to the presidency. Rachel Jackson was caught in the campaign acrimony, which un-nerved and hurt her. Shortly before the inauguration she heard women gossiping about her "vulgar" pipe smoking, how common she was, and her belated divorce and premature marriage. She became hysterical, wept all the way back to Jackson's Nashville estate, The Hermitage, and died a few days after suffering a breakdown (or a broken heart?) The official cause of death was a heart attack.

At her funeral Jackson mourned openly. "In the presence of this dear saint I can and do forgive my enemies. But those vile wretches who have slandered her must look to God for mercy!"[2] Not surprising, there were no civilities between the outgoing President Adams, and the President-elect, Andrew Jackson.

The second widower in the White House, Jackson had no relatives of his own to assist him socially, so he turned to his wife's family. He invited his unofficially "adopted" son, Rachel's nephew, Colonel Andrew Jackson Donelson, to live in the Executive Mansion with his wife Emily, who would serve as hostess. He also asked his daughter-in-law, Sarah, who was married to Andrew Jackson, Jr., his adopted son and heir, to oversee The Hermitage. Sarah and Emily were close friends, and after Emily died during Jackson's second term, Sarah broadened her duties to become mistress of the White House.

The Jacksons' residence in the White House began unpropitiously. On Inauguration Day, thousands of "Old Hickory's" supporters converged on Washington to meet their hero and enjoy the White House festivities. Daniel Webster wrote, "Persons have come five hundred miles to see General Jackson, and they really seem to think that the country has been rescued from some dreadful danger."[3] These were ordinary people, who traveled on foot, in wagons, by horse or mule; many women wore hickory nut necklaces in Jackson's honor. Unfortunately, the loyal admirers were not very well behaved and the Inauguration deteriorated into a mêlée. The ice cream, cake and punch soon disappeared. China was broken, fistfights and shoving occurred, people climbed on—and broke—fairly new tables and chairs to get a better view, and there were few security guards to maintain order. Margaret Bayard Smith, a contemporary author and chronicler of Washington society, described the crowd: "A rabble, a mob, of boys, negroes, women, children, scrabbling, fighting, romping, what a pity, what a pity!"

Some accounts say that over 20,000 people moved in and out of the White House that day.[4]

President Jackson was undeniably a "rough" soldier, but with Emily's help he made some luxurious and historic expenditures for the White House, including new decorations for the East Room, gilt chandeliers, bronzed and gilded tables, draperies of blue and yellow "moreen," a rich Brussels carpet and blue damask upholstery. He purchased new china, cutlery, and glassware—one French dinner and dessert set cost over $4,000; another blue and gold dessert service was decorated, to Jackson's orders, with the American eagle; and the crystal included decanters and an array of every known wine and champagne glass.[5]

In his two terms, Jackson spent over $50,000 refurbishing the White House, and, at the same time, removing *all traces* of the John Quincy Adams family. Jackson and his hostesses lavishly dispensed traditional southern hospitality—at many receptions there were a thousand guests. While Andrew Jackson preached the Spartan life, he lived a sumptuous one. At official dinners, the wines flowed into those beautiful crystal glasses; entrees included fish, duck, partridge, tongue, chicken, and delicacies the revered Rachel probably never tasted back in Tennessee.

Emily and "Jack" Donelson adored their uncle and were proud and happy (and undoubtedly, very comfortable) to serve as his host and hostess, but they did not approve of Andrew Jackson's sponsorship of Margaret "Peggy" O'Neale Timberlake Eaton, the wife of Secretary of War John Henry Eaton. Peggy and John Eaton were married after her first husband died at sea, purportedly committing suicide because of Eaton and Peggy's relationship. Although her husband was Secretary of War, congressional wives snubbed Peggy, and the only people who socialized with her were bachelors or the wives of Foreign Service ministers. Even Emily Donelson was temporarily banished to Tennessee because of her criticism, and during her absence, Peggy took Emily's place at the White House, heaping on more gossip that Jackson was her lover. Mrs. Smith, the society commentator, sniffed that Peggy was "one of the most...silly women you ever heard of," which Jackson countered by calling Peggy "The smartest little woman in America."[6]

The gossip became so heated, culminating with two ministers charging that Peggy had a miscarriage *before* her marriage to Eaton, that Jackson called a special cabinet meeting. He gathered testimonials from his cronies about Peggy's good reputation, and when a clergyman tried to present his case against Peggy, Jackson cut him off abruptly. Cartoonists picked up the story, and one depicted Jackson declaring "She is as chaste as any virgin."[7] (It doesn't take much psychological savvy to realize that Jackson's defense of Peggy was a reaction to the destructive slurs made about Rachel years earlier.) During the squabbling, Martin Van Buren, Jackson's Secretary of State, saw a chance for political opportunism and joined in Peggy's defense, in marked contrast to Vice President Calhoun. When the dust settled, the supportive Van Buren replaced Calhoun as Jackson's choice for Vice President during his second term. (And, Van Buren went on to become our eighth President).

For the rest of his years in office, Jackson's White House was filled with relatives, including his first grandchild, Rachel, who became the joy of his old age. As a gift for his last reception on Washington's Birthday, 1837, New York state dairymen sent Jackson a huge cheese, two feet thick, four feet in diameter and weighing over 1,400 pounds. The public had been invited to help itself to the cheese and they hacked off pieces, either eating it on the spot, or carrying away chunks. The smell of the cheese remained in the public rooms for weeks afterwards. Andrew Jackson left the White House as he had entered—a rough-hewn hero who allowed the people to share in his celebrations.

ANGELICA SINGLETON
VAN BUREN
(for Martin Van Buren)

Martin Van Buren, known as "The Little Magician," and "The American Tallyrand," had been a widower for many years when he was sworn in as the eighth President in 1837, after serving as Andrew Jackson's Vice President for four years.

Shortly after moving into the White House with his four sons, he faced a national crisis the luckier Jackson had avoided: The Panic of 1837. While grappling with economic disaster, he tried to set an example, despite his reputation as a gourmet and elegant man-about-town. His return to a "simpler life" in the mansion was also a good excuse to get rid of the *nouveaux riches* trappings the ebullient Jackson had accumulated.

Van Buren auctioned off some furniture for $6,000, repaired rugs and reupholstered furniture, cleaned and repainted the Mansion and replaced the opulent Jackson purchases with simpler accessories. Instead of Jackson's parties for 1,000, President Van Buren held small dinner parties, more in the style of Thomas Jefferson. Often the hostess was the celebrated (or infamous, depending on your point of view) Peggy Eaton, whom Van Buren had defended while she was under attack by Jackson critics. Although Peggy's presence renewed earlier criticism, Van Buren tried to mend political fences with Calhoun, Clay and other Jackson enemies.[1]

It was an uphill fight. Not only were his political moves challenged, but so was his White House lifestyle. Congressmen were annoyed by the infrequent invitations as a result of Van Buren's belt-tightening, and when they were invited, they were served neither a glass of wine nor punch, and sometimes, not even a piece of cake. In fact, Van Buren's decorous, refined White House was at the opposite pole from Andrew Jackson's "open" house, and ironically, the current President was criticized just as much for his austerity as his predecessor had been castigated for his excesses.

Martin Van Buren's four sons were equally well-mannered and refined to the point where one of them, John, was called "Prince John" by the President's political opponents. Moreover, all the polish and refinement and austerity did not make up for what veteran hostess Dolley Madison saw as the lack of the all-important "woman's touch." She set about to remedy that situation by arranging a match between the President's son, Abraham, and a pretty young relative of hers from South Carolina, Angelica Singleton. Angelica had a perfect oval face and classic features framed by black curly hair and set off by large black eyes. She had recently graduated from a fashionable Philadelphia boarding school (in those days called a "seminary") and was well trained to take over duties as a White House hostess.

It took Dolley a year to bring about the marriage, but by the New Year's Day reception of 1839, Angelica Singleton Van Buren was on hand to receive the President and his guests in the Oval Room, known then as the "Blue Elliptical Saloon."

Van Buren's White House, especially after Angelica began her "reign," was restrained, sophisticated and more "European" than his predecessor's but soon this improvement became political ammunition. William Henry Harrison, another war hero, was running against Van Buren for the election of 1840. Harrison portrayed himself as a humble Western farmer, perhaps playing on the public's wish for the return of a "common man" like Andrew Jackson to the White House. (Harrison's running mate was John Tyler, and their slogan became "Tippecanoe and Tyler, too".)

In the spring of 1840, a Harrison-Tyler supporter, Pennsylvania congressman, Charles Ogle, gave his famous "Gold Spoon Speech" before Congress. Ogle condemned Van Buren for his luxurious tastes, waved bills and vouchers to make his point (even though some of his "evidence" dated back to James Monroe's time). Van Buren wasn't at the session, but Ogle addressed him directly:

Your house glitters with all imaginable luxuries and gaudy ornaments...will they (the citizens of the United States) longer feel inclined to support their chief servant in a Palace as splendid as that of the Caesars, and as richly adorned as the proudest Asiatic mansion?[2]

Ogle left no dish or goblet unturned, as it were, while he touted the simple pleasures and democratic ways of the would-be President. "Harrison would scorn to charge the people of the United States with foreign cut wine coolers, liquor stands, and golden chains to hang golden labels around the necks of barrel-shaped flute decanters with cone stoppers." In Ogle's view, the continental fare served at the White House was atrocious. He, and it was assumed, Harrison, much preferred "fried meat and gravy, or hog and hominy." He even joked about Van Buren's tepid baths and his habit of spraying his whiskers with a French import, "Triple Distillé Savon Mons Sens."

It was the "Golden Spoon" versus the "Log Cabin." And although Log Cabin Harrison won the election, the always-gentlemanly "Little Magician" showed no rancor toward his successor and orchestrated a cordial change-of-office, not often repeated in subsequent Presidential elections.

HARRIET LANE
(for James Buchanan)

J ames Buchanan was 65 when he became the nation's fifteenth President, and the only President to enter and leave the White House as a bachelor. Aside from his political goals, he sought to change the rather melancholy air, which pervaded the White House during the terms of his three predecessors—Taylor, Fillmore and Pierce. Not only was he more worldly and more courtly than they, but he had a secret weapon: his niece and ward, Harriet Lane, a tall, charming blonde with violet eyes and a social background and experience any First Lady would envy.

After Harriet Lane was orphaned at the age of eleven, she chose to live with her mother's brother, James Buchanan. Her choice provided her with an excellent education and the opportunity to serve as her uncle's hostess, first at his "Wheatlands" estate in Pennsylvania, and then at the American Embassy, when Buchanan served as Ambassador to England. Reportedly, many years earlier, Buchanan had been engaged to a beautiful, wealthy young woman; they had a lover's quarrel, she died (or committed suicide) soon afterwards, and he never loved another woman. (When he became President, some shark-like Washington commentators called him "Betsey Buchanan" and implied that he was a homosexual.)[1]

When James Buchanan was inaugurated in 1857, Harriet Lane, although only 27, took over her role as hostess with grace and skill. She was quite able to match wits with her guests and was so adept at sparring and returning clever exchanges that a song called "Listen to the Mockingbird" was dedicated to her. Among the fashions she established during her reign were wide, lacy "Bertha" collars, lower necklines and fuller, but stiffer skirts.

At Harriet's suggestion, the White House was expanded to include a greenhouse to provide flowers for state occasions; and she supervised the purchase of $20,000 of new furniture to replace some old, worn-out pieces from James Monroe's term, forty years earlier.

Under her aegis, receptions were well-organized and very elegant. When Edward Albert, the Prince of Wales, who later became King Edward VII, visited Washington in 1860 (marking the first time a member of the English royalty had come to the United States) his stay was so pleasant and smooth-running that Queen Victoria sent letters of praise to James Buchanan and Harriet.

During the last years of Buchanan's administration there was a great deal of national unrest because of the slavery issue and threats of secession, but Harriet continued to run the White House tastefully and efficiently and enjoyed widespread popularity.

Unfortunately, her uncle was not as popular; Buchanan lost the 1860 election to Abraham Lincoln. At the last White House reception, in March 1861, five thousand people came to pay their respects while the Marine Band played "Dixie," before concluding with "Yankee Doodle." In 1866, five years after leaving the White House, Harriet married Elliott Johnson, but still spent much of her time at "Wheatlands," where her uncle died in 1868.

MARY ARTHUR MCELROY
(for Chester Alan Arthur)

Chester Alan Arthur was another widower who became President, the nation's twenty-first. His wife, Nell Herndon Arthur, died of pneumonia in 1880, just before Arthur was elected Vice President. After her death he left orders that her room should remain forever untouched.

A few months later, James Garfield was assassinated and Arthur found himself President of the United States and resident of the White House; he would have preferred to be someplace else, doing something else. He needed help, not only to care for his young daughter and son, but also help with social duties at the Mansion. His sister, Mary Arthur McElroy, agreed to leave Buffalo and stay in Washington during the season. Mary and her brother were patrician, sociable, and sophisticated. Chester Arthur, a tall, handsome, powerful-looking man with a full mustache and lavish sideburns, dressed elegantly and impeccably. He was the first President to have his own valet.[1]

Like several of his predecessors, Arthur had been an officer during the Civil War, with the major responsibility of supplying New York troops. Although he had never held public office, he was nominated as the Republican Vice President in 1880. None of his supporters—or he—ever thought he would become President. For almost three months before he took the oath of office in September 1881, his fate was in limbo while Garfield lingered between life and death. After inspecting the neglected White House, Arthur described it as "a badly kept barracks," and didn't move in until

December 7, 1881, when renovation, including two new bathrooms and an elevator, were completed. Not only did Arthur want to improve the appearance of the mansion, but he also wanted it to be more comfortable. He had twenty-four wagonloads of broken furniture, ripped curtains, cuspidors, moth-eaten carpeting, hair mattresses, children's chairs and assorted junk carted away.

Arthur also supervised the furnishing of new decorations, some provided by the famous Louis C. Tiffany, who wrote:

> *At that time we redecorated the Blue Room, the East Room, the Red Room, and the Hall between the Red and East Rooms, together with the glass screen...The Blue Room, or Robin's Egg Room—as it is sometimes called—was decorated in robin's egg blue for the main color, with ornaments in a handpressed paper, touched out in ivory, gradually deepening as the ceiling was approached.*[2]

Mary McElroy, of course, was scrutinized by the Washington social writers and judged favorably. One writer reported: "(Mrs. McElroy) made her home in Washington in the winter season, and dispensed the hospitalities of the White House with rare social tact, the place being one for which she was peculiarly fitted by her personal character and previous associations."

President Arthur loved music and most of his social events featured musical interludes. But as debonair and cultured as he was, he did not accord his obliging sister the same status as the bachelor President Buchanan had given his niece, Harriet. In fact, at the New Year's Day reception in 1884, the President entered the audience room with the House Speaker's wife (Mrs. Carlisle) on his arm. Mary McElroy was patient about such slights, and for the 1885 New Year's reception, when President Arthur asked her to act as hostess, she in turn, asked *sixty* other women to help her in what would be her brother's last public reception. One reporter describes the event:

> *Ms. McElroy, who stood at the President's right, and the ladies were not introduced, but stood in their places for the two hours in a line across the Blue Room between the two doors. The attendance must have numbered about 3,000, but the handshaking was done so expeditiously, and the people passed on by the ushers to the East Room so quickly that the number was easily disposed of before 11 o'clock had struck.*[3]

During the re-election campaign, the Stalwarts, who had been his strongest supporters (one of the Stalwarts had shot President Garfield), turned against him, and Chester A. Arthur lost the election. He left the White House rather ignominiously, with very few supporters, and died in New York City, just a year later, in 1886.

THE
SPOKESWOMEN

Jacqueline Bouvier Kennedy
1929-1994

Claudia Alta "Lady Bird" Johnson
1912-

Elizabeth Anne "Betty" Bloomer Ford
1918-

Barbara Pierce Bush
1925-

Laura Welch Bush
1946-

For two hundred years a number of First Ladies have had "causes" which they were willing to speak about and fight for, beginning with Abigail Adams and her admonishment to her husband to "Remember the ladies." Eleanor Roosevelt had many causes which she championed on her own...and a good many others she promoted to FDR via not so subtle hints.

But the idea that each First Lady should have a major interest, some voluntary effort for which she was willing to donate hundreds of hours for the good of her country really became 'fashionable" in 1960, when President John Fitzgerald Kennedy became President. When Americans were told "ask not what your country can do for you, but what you can do for your country" there was an enthusiastic response to the Peace Corps and a new pride in being an American.

In that spirit, Jacqueline Kennedy pledged to restore the White House as a "museum of our country's heritage" and searched the storerooms and records of the Mansion for old furniture, authentic wallpaper, paint colors and china patterns to recapture the historical décor and atmosphere of the White House. Every First Lady since then has had a "cause."

Lady Bird Johnson's was to restore beauty to the nation's countryside and highways, and she worked diligently to remove scene-spoiling billboards and plant attractive wildflowers. Pat Nixon was concerned about volunteerism and poor and sick children. Betty Ford talked about drugs and mastectomies, while

Rosalynn Carter espoused rebuilding neighborhoods so that disadvantaged people would have better housing. Nancy Reagan was first interested in a "Foster Grandparents Program," and during her husband's second term, spearheaded the drive against drugs with the slogan, "Just say NO!" Hillary Clinton initially poured her efforts into developing a health care program that would protect every American; when that plan failed to make it through Congress, she fought for better health programs and the rights of women and children on a world-wide basis. Both Barbara Bush and her daughter-in-law, our current First Lady, Laura Bush, continued their lifelong battles against illiteracy from their White House soapboxes.

Unquestionably, the media coverage of First Lady projects has a pervasive and positive influence on the public. Betty Ford's openness about her drug and alcohol dependencies has undoubtedly inspired countless women to seek help. Equally significant, her candid comments about her mastectomy (and Nancy Reagan's statements about her surgery and treatment for breast cancer) encouraged thousands of women to get breast examinations, thereby indirectly saving thousands of lives.

In the next chapters, we'll examine the work of Jacqueline Kennedy, Lady Bird Johnson, Betty Ford and Barbara and Laura Bush. Other First Ladies, who were active as spokeswomen played even stronger roles as their husbands' Eyes, Ears and Voices, and will be profiled in Part VII.

JACQUELINE
BOUVIER KENNEDY

When Jacqueline Bouvier graduated from the exclusive Miss Porter's school, her yearbook message was "Not to be a housewife." And she never was. The beautiful, wide-eyed brunette married the handsome young senator, John Fitzgerald Kennedy, at a lavish wedding in Newport in 1953, and seven years later, at the age of 31, moved into the White House as the thirty-fifth President's First Lady.

Millions of Americans considered her a princess or a queen; all over the world the press regaled Jacqueline Kennedy. Even the Soviet media called her "beautiful," and a Polish magazine, *Swiat*, said she gave the West new "tone and style." During 1961 and 1962, her fan mail averaged 8,000 letters a week, handled by a staff of thirteen. Not all the attention was favorable. She was criticized for what she wore, what she spent on clothes and how she acted as First Lady. Reporters became "Jackie-watchers;" one writer estimated that she had worn 400 different outfits in 1962 alone.

The "Jackie-look" was copied by women of all ages: pillbox hat, bouffant hairdos, sleeveless, two-piece sheaths, simple ball gowns in luxurious fabrics. Poet Laureate Robert Frost, hardly a devotée of fashion, and known more for his interest in New England landscapes than Washington social life, observed "There have been some great wives in the White House—like Abigail Adams and Dolley Madison—so great that you can't think of their husbands, Presidents, without thinking of *them*. It looks as though we are having another one now."

Regarding her new position, Jacqueline said, "It's frightening to lose your anonymity," a fact she realized soon after the birth of John, Jr., when she was still in the hospital recuperating from a cesarean, and a stranger said, "You're Mrs. Kennedy, aren't you? I recognize you from your pictures." And Jackie responded, "I know. That's my problem now."[1]

There were many "firsts" or precedents set by the young Presidential couple. At 43, JFK was the youngest President to be elected (Theodore Roosevelt became President at 42 after McKinley was assassinated), and the first Catholic President. He held the first "live" television news conferences, and his doctor, Janet G Travell, was the first woman named as White House physician. In her own right, Jacqueline Kennedy was the youngest First Lady since Frances Folsom Cleveland.

As a family, the Kennedys generated nationwide interest in spite of Jacqueline's efforts to shield three-year-old Caroline and baby John from public glare. Even Caroline's pony, Macaroni, and other pets were known to Americans of all ages and political backgrounds. Although much of the publicity about Jackie focused on such superficial subjects as her wardrobe and her glamorous lifestyle, she later won the country's respect for her courage and dignity when JFK was assassinated.

Jacqueline Bouvier was born on July 28, 1929, and grew up in New York City, Southampton and Newport, Rhode Island. She was named 1948 Debutante of the Year, went to Vassar for two years, studied at the Sorbonne, and then landed a $42.50 a week job as an inquiring photographer for the *Washington Times-Herald*. One assignment was to interview freshmen congressman Richard M. Nixon and his colleague Jack Kennedy. About their courtship she once said, "He was not the candy-and-flowers type, so every now and then he'd give me a book."

After he was elected President, JFK was demonstrably proud of his wife and liked the celebrity attention she generated on their trips together. During a visit to France he commented that he was "the man who accompanied Jackie Kennedy to Paris."

According to Chief Usher J. B. West, the White House management changed from a very regimented household to one that was impromptu and informal. "I would find myself dealing with Empire tables and rabbit cages; housing Maharajahs and ponies; streaming down the Potomac and wearing disguises; and thoroughly enjoying the most creative and challenging work to which the Chief Usher had ever been put."[2]

Soon after the inauguration, Jacqueline Kennedy announced that her major project as First Lady would be to restore the White House as a "museum of our country's heritage." Her project became a whirlwind effort that took on the same sense of urgency as the President's New Frontier programs. One cabinet member described the deadline for action on JFK's priorities as "the day before yesterday," and the description was equally appropriate for Jacqueline Kennedy's restoration goals. But first, she initiated more immediate changes to make her own family more comfortable, including a playroom for the children, and a daily play school for Caroline and other toddlers.

The Kennedy style of entertaining was different, too. Like Thomas Jefferson, the Kennedys had a French chef for state (*and* family) dinners. Jackie often eliminated receiving lines, preferring more informal ways of greeting her guests, and she reduced the number of formal courses served at official dinners from six, with 21 items, to four, with eight items. The young First Lady substituted fifteen round tables, each seating ten guests for the stiff E-shaped banquet table. (Additional guests were served in the Blue Room).

After dinner entertainment in the Kennedy White House was more sophisticated than it had been in decades. Some of the guests included violinist Isaac Stern and cellist Pablo Casals. (At Casals' performance, one guest, Alice Roosevelt Longworth remembered that Casals had played at the White House when her father was President in 1904.) There would be ballet, chamber music, opera, even Shakespearean drama, all arranged by Jackie's efficient social secretary, Letitia (Tish) Baldridge, an authority on protocol and etiquette, who has since written several books on such subjects. One particularly successful reception was held on April 29, 1962, when 49 Nobel Prize winners were White House guests. Other visitors that evening included John Glenn, the first American to orbit the earth, and the writers Pearl Buck, Robert Frost, Katherine Anne Porter, and Van Wyck Brooks. After dinner, actor Frederic March read from the works of three deceased Nobel Prize medallists—General George C. Marshall, Sinclair Lewis, and Ernest Hemingway.

Although she could have rested on her laurels as a chic and sophisticated hostess, Jackie moved full speed ahead on her restoration program. Several predecessors had also dreamed of refurbishing the White House with authentic furniture (as did several successors, including Pat Nixon). Grace Coolidge had been able to garner only a few pieces in her appeal for donations and Lou Hoover had concentrated on restoring many of the Monroe furnishings. After the Truman re-construction, the Executive Mansion was structurally sound, but hardly museum-like in décor, and Mamie Eisenhower's subsequent redecorating was pedestrian, lacking even good copies of the real thing.

The $50,000 appropriated by Congress was used on refurbishing the family rooms and replacing some accessories in the public rooms. Although Jacqueline made the final choices for new furnishings, fabrics and accessories, President Kennedy was interested in any of her decisions and wanted the house to mirror issues and people who concerned his administration. One of her purchases, for example, was new crystal made in West Virginia, where Appalachian poverty was miserably apparent. The crystal purchase was therefore not only a salute to American craftsmanship, but it was also a symbol of the President's awareness of West Virginia's economic hardships.

Jackie hoped to find many treasures in the vast White House warehouse, but generally, the furniture there was broken or no longer usable. (She did find parts of the china services used by Lincoln, Polk, and Harrison, as well as a fine Monroe pier table.) She would walk around the mansion with a yellow legal pad, making notes on possible furnishings, colors, fabrics, and then return to her own antique desk (an ornate French Empire piece which had belonged to her father, John Vernou Bouvier III) to write memos, ideas, instructions.

On her note-taking inspections, usually dressed in pants and comfortable shoes, she would banish "horrors," especially Victorian mirrors, and laughingly tell Mr. West,

> *They're hideous. Off to the dungeons with them...She had a total mastery of detail—endless, endless detail—and she was highly organized, yet rarely held herself to a schedule...We all had fun along with her. Yet she also drew a line against familiarity which could not be crossed.*[3]

When it was clear the warehouse would yield few authentic pieces, the First Lady found another way to refurnish the official rooms with antiques. She formed a Fine Arts Committee to collect furnishings of "museum quality." At the first meeting of the 14-member group, she announced "My main project here will be to make this a truly historic house." Through the committee, chaired by Henry Francis du Pont, an expert on American furnishings, and including such members as Mrs. Henry Ford II, Mrs. Albert Lasker, Mrs. Paul Mellon, John L. Loeb and John Walker, not only were period pieces collected, but the funds to purchase expensive antiques were donated. Stephane Boudin, of a distinguished Paris firm was named decorator.

Jackie also decided to publish a White House guide book, to provide additional renovation funds. She rejected suggestions by the *National Geographic* because she wanted photographs of rooms and articles, *not* people, so that the guidebook could last from one administration to the next with minimum changes. Throughout the project, she checked every photograph and word of copy. Her editorial efforts (later demonstrated in her subsequent publishing career) were very successful. Ultimately, sales of the book paid for many of the White House restorations. By January 1962, the renovations were almost complete and she celebrated the results over a daiquiri with M. Boudin and Mr. West, and announced: "I'm going to be a television star."

On February 14, 1962, the normally publicity-shy Jacqueline, escorted by CBS correspondent Charles Collingwood, took a nationwide television audience on a tour of the refurbished White House. The *New York Times* reviewer wrote, "Her effortless familiarity with dates and names attested to homework done for the occasion." Not only did 46 million Americans have a close glimpse of the historic "facelift," but CBS also donated $10,000 to the Committee for ongoing restorations. Mr. West recalled that JFK was so pleased with his wife's performance, he said, "It's terrific. Terrific. Can we show it in 1964?"[4]

In 1963, Jacqueline became pregnant, and when she left for Hyannis in May, she gave West instructions for converting the children's dining room into a nursery for the new baby. On August 7, Patrick Bouvier Kennedy was born prematurely and died two days later. It was Mr. West's sad job to dismantle the nursery, as if it had never existed.

A few months later, Jacqueline, the Kennedy family, and the nation experienced the tragedy an entire generation still remembers with horror and grief. Hours after President Kennedy was assassinated in Dallas on November 22, 1963, family friend Bill Walton called the Chief Usher to say that the First Lady wanted the White House exactly as it had been for Lincoln's funeral. The Lincoln catafalque was found; once again, the East Room chandeliers and windows were covered with black fabric. At 4:30 in the morning, a devastated family group, led by Jacqueline, still wearing the blood-stained pink skirt, escorted the President's body to the East room, where the coffin was placed on the historic Lincoln bier.

There were two things Jackie Kennedy wanted done at the White House in her husband's memory. The first was to have a simple plaque placed on the mantle in her bedroom, inscribed "In this room lived John Fitzgerald Kennedy with his wife Jacqueline, during the two years ten months and two days he was President of the United States." (The plaque was removed by the Nixons.) She also presented a painting by the Impressionist Claude Monet, "*Matinée sur la Seine, beau temps*," with a plaque which read "In loving memory of John Fitzgerald Kennedy, 35th President of the United States, from his family."

As a First Lady, Jacqueline had her own set of rules: she did not attend official lunches; she did not pour tea or appear at events and ceremonies which previous First Ladies felt obliged to participate in. Although she was never enthusiastic about such appearances, the reason she declined was to spend time with her children. She was backed in her refusals by JFK, who told Marianne Means, "Any First Lady will do all right if she is herself…each First Lady (must) do what best fits her temperament and personal inclinations.[5] (This opinion contrasted strongly with Cleveland's advise to his wife that she would get along as First Lady if she did *not* try anything new). In an ironic interview shortly before Dallas, Jackie explained she didn't accompany the President on trips because "the official side of my life takes me away from my children a great deal. If I were to add political duties, I would have practically no time with my children, and they are my first responsibility. My husband agrees with this. If he felt I should go on these trips, I would."[6] Jacqueline Kennedy made an exception to accompany her husband to Dallas.

After the assassination, she moved to New York City, where she felt she and her children would enjoy more privacy—a dream that eluded her for the rest of her own life. Her 1968 marriage to Aristotle Onassis, one of the world's wealthiest men, put her back in the headlines again—especially for her seemingly endless purchases of clothes and jewelry. When Onassis, who was 23 years her senior, died in 1975, Jackie began a new career as an editor for Doubleday. During those years she was frequently spotted in less than high fashion attire—often wearing pants, a trench coat and a kerchief, hailing a cab on the way to work, or walking in Central Park. Early in 1994 she was diagnosed with non-Hodgkin's lymphoma, a cancer of the lymphatic system. At that time she told a friend she was optimistic and hoped to live 20 more years. "But even if I have only five years, so what, I've had a great run."[7] She died in May 1994 and was buried beside President Kennedy at Arlington National Cemetery.

At her funeral her son John (who was to die in a tragic plane accident just five years later) described three of his mother's attributes: "love of words, the bonds of home and family, and her spirit of adventure."

Ironically, today she is remembered most of all for her sense of fashion and good taste. Oleg Cassini, who was the principal designer of her wardrobe while she was First Lady, talked about his relationship with Jackie in his autobiography, *In My Own Fashion*.

Jackie had a great wit combined with an intellectual intensity. She would listen carefully to what you were saying...(Although) she demanded excellence...she had the ability to make everyone around her feel part of a small privileged circle...Jackie was famous for her elusiveness, her shifting moods...She perplexed the Kennedys; she seemed quite a challenge to me. Some people who handle themselves well age so slowly that it's almost impossible to discern a difference. She had such innate class that the transition from her private life to the White House was imperceptible...She certainly belongs to the pantheon of the goddesses.[8]

A few days after John, Jr. was born in 1960, Cassini arrived at Georgetown Hospital with sketches and swatches. Jackie especially praised his suggestion for the Inaugural Ceremonies. Her costume that day—a fawn wool coat with a sable collar and matching muff, and high-heeled black boots to ward off the cold Washington weather—impressed people all over the world, men and women alike, especially since most of the other women attending the ceremony wore luxurious fur coats. That simple, elegant ensemble and the ivory satin gown she wore for the Inaugural Gala, as well as some 80 other dresses and ballgowns and coats and accessories—yes—even the famous pillbox hats, were the focus of the Costume Institute of New York City's Metropolitan Museum of Art's major exhibit for 2001. Even after her death, millions of women (and men, too) were fascinated by what she wore.

Time, in its coverage of the exhibit, reported that when she was 20 Jackie wrote that her goal in life was to be "a sort of Overall Art Director of the Twentieth Century."

Yet her attention to her wardrobe doesn't jibe with her life-long insistence that she had "no desire to influence fashions—that is at the bottom of any list."[9] Whether she wanted this label as the "First Lady of Fashion," or not...it stuck.

Family and friends prefer to remember her in a different light. The noted artist Bill Walton, a close family friend, described her more simply as "A strong dame."

CLAUDIA ALTA "LADY BIRD" TAYLOR JOHNSON

Lyndon Johnson, like the earlier President Johnson, Andrew, our seventeenth President, did not enter the White House triumphantly, as winner of an election, but tragically as a result of assassination. John F. Kennedy's death left the nation shocked and horrified; in addition, while the "King of Camelot" and his family had been widely known and had captivated the nation's hearts, LBJ, his wife and two daughters, were strangers to most Americans, even though he had been in politics for thirty years.

Lyndon Johnson gave his first Presidential address at Andrews Air Force Base on November 22, 1963, after the mournful return from Dallas. "This is a sad time for all people. We have suffered a loss that cannot be weighed. For me it is a deep personal tragedy. I know the world shares the sorrow that Mrs. Kennedy and her family bear. I will do my best. That is all I can do. I ask for your help—and God's."

And he could rely on his wife's help. Lady Bird had always acted as her husband's partner, in the same way as Eleanor Roosevelt had in the past, a pattern most First Ladies would admit to in the future. Christened Claudia Alta Taylor, but always called "Lady Bird," the shy, intelligent daughter of a wealthy Texas businessman met LBJ in 1934. He proposed on their first date, and they married two years later. Lady Bird managed the home life and business affairs, while LBJ concentrated on politics. A graduate of the University of Texas, with a double degree in liberal arts and journalism, Lady Bird was and is a shrewd woman who used her inheritance and business acumen to build the communications empire that provided most of their money.

The Johnsons had been married twenty-nine years by the time LBJ became the nation's thirty-sixth President. During those years, Lady Bird raised two daughters, managed houses in Washington and Houston, as well as their huge Texas ranch, ran the family business enterprises, and seemingly inexhaustible, made frequent and arduous campaign appearances on her husband's behalf. (During her first year in the White House she traveled to 35 states, giving speeches for LBJ). When they moved into the Executive Mansion, Lady Bird had the backbone and the background to be an effective, efficient First Lady, despite the tragic circumstances that brought her there. Chief Usher West says she ran the White House "rather like the chairman of the board of a large corporation," with her two generals, Bess Abell (Social Secretary) and Liz Carpenter (Press Secretary) serving as the corporation managers. (Lady Bird was the first First Lady to have a press secretary.[1]

Lady Bird made sure little things, as well as major projects, got done. One of the first not-so-little things was to change the shower head in LBJ's bathroom—no simple matter as it turned out. Plumbers and engineers tried more than half a dozen times to get the pressure high enough. (Ironically, this elaborate shower, with six nozzles at different heights, was one of the first things eliminated when Richard Nixon inherited the bathroom a few years later.) While thousands of dollars were spent on Johnson's shower, the President was obsessed with reducing lighting costs, perhaps an indication of a penny-wise/pound-foolish attitude. The outdoor lights Mrs. Eisenhower had been so proud of were extinguished early in the evening, and President Johnson would go from room to room in the mansion, turning off the lights. He scolded servants as well as family members who left a room without turning off the lights as they exited.

As methodical as he was about reducing lighting costs, the workaholic LBJ was erratic about eating habits, which, in addition to possible health problems, concerned his wife because sometimes the staff was kept waiting until after midnight to serve his dinner. Finally, a split shift was organized so that the proud staff could serve dinner at *any* time the President was ready to eat.

Lady Bird was very patient with her husband, but sometimes his spontaneity and irregular schedules could be exasperating. He thought nothing of inviting guests to dinner or lunch or breakfast on the spur of the moment. On December 23, 1963, just as the official mourning period for President Kennedy was about to end, he invited the *entire* Congress *and* their wives to the White House *that very same day*. Although the White House staff had always been flexible, this time they were a bit overwhelmed. They had only a few hours to make the Mansion ready for this huge party and prepare enough food to serve hundreds of guests. Maids, ushers, butlers, housemen—anyone who could help—were recruited to make thousands of finger sandwiches; other staff members drove around Washington to buy dozens and dozens of cookies; the mourning crepe was removed; a Christmas tree was found and decorated. The White House staff successfully pulled off this impromptu party attended by over a thousand people and superintended by the unflappable Lady Bird.

One of the new First Lady's initial official projects was to finish what Jacqueline Kennedy had started. She wanted the work of the Fine Arts Committee to continue and persuaded LBJ to sign an Executive Order allowing for a permanent curator of the White House (replacing the Smithsonian volunteer), and establishing a Committee for the Preservation of the White House.

Mrs. Johnson organized the same type of receptions at the White House as Jackie Kennedy had, with one difference: LBJ loved to dance—with his wife, his daughters, pretty guests. Since protocol demands that no guest leave before the President and his wife, many guests at State dinners stayed on long past their preferred departure time as the President continued to dance the night away. The Johnsons were also openly friendly, always exhibiting Texas-style hospitality. LBJ would tell jokes and engineer pranks, and even at one point, showed reporters his scars from a recent operation and allowed them to be photographed.

The Johnson girls, Lynda Bird and Lucy Baines, were active teenagers who lobbied for a special recreation room where they could play records, dance, and get away from the observing, dutiful eyes of their Secret Service escorts. Lyndon Johnson was a very outspoken man and sometimes outraged even his wife and daughters by his comments. Once he said, "I will never have to worry about either girl. Lynda Bird is so smart that she will always be able to make a living for herself. And Lucy Baines is so appealing and feminine that there will always be some man around wanting to make a living for her."[2]

In 1964, LBJ ran for election on his own. His goal was to build a "Great Society" by improving education as a way of wiping out poverty, and providing health programs for all Americans. He said: "Not how much, but how good; not only how to create wealth but how to use it...It (The Great Society) proposes as the first test for a nation, the quality of its people."

Lady Bird had a goal of her own, in addition to speaking out on behalf of her husband's aims during the election campaign. She planned to restore and protect the charm of America's towns and the countryside, to create an environment of "beauty, joyousness, and liveliness as well as dignity."[3] In the next four years she gained attention from conservationists and the public. She scheduled numerous trips to plant trees and flowers, spoke out against the defacing of the nation's highways with ugly billboards, became an effective speaker for maintaining ecological balances, launched new parks, and recorded a guide for White House tourists documenting the trees, flowers and special plants on the Mansion's grounds.

In 1964, Lady Bird Johnson became the first President's wife to embark on a whistle-stop tour of her own, traveling 1,700 miles to southern cities from Virginia to Louisiana. Her caravan—ten red, white and blue railroad cars called "The Lady Bird Special"—made 180 stops. She also acted as her husband's spokeswoman for programs of the Great Society, including visits to Head Start classes and job centers, and, with her daughters, flew to dozens of cities, while LBJ covered 50,000 miles, to tell the nation about his dreams for his war-on-poverty and the Great Society.

On November 3, 1964, Lyndon Johnson won a landslide victory (with the greatest popular vote in history until that time) over Arizona's conservative senator Barry Goldwater. In typical Texas fashion, Johnson invited anyone close enough to hear him to a grand Texas barbecue at the Lyndon Johnson ranch.

Lady Bird Johnson's duties as First Lady were not all "business as usual," however. On December 9, 1967, Lynda became the first President's daughter in 53 years to be married in the White House. But her marriage to Color Guard Captain, Charles Robb (who later became a U.S. Senator), was much more complicated than those of her predecessors. The confusion came with the expanded press corps, and most of all, television. Although she initially resisted TV coverage, finally, the mother-of-the-bride permitted the networks to shoot for twenty minutes during the procession and the beginning of the reception, and then gave them exactly five minutes to clear all equipment from the rooms.

Aside from his national goals, hanging over Lyndon Johnson's head after his election was the increasingly unpopular Vietnam War. In 1968, with the Great Society stalemated and almost forgotten by bitter opposition to the war, LBJ decided not to run for re-election. He felt his divisive presence in the race would only create additional national unrest and hamper him in bringing the Vietnam crisis to a conclusion.

In 1969, when Richard Nixon succeeded him as President, the war was still not over, and LBJ retired to his ranch in Texas, disheartened and in ill health, where he died of a heart attack in 1973. In the thirty-plus years since she left the White House, Lady Bird Johnson has continued her efforts toward beautifying the countryside and protecting the environment. In 1988, on her 75th birthday, she received a Congressional Gold Medal for her work with the National Wildflower Research Center in Austin, Texas, which she founded in 1982. The always gracious Lady Bird was typically modest about accepting kudos for what LBJ used to call "Lady Bird's Weeds."

ELIZABETH ANNE "BETTY"
BLOOMER FORD

Congressman Gerald R. Ford promised his wife, Betty, he would leave politics for good by the time his term ended in 1974. He was not able to keep that particular promise, because in 1973, he became Vice President, and then in August, 1974, when Richard M. Nixon resigned, he became the thirty-eighth President of the United States. Once again, the presidency was determined as a result of tragic circumstances.

In this case one might say that Ford was very lucky. But for Betty Ford the new responsibilities often outweighed the glory of being First Lady, and as time would tell, led to a very serious emotional and physical breakdown.

Betty Bloomer was born in Chicago and grew up in Grand Rapids, Michigan, as did Jerry Ford; she was pretty, pert, smart and graceful. After studying dance at Bennington College, she joined the famous Martha Graham group in New York, supporting herself as a model for John Robert Powers, at that time one of the top New York fashion agencies. Unfortunately, after a few years, the dancing career hadn't materialized and Betty returned home to Grand Rapids, where she ultimately embarked on a successful career as fashion coordinator for a department store. She had also been briefly and unhappily married to a traveling salesman, an experience, she said, "I could just as well have skipped."[1]

Shortly after her divorce became final, old acquaintance Jerry Ford reappeared, after having some unsuccessful romantic liaisons of his own. Ford, too, had done some modeling to help pay expenses at Yale Law School, and he had dated several models (one for four-and-a-half years). But in 1947, following his discharge from the Navy at age 34, he returned to Grand Rapids to begin his legal career. After dating for about a year, he proposed and Betty accepted; they were married in October 1948, just before he was elected to Congress. (Jerry Ford was re-elected twelve times in a row, and in 1965, became the minority leader of the House of Representatives).

In Washington in the years that followed, Betty was busy raising three boys and a girl and managing her household almost as if she were a single parent. Ford often accepted as many as 200 speaking engagements a year, which meant he didn't have time to mow the lawn or put up screens, much less pay attention to his children or wife. Betty once said, "I wish I had married a plumber. At least he'd be home by 5 o'clock."[2] The strain began to show, and Betty developed a pinched nerve. Her doctor prescribed tranquilizers to ease the pain, and she was advised to "gear down" from all her chauffeuring, cooking, cleaning, mothering, and wifing. Ford, after some psychiatric counseling sessions dealing with Betty's problems, agreed to quit political office after 1974.

In 1973, Nixon's Vice President, Spiro Agnew, resigned in the wake of financial scandals, and Ford, who had always supported Nixon, was named Agnew's replacement. After two months of hearings, his nomination as Vice President was confirmed, but by then the disastrous Watergate affair had undermined Nixon's presidency. Faced with imminent impeachment, he resigned in August 1974. Ford succeeded him and less than a month later, the new President Ford pardoned the ex-President Nixon. He said then, and has repeated through the years, "The only way to clear the desk in the Oval Office was to get Mr. Nixon's problems off my agenda and get my total attention on the problems of the country."

Betty, as First Lady, was soon charming the country with her candor and inspiring sympathy for her problems. In the fall of 1974, she had a mastectomy, and went public to tell Americans about it, imploring women to have their breasts checked regularly, and undoubtedly saving thousands of lives. She also talked openly about problems with her children, and discussed telling teenagers about birth control and premarital sex. Women of all ages and backgrounds identified with and related to her, in the same way they had found a kindred spirit in Mamie Eisenhower.

Despite his arduous campaigning efforts in 1976, Ford did not win. With a nation eager for a change from Republican scandals, he lost the election to Democrat Jimmy Carter. Some political observers and historians believe his pardon of Nixon cost him the election to the presidency in his own right. (In fact, he had uniquely attained this highest office in the nation without having been elected either Vice President or President.)

In retirement, Jerry Ford was in demand as a Republican speaker, and Betty came forward with her usual candid admissions, showing and telling the world about her face lift, and then, much more seriously, admitting that she had abused drugs and alcohol. Suddenly, the two or three martinis the Fords used to enjoy together were no longer a pleasant prelude to dinner, but in Betty's case, had become part of a dangerous addiction. Betty Ford went through a rigorous detoxification program, and could have gone on to a carefree retirement, enjoying her rich family life with her husband, children, and grandchildren. Instead, she turned her bad experience into a good one by establishing the Betty Ford Center for substance abuse at the Eisenhower Medical Center in Rancho Mirage. In the decades since then her hands-on efforts and supervision of the program have helped thousands of drug and alcohol abusers overcome their problems and begin new lives.

Although her tenure as First Lady was among the briefest, she has always remained one of America's favorite White House ladies. She shared her experiences with her thousands of fans in two best-selling books, *The Times of My Life* and *A Glad Awakening*.

In 2001, the very action that may have cost Gerald Ford the 1976 election—his pardon of Richard Nixon—earned the former President the John F. Kennedy Profile in Courage Award. Jerry Ford's graceful acceptance speech was widely reported: "President Kennedy understood that courage is not something to be gauged in a poll or located in a focus group. No adviser can spin it. No historian can backdate it. For, in the age-old contest between popularity and principle, only those willing to lose for their convictions are deserving of posterity's approval."

BARBARA PIERCE BUSH

arbara Bush, wife of the first President Bush, is very much like
Bess Truman in her assessment of the role. She was—and still
is—totally family oriented, worries about her husband's health
and well-being, and during her time as First Lady, had little interest
in the high-fashion position of her predecessor, Nancy Reagan.
However, as First Lady, she was a bit of an enigma: well-traveled,
but definitely a homebody; well-educated, but not a sophisticated
snob; politically oriented, but not, ostensibly, a woman who tried to
influence her husband's decisions during his term. Barbara Bush
maintained a unique but difficult position of juggling private life
with public presence, even with more exposure than any other
"private" First Lady had before her.

Barbara Bush is one of those Presidents' wives who actually look
forward to residency in the White House and worked vigorously to
help her husband get there...even though their stay in the Executive
Mansion meant one more delay in establishing a permanent home.
By the time George Herbert Walker Bush became the forty-first
President, he and Barbara had been married forty-three years and
had lived in twenty-nine houses in seventeen different cities from
Houston to Beijing. She told *People* their summer home in
Kennebunkport, Maine (built in 1903 by George's maternal
grandfather) "has come to mean roots. When I'm in my garden
there planting peonies that will last a hundred years, I'm doing that
for my children and grandchildren."[1]

As a young woman, Barbara thought her roots would be planted somewhere in the affluent suburban area where she grew up in Rye, New York (Bush's hometown was nearby Greenwich, Connecticut). One of four children of Marvin Pierce, publisher of *McCall's* magazine and Pauline Pierce, daughter of an Ohio Supreme Court justice, she had a privileged, upper-class childhood and went to boarding school at Ashley Hall in Charleston, South Carolina. At a Christmas dance in Greenwich in 1942, she met seventeen-year-old George, home on vacation from Andover, and she knew immediately, and has told the story many times, that she wanted to marry him. They became engaged a year later, just before George went off to fight in World War II as a Navy pilot. In January 1945, several months after his torpedo bomber "Barbara" was shot down, Barbara dropped out of Smith and they were married, George in his uniform, she in a white satin gown.

After the war their first move was to New Haven, where George was a star student and star baseball player at Yale. They next moved, in 1948, to Odessa, Texas with their two-year-old son, Georgie. In Texas, George worked hard building a successful oil company and Barbara worked hard nurturing the Bush family, which eventually included six children, four boys and two girls. When the first daughter, Robin, died of leukemia in 1953, just short of her fourth birthday, Barbara says, "I nearly fell apart. I couldn't put my right foot in front of my left, but George didn't let me retreat (and) I realized you either pull together or you shatter."[2] Following her daughter's death, thirty-five-year-old Barbara's hair turned white overnight. Our current President recalls that after Robin died, he sensed his mother's loneliness and often wanted to keep her company, but she would shoo him outside so he could play baseball with his buddies.

In 1959 the Bush family moved to Houston where George made his first political bid, an unsuccessful race for the Senate. They then re-located to Washington when George won a seat in Congress in 1966 and Barbara won her reputation as Super Mom, not unlike that of Betty Ford, teaching Sunday school, running car-pools, serving as Scout mother, supervising the kids' homework. In her view, she has attended "more Little League games than any living human" and her second son, Jeb, (full name, John Ellis Bush), who is currently Governor of Florida, says his father was the chief executive officer of the family, but mother was the chief operating officer. "We all reported to her. She did a good job of keeping the family intact."[3]

Her job was not made easier when George was named Ambassador to the United Nations in 1971 and the family moved to New York City. Two years later she shifted gears once again and resettled the family in Washington when her husband became Republican National Chairman. The most drastic move, however, occurred the following year when Bush was named the United States Ambassador to China, based in Beijing. By then, the children were almost grown-up, so they stayed in the States and Barbara, for the first time in almost twenty years, had George all to herself. She has always said she loved her time in China. That idyll ended within a year when President Ford named Bush Director of the Central Intelligence Agency, and they returned to Washington.

In 1980, George Herbert Walker Bush made his first run for the Republican Presidential nomination. Ronald Reagan got the nod instead and named George as his running mate; the Reagan-Bush ticket won the elections of 1980 and 1984. As the Vice President's wife for eight years, Barbara rivaled Pat Nixon in travel and hostessing records, excellent training for her role as First Lady.

When George ran for President in 1988, some of his "handlers" thought Barbara should change her image, become more svelte, more chic, more patterned after some of her predecessors. She told chief advisor Roger Ailes, "I'll do anything you want, but I won't dye my hair, change my wardrobe or lose weight."[4] Her white hair became her trademark and she often cut and blow-dried it herself, even with all the resources available to her as mistress of the Executive Mansion. She became known for her "Barbara Blue" dresses by designer Scassi and her faux pearl choker from jeweler Kenneth J. Lane.

Barbara Bush has always been proud of her athletic skills and during her White House years frequently played tennis with such high-profile doubles partners or singles opponents as Supreme Court Justice Sandra Day O'Connor, "the same girls I've been playing with for sixteen years," as she told *Life*.[5] When she played, she played to win. Her sister-in-law, Nancy Bush Ellis, said, "If you irritated or double-crossed her, she'd let you know." Mrs. Ellis also reported that Barbara could mimic anybody—her children, her siblings, her husband, even Gorbachev—and does."[6]

As First Lady, Barbara Bush usually had more important things on her mind. During her time in the White House (as well as the years afterward), she continued to fight against illiteracy, an interest she developed more than two decades earlier when Neil, her third son, was diagnosed as dyslexic. During her eight years as the Vice President's wife, she attended over 500 fund-raising receptions on behalf of literacy, and wrote an amusing book, *C. Fred's Story*, as "written" by her late cocker spaniel, with all royalties channeled to literacy groups. Barbara has often said that illiteracy is the most important issue we have. "If we can get people to read, we can get them out of jails and shelters and off the streets and get them back to work."[7] Other charitable concerns included research on leukemia, improving education, and boostering volunteerism, a reflection of George Bush's campaign goal of a "thousand points of light."

The White House under the Bush administration was very different from that of the Reagan years. The ten grandchildren (at that time) visited frequently and their toys and "big wheels" were often seen on the grounds. Entertaining was not as formal as during the Reagan administration, but when key receptions were held, the pattern followed Nancy Reagan's. Barbara has said several times that her predecessor made the job of First Lady easy: all you had to do was say "ditto" to the way Nancy did it.

All First Ladies will always be compared to one or more of their predecessors...and retroactively to their successors. But there is only one precedent that two First Ladies have shared: the dual role of *wife* of the President...and *mother* of the President, a woman who married one President and changed another one's diapers. Abigail Adams, wife of John Adams, our second President, was the mother of John Quincy Adams, the sixth to hold the office. But Abigail died in 1818, seven years before her son was elected in 1825. One hundred and seventy-five years later, Barbara Bush danced at *her* son's inauguration as the forty-third President of the United States. Aside from her ongoing status as Americans' favorite "modern" First Lady, repeated year after year since the Bushes left office in 1992, Barbara Pierce Bush may remain unique as the only woman who married a President and graduated to the rank of "Queen Mother" (or the closest position we have to that honor in the United States) during the "reign" of her son, George Walker Bush.

LAURA WELCH BUSH

When Laura Welch Bush, as wife of the forty-third President, became our current First Lady, she had *two* tough acts to follow: her mother-in-law, Barbara Bush is consistently rated one of our most popular "modern" First Ladies, and her predecessor, Hillary Clinton, now Senator Clinton, indisputably is the most talked about, most written about First Lady in history (far out-ranking Jacqueline Kennedy Onassis).

But the mild-mannered, soft-spoken Midland, Texas, native brings her own strengths to the role, not the least of which is her influence over the man we call "President," and the husband she sometimes calls "Bushie," or even "Bubba," or on more than one occasion, when he garbles his words, "You idiot, " (spoken affectionately). President Bush, famous for his penchant for nicknames calls her "First."[1]

Growing up in the West Texas oiltown (where George also spent part of his childhood), Laura, an only child, dreamed of being a teacher and a housewife, not a President's wife. According to her mother, Jenna, her daughter loved all the things little girls love. She enjoyed "teaching" her dolls, lining them up in a row for "class;" cooking muffins and cookies and casseroles, and most of all reading books, first with her mother, and then on her own. She enjoyed happy times in high school with a wide circle of friends, cruising the local scene, listening to records, and enjoying the special freedom of growing up in a small town.

The idyllic adolescence was marred, however, on November 6, 1963, when Laura, driving her Chevy sedan missed a stop sign at an intersection and hit a Corvair driven by her close friend, high school track star, Mike Douglas. The young man died of a broken neck at the scene; Laura was not charged—the collision was ruled an accident. During the Presidential campaign, when the accident once again came to public attention, she recalled that this was a very sad time and it took many months before she got over it. But she was supported by a loyal group of friends, some of whom she still counts on as her closest confidants.

A year later, Laura left home for Southern Methodist University in Dallas, joined a sorority, played bridge, listened to—and loved—the Beatles, and was known as a cut-up. One of her friends remembers her practicing her "Miss America wave," (middle fingers together, hand moving robot-like back and forth), "because you never know when it will come in handy."[2] And the gesture did come in handy years later during George's various political campaigns. Although Laura grew up in the rebellious 60's, she was not an activist (nor was her husband). In fact, she has no recollection of Martin Luther King Jr.'s historic 1966 visit to SMU.[3] During those years, like most Texans at that time, she considered herself a Democrat.

After graduating with a bachelor's degree in education, Laura taught elementary school for a few years and then earned her master's degree in library science from the University of Texas at Austin in 1973. In the summer of 1977, she finally gave in to friends who had been trying to play matchmaker for two years, and agreed to attend a cookout where she once again "met" George Bush, whom she had known briefly in seventh grade back in Midland. The fix-up worked beautifully, and George and Laura were married just three months later. Her brother-in-law Marvin has described her entry into the frenetic and disorganized Bush lifestyle: "It was like Audrey Hepburn walking into 'Animal House.'"

Barbara Bush tells another story about Laura's early days in the marriage. She says that former President Bush's mother once asked Laura, "And what do you do?" According to her mother-in-law, Laura replied "I read, I smoke, and I admire." In an interview with the *Washington Post*, Laura said she doesn't recall using the words "admire" or "smoke."[4] She quit smoking a few years later, but admits sneaking a few cigarettes during her husband's 1994 run for governor).

Eventually the calm and disciplined Laura, a self-described introvert, was able to establish order and direction in her freewheeling, extrovert husband's world. She attributes the turning point in their lives to the 1981 birth of their twin daughters, Jenna and Barbara (named for their grandmothers). In 1986, she gave her husband an either-or ultimatum about his drinking, and he quit, an event he talked about frequently when he was campaigning for President. Laura herself still enjoys salt-rimmed margaritas on the rocks.

Although Laura Bush has always insisted on her own privacy and has always resisted too much attention, there was not much she could to do maintain this. Actually, her public life began even while she was on her honeymoon in 1977 when George made his first (unsuccessful) bid for Congress. Then beginning in 1981, she was on the road during four national campaigns for her father-in-law when George, Sr., ran as Vice President or President. Following in her mother-in-law's footsteps, she uprooted her family frequently. In 1987, the young family moved to Washington so her husband could work on his father's 1988 campaign. Then they moved back to Dallas when Bush took over the Texas Rangers baseball team. It was back to Washington in 1992 for George, Sr.'s unsuccessful run against Bill Clinton, and finally, they moved back to Texas where George W. embarked on his successful campaign to become Governor of Texas in 1994, and Laura began her six-year tenure as First Lady of Texas. All these moves and all this campaigning demanded that Laura become a "public person," even though her husband had promised when they married that she would never have to give a speech.

It takes a steady and unflappable woman, one who is not easily flustered, to survive all these changes. And, unquestionably, Laura is more organized, intellectual, independent, and insular than her outgoing husband. She has been known to read entire collections of particular authors (her favorites are Dostoyevsky and John Graves), and she shelves the books in their library using the Dewey system.

During the tumultuous post-election days when America did not know just who the forty-third President of the United States would be, Laura Bush kept a fairly low profile and worked steadily to finalize the construction and details of the 1,600 acre ranch they were developing in Crawford, Texas. When the Supreme Court brought the recounting and recounting of the votes in Florida to a final, decisive end, and George W. Bush became President as a result of his 271 to 267 victory in the electoral college over Al Gore, Laura, ever resourceful and organized, switched gears to move out of the Governor's Mansion in Austin, and transform the White House into their new home.

She enlisted a Texas decorator to re-do the private rooms and moved the First Lady's office back to the East Wing, where it had been prior to Hillary Clinton, sending a clear message she would not be following Hillary's path. For the President's Treaty Room, which serves as his office upstairs in the residence, she re-installed President Grant's furniture, and she unearthed Jackie Kennedy's French desk (which had belonged to her father, Jack Bouvier) to use in her own office. Upstairs in the utility kitchen installed by Hillary, she makes sure the fridge is stocked with her husband's favorites—including egg salad and peanut butter and jelly, and diet Coke. The quiet woman often described as always having her head in a book, now heads a 25-person staff in a house of some 150 rooms.

At the Crawford ranch, she continues the informal entertaining the Bush's favor and has been known to whip up her legendary chili, or sandwiches and soup, plus brownies and cookies when cabinet members come to visit. In the White House, entertaining has become less formal than it was during the Clinton years. There is more Tex-Mex on the menu and more barbecuing and grilling, in keeping with the President's favorites and her own style established when she was First Lady of Texas.

In terms of her wardrobe, Laura Bush ranks someplace in the middle between her mother-in-law Barbara and Hillary Clinton. She is definitely not a Jacqueline Kennedy or Nancy Reagan *fashionista*. By her own admission, she is a jeans and T-shirts lady, but during her years as the Texas First Spouse, and even more so now, she has had to change her outlook—select the suits and the gowns and the rest of the wardrobe required for the job. Although she had relied on Texan designers before her husband became President, a few months after the election, Arnold Scaasi, the designer famous for dressing Laura's mother-in-law in "Barbara Blue," took over the fashion detail and announced a change to very bright colors (reds, turquoises, bright blues), shorter skirts (mid-knee) and higher heels. Whatever direction her new look takes, the always organized First Lady stores her shoes by color in their boxes, and is now using a computer to keep track of her outfits.

For the most part though, all of this is secondary to her major role as someone in the public eye—a spokewoman for literacy, education, and the teaching profession…the causes she has championed all her life. In Texas in 1997, she established Reach Out and Read (ROR), and she has remained involved in The New Teacher Project, Teach For America (which benefits recent college grads who commit to teaching at least two years in inner city areas), and Troops to Teachers (which pays tuition for retired military personnel to get teaching certificates, a program, incidentally, also backed by Senator Clinton).

In an op-ed piece in the *Washington Post* in April, 2001, Laura referred to libraries as "palaces of all the people." "The key to these palaces (and the treasures within)," she wrote, "is a library card. I am fortunate that my mother took me to get my library card at an early age. In fact, that was the first card I carried in my wallet, and I used it throughout my childhood and into my adult life."[5] In July the White House announced two new efforts to promote reading and literacy, spearheaded by the First Lady. The first was the establishment of the Laura Bush Foundation, formed to provide support to school libraries around the country, and in September, 2001, Laura Bush launched the first National Book Festival held on the Capitol grounds and in the Library of Congress, featuring readings and panel discussions by well-known American authors.

Six months into her new post, the First Lady also sponsored a seminar on pre-school education, showcasing programs such as Head Start, that help disadvantaged children prepare to learn to read. She told her audience, "Language development begins long before a child speaks his first words, and learning how to read begins long before a child reaches school age." Although President Bush's proposed budget for Head Start included a modest $125 million increase, Laura Bush believes so strongly in the value of such programs that hopefully, she will work behind the scenes, as many First Ladies have, to influence his direction.

Although Laura usually keeps her opinions private, she is not timid about expressing them, either. When Katie Couric interviewed her on NBC's "Today" show shortly after the election, she said that she did not believe a woman's constitutional right to an abortion should be overturned, even though she is adamantly "pro-life." Aides quickly complained that she wasn't supposed to be asked such questions, but Laura stood her ground. She subsequently said about abortion "Don't think that because I don't speak I'm stupid...It just means I have self-control and a sense of propriety." Her candor reminds us of her mother-in-law's outspoken comments on issues. Recently, however, she backed off a little from expressing her opinions. In a July 2001 interview with CNN's Judy Woodruff on "Inside Politics," while she admitted she had her own viewpoint about stem-cell availability for research, "a very serious moral and ethical issue," she made it clear that when her husband made up his mind on this controversial subject, it would be *his* decision, and she chose to keep her own conclusions to herself.[6]

Balancing her public persona is her involvement and dedication to her husband and daughters. As a columnist for the *Houston Chronicle* wrote: "People who dismiss Laura Bush as a mousy librarian are missing her key role. She's the iron rod at her husband's back. She keeps him from going too far off the deep end when he gets all caught up in his cock-of-the-walk behavior."

The President and First Lady are obviously devoted to each other—often tears well up in his eyes when he speaks of his wife.

They don't like to be apart, and during the last months of the campaign—although she could have been an effective campaigner traveling on her own agenda—they opted to travel together full-time. During the first few weeks in office, when she had to go back to Crawford to oversee final details on that home, on Valentine's day, he sent roses and she sent him a heart-shaped coconut cream pie, his favorite.

The early months in the White House also represented another transition for the couple—the empty nest syndrome, with Barbara away at Yale and Jenna at the University of Austin. The girls were never particularly keen on their father running for President to begin with—they felt it would be the end of their privacy and an unwanted spotlight on their activities. Their worst fears came true as Jenna first attracted attention in February 2001 when her secret service agents were called on to rescue a drunken pal from jail. Then, in April she was caught drinking a beer at an Austin bar (In Texas, the legal drinking age is 21, and the penalties for breaking the law include strict zero tolerance policies signed into law by Governor Bush in 1997). A few weeks later, both Jenna and Barbara were charged with breaking the law at an Austin Tex-Mex college hang-out, Jenna for trying to use a fake i.d, Barbara for possession of an alcoholic drink. The press for the most part treated them gently—who among us hasn't at one time or another broken the underage drinking rule? Like the Clintons, the Bushes asked the press to keep their children off limits.

The bottom line among observers is that the girls took foolish chances in a town where they are known by sight. In short, many observors felt they brought this on themselves. Still, it's one more thing White House parents—and their children - have to bear. When the Bush twins hit the headlines, other former Presidents' kids spoke publicly about their visibility. Gerald Ford's daughter Susan said: "Children in the White House have to understand they are in a glass cage." Jack Carter, Jimmy Carter's son, observed, "If you walk into a bar with two secret service agents next to you and you think no one will notice you you're just plain naïve." For those who ask why the secret service agents didn't stop the girls, one agent said publicly, "we're not baby-sitters." Barbara Bush, commenting on the news about her granddaughters to an audience of Junior Leaguers in Indianapolis, said, "He (the President) is getting back some of his own."[7]

In a way the Bush girls are lucky because they will actually only be visitors to the White House, unlike Chelsea Clinton who lived there from the time she was 13, or Amy Carter, the focus of press attention from the day she started elementary school in Washington. Or the Johnson girls, Luci and Lynda, and the Nixon girls, Julie and

Tricia, who lived there during their teen and early adult years; Lucy, Lynda and Tricia were all White House brides.

Despite these personal trials and the normal rough spots that come with moving into a new home and a new "job," Laura Bush is obviously enjoying this unplanned career. When she was asked which First Lady role model she would follow, her mother-in-law's traditional pattern or the one set by Hillary Clinton, she answered. "I'll just be Laura Bush." And she is enjoying a few other firsts: She is the only First Lady *People* magazine has named "one of the world's most beautiful people," and she has a horticultural first, too: The Laura Bush Petunia (*Petunia X violacea 'Laura Bush'*), a hybrid between the VIP and old fashioned petunia which was born and bred in Texas.

As Anna Perez, former press secretary to Barbara Bush told the *Los Angeles Times*, "She had a life when she got to Washington, she's going to have a life when she leaves and, by George, she's going to have one while she's there."[8]

NOTE: On September 11, 2001, as *The Presidents' First Ladies* went to press, our nation was devastated by the horrific terrorist attack on New York's World Trade Center and the Pentagon, which killed almost 6,000 people in the deadliest assault on American soil in our country's history. President Bush called this the first war of the twenty-first century and vowed, "We will smoke them (the terrorists) out of their holes...We will bring them to justice." The government mobilized for full-scale action against Osama bin Laden, the "prime suspect" of the barbaric action, at home, in Afghanistan, and other Islamic terrorist strongholds throughout the world. And Americans wept at the catastrophic loss of life and the unbearable visual evidence of the destruction caused when four American planes were hijacked and literally turned into guided missiles. We rallied behind our President whose wavering popularity suddenly rose to 90%, we bought and displayed every flag that could be found, and we steeled ourselves for what President Bush and his advisors and political pundits told us was going to be a very long fight. "You will be asked for your patience," said the President, "For the conflict will not be short. You will be asked for resolve, for the conflict will not be easy. You will be asked for your strength, because the course to victory may be long. This is a conflict without battlefields or beachheads, a conflict with opponents who believe they are invisible," President Bush said. "Yet they are mistaken. They will be exposed (and) we will bring them to justice."

Just as George W. Bush changed—overnight, it would seem—as he tackled the greatest challenge for any President since

Pearl Harbor, so too did Laura Bush, as she joined the ranks of other First Ladies before her who were faced with war...or the threat of war. While Eleanor Roosevelt was "seasoned" for her strength in World War II by her experiences nursing FDR through his bout with polio, and then the hard times for the country during the depression, many of her predecessors were not prepared to play a major role during a national disaster. President Wilson's illness turned the protective Edith Wilson into "Madame President." The shy and private Bess Truman provided valiant support for Harry, when he made his decisions about dropping the atom bombs on Japan, conclusively ending World War II. Another shy First Lady, Jacqueline Kennedy, gave behind-the-scenes comfort to JFK during the Cuban missile crisis, as did Pat Nixon and Lady Bird Johnson, while their husbands endured the seemingly never-ending problems of the Vietnam War.

For Laura Bush, who had expressed a wish to spend as much time as she could at the Crawford ranch, the days after September 11th were spent in a new role as a national comforter. She went from bedsides comforting the wounded, to benefits comforting the victims in Washington and New York. She posed for photo ops, addressed volunteers and firefighters, appeared on "60 Minutes" and Oprah Winfrey, speaking about our national grief and how to cope with loss and future threats of terrorism. We know she was there to comfort President Bush as he dealt with disaster and took the steps necessary to fight this "New War." And she gave her attention to the youngest "victims" of the events that changed all our lives—children bewildered and frightened by the terrorist attacks. After spending an hour and a half reading "I Love You, Little One, " to a group of public school kids in New York City, she told Governor George Pataki's wife Libby, "That's my favorite thing, reading to the children. It's because that's what I used to do."[9]

EYES, EARS, VOICES

Sarach Childress Polk
1803-1891

Helen "Nellie" Herron Taft
1861-1943

Ellen Axson Wilson
1860-1914

Edith Bolling Galt Wilson
1872-1961

Florence Kling Harding
1860-1924

Anna Eleanor Roosevelt
1884-1962

Thelma Catherine "Pat" Ryan Nixon
1912-1993

Rosalynn Smith Carter
1927-

Nancy Davis Reagan
1921-

Hillary Rodham Clinton
1947-

Although we tend to think that it is only recent First Ladies who had influenced their husbands' actions, history proves us wrong. Abigail Adams, the second to hold the post was derisively called "Mrs. President" because she often gave her husband advice—which he often took. Among her causes were "women's rights," and she was arguably the nation's first feminist.

Sarah Polk, Helen Taft, and Florence Harding not only acted as their husbands' "eyes and ears," but often as their "voice," working to get them elected and then helping to get their programs across to the public. Much more vocal—by necessity—than any of these First Ladies was Edith Wilson, who literally took over the presidency when Woodrow Wilson had a stroke. She truly acted as the "First Lady-President," which incidentally no other First Lady had done before or would be able to do now. The passage of the Twenty-fifth Amendment in 1967 clearly defines the succession of authority when the President is incapable of governing, and insures that a First Lady could not act as President.

Lady Bird Johnson, Pat Nixon, Rosalynn Carter, and Nancy Reagan also served as their husbands' strong supporters and advisors, even voicing their opinions (albeit often behind the scenes) about important Presidential appointments and decisions.

Until recently, the one First Lady who played the strongest role as her husband's partner was also the woman who served as First Lady the longest: Eleanor Roosevelt. She was so dynamic that reporters called her "Public Energy Number One," and she set precedents that few of her successors chose—or were equipped—to follow...until the last First Lady of the twentieth century took on the challenge. Hillary Clinton was adored by many, and abhorred by just as many, but unquestionably, she was her husband's political as well as domestic partner.

SARAH CHILDRESS POLK

S arah Polk was the daughter of a prosperous Tennessee farmer; a very religious Calvinist, she was totally devoted to her husband, James Polk, the nation's eleventh President.

From the time they were married, when she was 20, Sarah was literally at his side as his "confidential secretary" during fourteen sessions in Congress and his term as President, a role made easier by the fact that the couple had no children. Some observers thought Polk's "guardian angel," as she was sometimes called, was very attractive as well as very devoted. One visiting Englishwoman described her:

> *Mrs. Polk is a very handsome woman. Her hair is very black, and her dark eyes and complexion remind one of the Spanish donnas. She is well read, has much talent for conversation...her excellent taste in dress preserves the subdued though elegant costume* (of) *the lady.*[1]

Sarah Polk was slim and graceful, but despite this pleasing description, portraits reveal a rather unattractive strong jaw and a somewhat menacing expression, and her hands are folded *very* firmly in front of her.

She could not dictate what went on in the embassies, or at the parties at the home of the eighty-year-old Dolley Madison, but at the Polk White House, wine was banned, card playing was out, and dancing was verboten. Sarah said, "To dance in these rooms would be undignified, and it would be respectful neither to the house nor to the office."[2] However, she entertained regally, and insisted on formal reception lines where she sat, dressed in a "rich but chaste" velvet or satin gown, while guests were properly presented. Her parties were surprisingly popular. "Madam," said a prominent South Carolinian at one of her levées, "there is a woe pronounced against you in the Bible." When she asked what he meant, he said, "The Bible says, 'Woe unto you when all men shall speak well of you.'"[3]

Since John Quincy Adams, there hadn't been an official First Lady in the White House except for the brief reign of Julia Tyler. President Polk and Sarah, who did not look kindly on time that was "unprofitably spent," adopted a new austerity which remained in effect for the next three administrations—those of Zachary Taylor, Millard Fillmore and Franklin Pierce.

Among President Polk's major concerns were the Mexican War and the problem of dealing with gold miners and their bounty in the California territory. In addition, he was not in good health, and his doctors recommended that he vacation at the ocean and eat crabs and oysters to rebuild his stamina. Polk did not take any of this advice and never took a vacation anywhere during his term; instead, he harnessed himself to his responsibilities.

During his first year in office Polk made only three social calls: two to members of his Cabinet and the third to Dolley Madison. Sarah made *no* social calls. In addition to working twelve to fourteen hours a day as her husband's confidential secretary, she made some changes in the White House, including the installation of gas lights, replacing the old oil lamps and candle-lit chandeliers.

Sarah was one of the First Ladies who had always wanted her husband to forge ahead and become President of the United States. In fact, Polk once said that if he had continued his job as clerk of the Tennessee state legislature his wife wouldn't have married him. She was very much James Polk's equal—politically shrewd and ambitious. If she had been born in another time, her strengths might have gone into establishing her own career. Sarah always preferred to talk about political affairs and current events with the men, *not* their wives. She regarded "perfect wives" as those who stayed in the background and never bossed or contradicted their husbands in public, contrary to her own role as a wife. She was astute about politics and could cite the vote counts, and who had voted for whom or what in Congress. The President's wife seemed to consider it her personal mission in life to ensure her husband a secure place in history; she was so serious, in fact, that she deeply believed that God had pre-destined her position as the First Lady.

Sarah also had a strong and unwavering sense of equal rights, as reported by a member of the White House staff. One day she drew her husband to the window and pointed out the black workers. "The writers of the Declaration of Independence were mistaken when they affirmed that all men are created equal," she said. When the President tried to dismiss her "foolish fancies," she told him, "These are men toiling in the heat of the sun, while you are writing, and I am standing here fanning myself, in this house as airy and delightful as a palace...Those men did not choose such a life."[4]

Although the Polks had a private income, they did not use their own funds to run the White House, and Sarah was proud about staying within their $25,000 salary. President Polk once said, "None but Sarah knew so intimately my private affairs." She tried to diminish his workload by doing some of it herself, and would read all the newspapers, mark the pertinent sections for him and leave the edited papers beside his chair or on his desk.

James Knox Polk survived his presidency by only three months. In June, 1849, at the young age of fifty-three, he died of what was listed as "diarrhea." On his deathbed, President Polk said, "I love you, Sarah, for all eternity. After her husband died, Sarah Polk, 46, wrote, "And life was then a blank." Although she lived another 42 years, she never again accepted a social invitation and left her house only to attend church; she devoted all her energies to perpetuating his memory. Sarah Polk died just before her eighty-eighth birthday in August, 1891.

HELEN "NELLIE"
HERRON TAFT

Two people were responsible for William Howard Taft's election as twenty-seventh President of the United States: Teddy Roosevelt and Helen "Nellie" Taft. She wheeled, dealed, argued, charmed, cajoled, discussed, debated, and finally *convinced* President Roosevelt that instead of appointing William Howard Taft as Chief Justice, he should sponsor him for the presidency.

But then, the affable, ebullient, and corpulent William Howard Taft always relied on Nellie for advice and advancement. Before they were married in 1886, he wrote her a love letter (May, 1885) : "Do say that you will try to love me. Oh, how I will work and strive to be better and do better, how I will labor for our joint advancement if you will only let me."

Helen Herron grew up in Cincinnati, the daughter of cultured, wealthy parents. She was well educated and at 18, started a "salon" to discuss politics, economics, education, music, and literature. Among the young men invited to this salon were William Howard Taft, who was already becoming a notable young lawyer in Ohio, and his brother, Horace.

In 1900, after Taft had served as an Ohio Judge and had become influential in Republican circles, President McKinley named him to head a commission to the Philippines, which ultimately led to his appointment as governor of the islands. Taft hesitated, but his wife was eager for him to take the job. She said, "I wasn't sure what it meant, but I knew instantly I didn't want to miss a big and novel experience."[1] (By then they had three children, Robert, Helen, and Charles, who accompanied them to the islands). Nellie enjoyed her luxurious lifestyle in the Philippines and retained many of the gracious traditions she adopted there.

When they returned to the States, Taft was so well regarded that he was a contender for either an appointment to the Supreme Court or the Republican nomination for President. Nellie pushed vociferously and ardently for the Republican nomination. (As a young guest in the Hayes' White House, she had vowed to return some day as First Lady.) Even though it was evident that her mellow, good-hearted husband had his heart set on being a Supreme Court Justice, she hounded Taft to strive for the top job in the nation and pressured Roosevelt for his support. One would not readily believe that the stalwart, macho Roosevelt could be swayed by a woman, but it was Nellie who won the bout: By the late spring of 1905, Roosevelt agreed that Taft would be the best candidate. Taft gave up his judicial dream, but did not do very much to further his Presidential goal; his brothers and his wife moved the cause ahead, and he was elected.

Nellie's experience as the Philippines Governor's wife was excellent training for her new role as mistress of the White House, and, with characteristic energy, she set out to put her own stamp on the Mansion. She immediately hired Mrs. Elizabeth Jaffray as housekeeper to replace the male steward (she felt a woman should handle what were after all, *her* affairs); had vaults built to hold White House silver; and housed a cow named "Pauline Wayne" on the White House lawn to provide the family's milk.

Nellie also paid a great deal of attention to the food served, and although the full-time cook was Irish, she brought in a special chef for official dinners to make terrapin soup—and nothing else, according to Lillian Parks.

> *I think the cook was given $5 each time. Mrs. Taft was very particular about the terrapin soup and would come to the kitchen to taste it, and make sure it had reached the peak of perfection. She was one of the few First Ladies who ever came into the kitchen. Bess Truman, years later, was another.* [2]

Nellie followed Edith Roosevelt's practice of having attendants in blue livery at the main entrance to the White House. And with the help of Archie Butt, who had been an aide to the Roosevelts, she devised an outdoor reception area, with grandstands and a stage, similar to the "Luneta Park" in the Philippines. During the spring and summer, lavish musicales and entertainments were scheduled, orchestrated brilliantly by the First Lady. Even though Nellie was a seasoned hostess, all this new activity proved a bit too much for the 48-year-old woman. During a cruise on the Presidential yacht, the "Mayflower," she suffered a stroke and was incapacitated for a year. (Her four sisters stood in for her as hostesses during that time.) The President, who had always relied so much on his wife's help and advice, neglected his own responsibilities, spent hours at her bedside, and helped her learn to speak again. Archie Butt observed that the President "would be about three years behind when the fourth of March, 1913, (the end of his term) rolls around."[3]

After she recovered, Nellie gave twice as many social affairs as any other President and First Lady until then. One of the most gala events was their twenty-fifth wedding anniversary, which was celebrated by 2,000 guests at a garden party in the Luneta area. She was also responsible for one contribution as First Lady that was far more enduring than all her parties. Nellie Taft arranged for the shipment of 2,000 Japanese cherry trees to Washington, where they were planted along the Tidal Basin and Capitol grounds; the trees are still a glorious sight every spring when they bloom.

Despite her gracious entertaining skills, Helen was not a popular First Lady; perhaps the public sensed that she had manipulated her husband into his job, and she was criticized for her "pushy" role in her husband's affairs. Even worse: the sharp-tongued Nellie was not above criticizing Taft in public. Not only did she challenge his political stands, but she also rebuked his eating habits and his disastrous habit of falling asleep in public, a condition now recognized as "narcolepsy." As one observer wrote, "sometimes she would carry on the conversation for him, for she was a brilliant woman, and she did know his views."

More serious, in the view of some critics, was the fact that Helen Taft sat in on meetings between the President and his Cabinet, unasked and unannounced. She didn't give opinions during the sessions, but as soon as they were over, she made her positions *very* clear to her husband.

The Republican Party did not regard Taft as a very effective President, and when Roosevelt returned from an extended trip to Africa, he was touted as their Presidential candidate. In order to hold on to his job, Taft, in return, sided with Roosevelt's enemies. The more Taft worried, the more weight he gained; the pounds did not diminish despite horseback riding, walks, golf and other exercises. The President also suffered from agonizing pains in his foot, which attentive Archie Butt correctly diagnosed as gout. But Taft wouldn't get medical aid until the pain became excruciating. The President was so overweight he required an oversized bathtub, and a famous picture of the time shows four workmen sitting in this especially manufactured tub.

Butt was caught in the middle between Roosevelt and Taft, and Alice Longworth warned him to break connections with Taft before it was too late. Butt decided to neutralize the situation with a trip to Europe, and after a month abroad, he sailed home on the "Titanic." He was not among the survivors.

The feud between Roosevelt and Taft split the Republican Party. After Taft was nominated to run for re-election, and Teddy Roosevelt launched his own third party, the Progressive Party, Helen Taft told her husband, "I told you so four years ago, and you would not believe me." Taft replied, "I know you did, my dear. I think you are perfectly happy now. You would have preferred the Colonel (Roosevelt) to come out against me than to have been wrong yourself."

The result of the three-way race (with Republican votes split between Taft and Roosevelt) was that Democrat Woodrow Wilson, former governor of New Jersey, won the Presidential election of 1912. Taft was not totally disappointed; he had not wanted to be President in the first place. Before leaving office he said, "The nearer I get to the inauguration of my successor, the greater the relief I feel."[4]

When Wilson was inaugurated, the unhappy, defeated Helen Taft wouldn't even say goodbye to the White House staff. Several years later, in 1924, President Warren Harding appointed Taft as Chief Justice (after he had served as a law professor at Yale), and this time Nellie Taft did not interfere. William Howard Taft became the only man in American history to hold the posts of President and Chief Justice of the Supreme Court.

ELLEN AXSON WILSON
AND
EDITH BOLLING GALT WILSON

Woodrow Wilson, twenty-eighth President, described his first wife, Ellen Axson Wilson, as a girl with a "tip-tilted little nose, sweetly curved mouth, and hair like burnished copper." The Wilsons had three daughters, Margaret, Jessie, and Eleanor, and regarded the White House, not as a public place, but as their own home. (Two daughters were married in the White House: Jessie married Francis B. Sayre in November, 1913; six months later Eleanor married William Gibbs McAdoo, Secretary of the Treasury.)

Ellen had been diagnosed with Bright's Disease and tuberculosis when Wilson was elected in 1912. In her brief time as First Lady, she left her mark by planting beautiful gardens with box trees, rose bushes and rose trees, and designing the Blue Mountain Room with arts and crafts made by poor women who lived in the Blue Ridge Mountains. Ellen was a professional painter and converted an attic room with a skylight into a studio. She also devoted a great deal of time to improving slum conditions in Washington, and persuaded Congressmen to accompany her on tours for a close look at the shacks and lean-to's of the poor.

As a result of her efforts, Congress passed a slum-clearing bill shortly before she died, at age 54, on August 2, 1914. That very day, Germany invaded France and Russia invaded Germany: World War I had begun. Although Wilson pledged neutrality, he was in a no-win situation. On one hand, he was criticized for dragging his heels and staying *out of the war*; and on the other, castigated for leading the country *into war*.

When Ellen was dying she asked Dr. Grayson, her friend and family doctor, to "take care of Woodrow." Dr. Grayson kept his promise by seeing that the President got enough fresh air, even playing golf with him. In addition, he inadvertently provided the President with the best medicine of all: a new love interest.

After Ellen died, a young cousin, Helen Bones, who had been brought up by the Wilsons, wandered around the White House with little to do. Dr. Grayson introduced Helen to Edith Bolling Galt, his fiancée's guardian. Edith, a ninth-generation descendent of Pocahantas, had grown up in rural Virginia, and although her parents lost everything in the Civil War, she was well educated by her father, a judge. At eighteen she visited her sister, Mrs. Alexander Galt, in Washington, and met Alexander's younger brother, Norman, the wealthy owner of a jewelry store. They married, lived very comfortably, and traveled to Europe frequently. Edith wore couture gowns and was the first woman in Washington to have an "electric" (a battery-powered car).

After Norman's death in 1908, Edith sold the store for a handsome profit. The childless widow "adopted" Altrude Gordon, Dr. Grayson's fiancée, and became friendly with Helen Bones. Edith and Helen would go for long walks or drives, and then have tea together, usually at Edith's house.

One March day in 1915, Helen asked Edith to tea at the White House since "Cousin Woodrow" was out playing golf. However, Grayson and the President returned early and joined them, and for the first time in months the President smiled and laughed. The courtship was on. Wilson proposed on May 3rd, two months after he met her. At first Edith, 47, said no, but she accepted his proposal in September. Wilson's political advisers were dead against his re-marrying so soon after his wife's death, and worried about the effect on the 1916 election.

In order to stall him, his closest adviser, Colonel Edward House, and his son-in-law, William McAdoo, told Edith about a woman friend with whom Wilson had allegedly corresponded for seven years. Edith was hurt by the story and wrote to Wilson, asking for an explanation. Edith's letters were somehow "lost," and the President was so shocked by her rejection he became ill. It wasn't until Dr. Grayson brought her to the White House and she reassured Wilson of her love and loyalty—and he assured her that there was no other woman—that he recovered.

After a brief engagement, they were married on December 18, 1915, at her home. Soon after, Edith discovered Colonel House's attempt to thwart their relationship, and she obviously and understandably never trusted him again...and remained very wary of McAdoo.

The new Mrs. Wilson took with her the furniture and accessories from her bedroom, her books, her piano, and her sewing machine, which became very useful a year later, when the First Lady and Congressmen's wives used it to sew pajamas and shirts for the Red Cross.

The newlyweds soon established a daily routine: breakfast at eight followed by a game of golf and a walk through the rose garden to his office. At noon they had lunch; he worked afternoons while she received visitors. They took a drive before dinner, and after dinner there would be a game of pool or reading or working on official business. Wilson adored his bride. During the re-election campaign, while he read his correspondence, Edith would place letters typed by his secretary in front of him to sign. Once he looked up and sighed, "When you are here, work seems like play."

A key issue during the 1916 campaign was women's rights, and suffragettes had become vociferously active, picketing the White House and other major locations and demanding the right to vote. Edith found the behavior of these activists distasteful and unfeminine; she called them "disgusting creatures" and wrote that the only speech by her husband that she failed to enjoy was one he gave at a suffragette meeting. "I hated the subject, so it was acute agony." Even so, she wore orchids presented by the ladies. It's important to remember that Edith was brought up as a traditional Southern belle. Wilson didn't sympathize with the suffragette's cause, either—but, eventually, he gave in to pressure and recommended a Constitutional amendment giving women the right to vote. (The Nineteenth Amendment was proposed in 1919 and ratified by the states in 1920).

In April 1917, Wilson declared war against Germany, in a speech which included the famous phrase "to make the world safe for democracy." The United States had entered World War I and for the duration there would be no more golf games or entertaining at the White House. Now, the Wilsons endured meatless, wheatless, gasless, and heatless days, along with the rest of the country. A flock of sheep grazed on the White House grounds and produced 98 pounds of wool, which was auctioned for $100,000, the proceeds going to the Red Cross.

During the war, only the President, his wife, and Colonel House knew the code for communicating with representatives abroad, and in the evening Edith would decode all messages to the President. One of the First Lady's more pleasant wartime jobs was to christen newly built American ships, as well as re-christen eighty-eight captured from Germany. She discovered the English had already appropriated the "good" names, so she referred to an American Indian dictionary, and gave the ships Indian names.

In November, 1918, the Armistice was announced, and President Wilson left for France to present his "Fourteen Points" for lasting peace as part of the Treaty of Versailles. A major goal was to establish a "League of Nations," a federation of countries dedicated to maintaining peace. However, Wilson's political opponents led by Senator Henry Cabot Lodge were adamantly against American participation in the League and the Senate voted against ratification of the Treaty.

Wilson opted to take his case to the people via a speaking tour in September 1919, hoping that public support would force the Senate to change its mind. (Today, of course, the President would simply ask for television time to present his views, a much less arduous task). Dr. Grayson warned Wilson against making the trip—Wilson was 63 and the pace might be too fatiguing. Unfortunately, his advice was ignored. The President traveled 8,000 miles, delivered forty speeches (most of them an hour long), took part in a dozen parades, shook thousands of hands, and attended luncheons, dinners and receptions. One reporter wrote:

> *The President can truly say that Mrs. Wilson sustains him. As Mr. Wilson, standing in his auto, bowed right and left, waving his brown fedora in answer to the cheering thousands, she constantly held her hand against his back supporting him against the possibility of a fall.*[1]

After twenty-two days, President Wilson collapsed and was rushed back to the White House. For several days he continued to have excruciatingly painful headaches, and then one morning, a few minutes after complaining of having no sensation in his hand, he lost consciousness. He had had a cerebral thrombosis—a stroke—which paralyzed his left side. He remained in critical condition for weeks, and the White House became a veritable hospital.

Dr. Grayson was aided by a team of medical specialists who warned the President might live for five days...or five months...or even five years, depending on protection from "every disturbing problem." Dr. F.X. Dercum urged Edith to screen visitors and weigh all problems before discussion with Wilson. "Every time you take him a new anxiety or problem...you are turning a knife in an open wound," he warned. (During this time Edith did a bit of letter-hiding herself and refused to show her husband Colonel House's affectionate letters offering help—although such help could have been advantageous to the President.)

A month after the stroke President Wilson was able to sit in a wheel chair; several months later, he was able to go for a short drive. Edith fended off requests from congressional leaders to visit and confer with the incapacitated Wilson for almost *a year and a half*, a time in which the nation was without an active leader. Not only did the White House take on the air of a hospital, in many ways it was a prison, to keep the public *away* from the President. Guards were stationed outside locked White House gates; some people said that bars had been put on windows because Wilson was a lunatic. (The bars had been placed in another bedroom during Theodore Roosevelt's term to keep his children from falling out the windows).

It didn't take long before critics accused Mrs. Wilson of standing-in as President. She called this time her "stewardship." Others had less kind words. Some bluntly said Edith ran the country, and others called her "acting President." One White House reporter labeled this period as "Mrs. Wilson's Regency." Another commentator wrote in *Liberty* magazine, "Edith Bolling Wilson is not only acting President, but Secretary to the President and Secretary of State." Some observers were more positive. Reporter Davie Lawrence wrote: "Between the President and the outside world stands Mrs. Wilson, as devoted and faithful a companion as ever nursed a sick man...it is doubtful if ever a woman in American history had such a burden." The comments were not limited to the American media. In London, *The Daily Mail* commented: "Though Washington tongues are wagging vigorously, no suggestion is heard that Mrs. Wilson is not proving a capable 'President'."

In Edith Wilson's book, *My Memoir*, she described doctors' orders to "act as a go-between" to save her husband's life. Every day, at the time she thought he felt most energetic, she presented a summary of pressing national problems as outlined by Cabinet members and Congressmen, and then conveyed the President's opinions or recommended actions. One of those important matters was the Treaty of Versailles, which had still not been ratified. Although very few visitors were allowed to see President Wilson, Senator Gilbert Hitchcock from Nebraska was granted a visit to plead for a compromise. The annoyed Wilson told him, "Let Lodge compromise." Edith appealed to her husband to give a little on his stand: "For my sake, won't you accept these reservations and get this awful thing settled?" She recorded his reply: "Little girl, don't you desert me. That I cannot stand."[2]

The Treaty and the League of Nations were rejected again by the Senate, and not long afterward, another subcommittee headed by Senator Albert Fall asked for a conference with Wilson about the situation in Mexico. The real purpose of the visit was to decide whether Wilson's mental capacities had diminished to the point where he could be judged incompetent to serve as President. When Fall told President Wilson "We have all been praying for you," the always sharp Wilson replied, "Which way, Senator?" Edith had been taking down every word of the meeting, and Senator Fall observed, "You seem to be very much engaged, Madam." She responded: "It (is) wise to record this interview so there may be no misunderstanding or miss-statements made."

Among the few visitors admitted to Woodrow Wilson's private chambers at the White House were King Albert and Queen Elizabeth of Belgium, the Prince of Wales, Secretary of State Robert Lansing, and finally, in April of 1920, the entire Cabinet, which met at his bedside. During his last months in office, Wilson was rarely seen in public. On March 4, 1921, a frail President, noticeably limping, climbed into an open-top limousine where he sat next to Warren Gamaliel Harding, the President-elect, for the inaugural ceremonies at the Capitol.

How strong was Edith? How weak was President Wilson? No one will ever know. At the height of his illness, did the President understand what he was signing? Did Edith Wilson, who had no political background, know what she was asking him to sign? There is no record, and there are no answers to these questions. One thing is clear: such a stewardship could never again happen in our country. In February 1967, almost fifty years after President Wilson's stroke, the twenty-fifth Amendment to the Constitution was ratified, specifying the proper succession of power should the President become seriously ill.

After the election of President Harding, Edith and Woodrow Wilson retired to their house on S Street in Washington, where Woodrow Wilson died in 1924, never fully recovering from the disastrous effects of his stroke. For many years afterward, his widow, Edith Galt Wilson, continued to work on behalf of the League of Nations (which the United States never joined), and other favorite causes of her husband's, until her death in 1961.

FLORENCE KLING HARDING

When Warren Gamaliel Harding became the twenty-ninth President, his wife turned to him and said, "Well, Warren, I have got you the Presidency; what are you going to do with it?" His reply was, "May God help me, for I need it." Harding always thought of himself as "just folks."[1]

Florence Kling Harding, however, was not "just folks." She was the daughter of the richest banker in Marion, Ohio, and at age 18, became a widow (some reports say "divorcée") with a young son. Her father opposed her second marriage to Harding, but she married him anyway. At the time, Harding ran a newspaper in Marion; initially, she helped him in emergencies and remained at his side for fourteen years, turning the paper into a paying proposition.

Many historians believe that Harding was our "worst President."[2] Maybe that's because he was not a self-made man, but a wife-made man. Unquestionably, his wife, whom he called "The Duchess," propelled him into the important positions of his life. She liked the idea of being First Lady, and after Harding served in state political positions and as a little-known senator, she gained the support of Ohio's political boss, Harry Daugherty, who persuaded Harding to jump into "the big circus." Harding was 55 and "seemed" like a Presidential candidate, with a sincere look, full black hair, well-chiseled features and a silvery voice, which his audiences responded to, even if he didn't have much to say. During the campaign, Florence was always at his side, always well dressed, but a little *too* well turned out, with a bit too much make-up, and hair just somewhat overdone.

Harding was elected in 1920 with over 60 percent of the popular vote. By the time Florence reached the White House, her health wasn't good, but her spirit was just fine, and she plunged into her role as First Lady. She was at least five to eight years older than the President, and she worked very hard to appear as young as her husband—or younger. She had a facial and massage every day, and wore a ribbon or "dog collar" around her neck to hide wrinkles. Two maids looked after her wardrobe; instead of Edith Wilson's dignified blacks, Florence Harding wore grays, pastels, rich brocades; special shoes to match each dress were kept in a glass case.

On Inauguration Eve, the new guardian of the Presidential Mansion welcomed thousands of sightseers to meet the President in the White House; her party was a change from the restraint of the World War I years and President Wilson's illness. At the first New Year's reception, she stood in line with Harding for six hours; by the time the reception was over, she had shaken hands with over 6000 people and her hands were so swollen her gloves had to be cut off.

Since Harding was President during Prohibition, alcohol was not served at formal White House events, but upstairs, the President had a bar well stocked with bourbon, scotch, fine wines, and brandies, which he served to his card-playing cronies.

In September 1922, Florence suffered a kidney infection and wasn't expected to live, but she recovered after six weeks and resumed her work as First Lady and the President's right hand. She spent hours visiting veterans and once gave them a garden party at which she insisted on wearing an old straw hat. She said, "The boys are accustomed to it, and as soon as they see it, they know where I am."[3] She was concerned about her relationship to "the people," as she called them, and made herself available for causes and entertainments on their behalf. Florence loved to play lighthearted music on the piano; her favorite song was "The End of a Perfect Day," which the Marine Band included in every official reception.

The days in the White House, however, were not so prefect, as the President's shortcomings, and his wife's heavy hand began to cause criticism. To echo Willy Loman's credo in *Death of a Salesman,* the most important thing for Harding was to be "well-liked." And Harding *was* well-liked. His wife was not. The First Lady was regarded as a strong-willed, vindictive woman, subject to temper tantrums and revenge, a person who wouldn't let go of grudges and sought pay-back. She listed the names of the people who had snubbed her in a red book, and according to Alice Roosevelt Longworth, Florence kept this list because "these people were to realize that she was aware of their behavior."

Not only did Florence plan White House social events, she also had her say about the political events of the country. She rewrote Harding's Inaugural Address, discussed major appointments, and, for her first White House Christmas, chose which convicts to pardon. Florence sat in on conferences and must have been disturbed that Harding never made up his own mind. He was generally successful when he followed *her* advice, but often he followed others' suggestions and was not as successful.

Most likely, if she could have attained the office in her own right, Florence would have made a strong President. She was more of a political "animal" than her husband. When she was compared favorably with Edith Wilson, she replied, "How happy I am to know that I am in the same case with that lovely woman." Florence was also equipped with a special trait that helps many people who seek power. Like Sarah Polk, she believed she was a "woman of destiny." Harding had no such belief. "I am a man of limited talents...oftentimes, as I sit here, I don't seem to grasp that I am President," he said. Unfortunately, in addition to his "just folks" attitude, he also had some ideas, which were decidedly against "home and hearth." He was known as a ladies' man, and although Florence tried to keep her husband home at nights, he tended to stray—to play poker with buddies, and to play other games in other places.

A notorious example was his liaison with Nan Britton, a twenty-ish blonde who had worked for him as a teenager, and later had an "assignation" with him at a New York hotel. There, according to her book, *The President's Daughter*, he "tucked $30 in my brand-new silk stockings and was sorry he had no more that time to give me." She chronicled secret meetings that lasted from 1916 until Harding's death and charged that their daughter was born on October 22, 1919. She alleged that Harding had never seen his daughter, although he continued to see Britton after the baby was born. No matter that her suit was thrown out of court; more to the point is that Harding was the kind of man who allowed himself to get into such a messy scandal. (a moral failing that cost Gary Hart his political career almost seventy years later, and was a major factor in the impeachment of Bill Clinton).

By the spring of 1923, other scandals were occurring which were much worse. Harding's administration was crumbling under rumors of graft. Interior Secretary Albert Fall resigned and two advisors, Charles Cramer and Jesse Smith, committed suicide. In July, to distance themselves from increasing scandal, an exercise in shutting the barn door after the horses escape, Harding and The Duchess traveled to Alaska. On August 2, on the way home, the President collapsed on a train and died in a San Francisco hotel. The first report was that he had been stricken by food poisoning, but later, doctors said he died of a blood clot in his brain, with complications of pneumonia. After Florence refused to allow an autopsy, gossips speculated that she had poisoned her husband in order to prevent his impeachment, but she was later cleared of all suspicious charges.

For the funeral, Florence selected flowers "Warren would like," and according to her friend, Evalyn Walsh McClean (of the Hope Diamond fame) said, "No one can hurt you now, Warren."

After his death, more and more scandals came to light. Eventually it was proved that Harding wasn't directly responsible, and the people involved were ultimately prosecuted. Florence Harding did not live long enough to see this justice. A year after the President's death, she returned to Marion for a visit and quietly died in her sleep. Years later, Alice Longworth wrote, "Harding was not a bad man. He was just a slob." Florence was "a nervous, rather excitable woman whose voice easily became a little high-pitched, strident," and Mrs. Longworth admitted in her memoirs that it was strange for her to have seen so much of a couple she had never really liked.

ANNA ELEANOR ROOSEVELT

For those growing up in the 1940's Eleanor Roosevelt was everybody's "aunt," and Franklin Delano Roosevelt was the patriarch, and perhaps, everybody's "grandfather." In a sense, Eleanor Roosevelt was the first "career woman" to live in the White House, and although she had about half a dozen careers—one of them as First Lady—she managed to juggle all her activities and supervise a family of four sons and one daughter. Eleanor was so energetic, so active, so involved and concerned with so many different interests, she may have unconsciously inspired Americans to think that someday there might even be such a woman who would be elected in her own right as President of the United States. Yet, she didn't start out with any of that potential.

Eleanor Roosevelt, who was born on October 11, 1884, was always self-effacing, and that may have accounted for her appeal to people of all classes. She described herself as "an ugly duckling," the "plain" daughter of a beautiful socialite mother and a socially prominent, alcoholic father. Anna Hall Roosevelt told her daughter she was "a funny child" and "not pretty." Looking back on her youth, Eleanor said, "There was absolutely nothing about me to attract anybody's attention." She grew up as a serious, shy, lonely and insecure girl; her mother died when she was eight, and her father a year and a half later. The orphan was brought up by her grandmother and other relatives who were big on discipline but short on love. She wasn't considered a good catch, didn't blossom at debutante parties (she called them "utter agony"), and she and her relatives feared she would become an unwanted old maid.

Enter the knight on a white horse, Franklin Delano Roosevelt, her fifth cousin. Maybe he felt sorry for her. Maybe he found qualities in her that no one else had seen. In any case, he danced with her at parties and accompanied her on trips to the slum district Rivington Street Settlement House, where she taught calisthenics and dancing as part of a Junior League volunteer program. Whatever the attraction between the young Roosevelts, in 1903, FDR, who was still at Harvard and had a reputation as a debonair "man about town," asked his shy cousin to marry him. And Eleanor, smart girl that she was, immediately accepted. FDR's very strong mother, Sara Delano Roosevelt, was not very keen on the match, and in typical fashion for those days (and perhaps even *these* days) sent her son on a West Indies cruise, hoping he would change his mind. He didn't, and Franklin and Eleanor were married on March 17, 1905. The bride was given in marriage by her uncle, President Theodore Roosevelt.

For the first ten years of their marriage, Eleanor concentrated on her own children instead of slum kids or other needy people. She had six children, of which five survived childhood. (After the birth of the sixth child, Eleanor opted for separate bedrooms; FDR found sexual companionship with other women during the next twenty-nine years, but that's another story). By her own admission, young Mrs. Roosevelt was "cowed" by the dictatorial Sara Roosevelt. Eleanor was so shy that she couldn't deal with servants and left the household management to her mother-in-law, who lived next door to the young couple in a townhouse in New York's Murray Hill district.

However, in 1911, FDR was elected to the New York State senate, and in Albany, Eleanor had to captain her own ship. She tried to be affectionate to her mother-in-law, and once wrote to Sara, "I do so want you to learn to love me a little." Eleanor accompanied her husband to political meetings and speeches, but said nothing and contributed nothing. She wrote, "It was a wife's duty to be interested in whatever interested her husband."

Eleanor was too shy to step far out of her shell. She was confused by FDR's closest advisor, Louis Howe (he later became her ally), and overwhelmed by duties as hostess, especially when FDR became Secretary of the Navy. Every time she went to a party she hoped "the ground would open and swallow me." FDR, however, was regarded as a promising Democrat and was nominated as James Cox's Vice Presidential running mate in 1920. Mrs. Woodrow Wilson thought FDR could "charm the birds off the trees." The Cox-FDR ticket lost, but a new triumvirate was emerging: FDR, Louis Howe, and, surprisingly, Eleanor Roosevelt.

Disaster struck the following spring when FDR contracted polio while the Roosevelts vacationed at their summerhouse in Campobello, Maine. Although he had the best care possible at that time, doctors were worried that he would not survive. He recuperated at Hyde Park, the Roosevelt estate in New York, and Eleanor and Louis Howe, who lived with the Roosevelts until his death in 1936, took turns massaging FDR's legs and "massaging" his spirits. Not only was Eleanor waging a war against her husband's illness, she had now begun to fight a war against Sara's dominance. Sara would have liked her son to live as a pampered invalid, but Eleanor wanted him to have a real link to the world, which she and Howe believed would keep him alive. This was the start of Eleanor's eventual emergence from her protective shell. She became active in the League of Women Voters, raised funds for Democrats, drove voters to the polls, and kept FDR's name in front of the public, even though in her words, she "died" when she had to give a speech.

The Howe/Eleanor Roosevelt team was effective, both politically and physically. By 1924, FDR had regained use of his arms, he resumed his law practice, and he managed Governor Al Smith's campaign for the Presidential nomination of 1924 (which Smith lost). In 1928, Franklin nominated Smith as the Democratic candidate for President, the nation's first Catholic Presidential nominee, presenting Al Smith as "The Happy Warrior." In turn, Smith supported FDR's run as Governor of New York. FDR was elected, while the "Happy Warrior" was defeated in the national election.

In 1932, the Democrats nominated Franklin Roosevelt as their Presidential candidate. His theme song was "Happy Days Are Here Again," and he promised a "New Deal" for "the forgotten man." The devastating Depression, coupled with Roosevelt's effervescent, optimistic charisma (a word which wasn't used in those days), resulted in his election as thirty-second President. Eleanor was a key promoter and spokesperson of that New Deal. When jobless veterans marched on Washington, the First Lady was there to greet them. President Hoover had driven them away with tear gas; the Roosevelt administration gave them tents and served them hot meals.

Driving her own car, taking trains, buses, subways, boats, planes, any kind of transportation, the First Lady criss-crossed the country, acting as the "eyes and ears" for the President, who depended on his wife to inform him about the reactions of the American people. She had her finger on the nation's pulse, and he listened closely to her suggestions. In her twelve years as First Lady she averaged 40,000 miles of travel a year. She became so popular that her correspondence amounted to over 300,000 letters the first year her husband was in office. By 1934, Hitler said of her, "Eleanor Roosevelt is America's real ruler."

The First Lady was not content simply to act as eyes and ears; she wanted action—she wanted her recommendations carried out. Her strident ways did not go un-noticed. Washington commentators gave her many nicknames, including "Lady Bountiful," "The Busybody," "The Meddler," and "The Gab."[1] Eleanor found the dinner table offered a good chance to express her opinions, to the point where her daughter Anna once objected, "Mother, can't you see you are giving Father indigestion?" Frequently, she left notes with her advice on her husband's bedside table.[2]

Forty-eight years old when her husband was elected President, Eleanor was healthy and energetic, a physically active woman who walked a good deal, rode horseback, did calisthenics and enjoyed square dancing. Her ability to outwalk, outtalk anyone around her was legendary. One White House usher couldn't understand Eleanor when she was walking *and* talking, and switched to a less confusing job in the engineering department, eventually becoming chief engineer of the White House. Eleanor's secretary, Malvina "Tommy" Thompson, was used to running after her boss and would follow her down the halls, taking dictation for the First Lady's daily syndicated newspaper column, "My Day." Once a week, when Eleanor wasn't traveling, she stopped fast-walking long enough to hold a press conference in the Monroe Room, where she discussed her husband's New Deal policies.[3]

The Roosevelts entertained thousands of visitors, and occasionally, Eleanor shook hands with 1,500 guests in the afternoon, and then, joined by FDR, another 1,500 visitors in the evening. Sometimes there were as many as five official functions listed on the First Lady's calendar. In addition to official entertaining, the Roosevelts had many "unofficial" parties: gala receptions for the press, parties for war veterans. More than a million members of the public were in and out of the White House each year, contributing to the wear and tear on the mansion, which was becoming a serious problem.

Henrietta Nesbitt, the Roosevelts' housekeeper, wrote in her memoirs, *White House Diary*, that sixty rooms and twenty baths had to be cleaned every day, and the entire house dusted three times a day. Mrs. Nesbitt eliminated the maids' feather dusters and replaced them with more practical dust rags, but she found it difficult to keep the house looking as it should while thousands of people trouped in, and hundreds more were working in the Executive Offices of the Mansion.

The Roosevelt household itself was more than a handful. Anna and her children "Sistie" and "Buzzie," lived in the White House, and James and Elliot (and their wives), and Franklin Jr. and John, who were still in school, were often in residence. In addition to

Louis Howe, another long-term "permanent" guest was Joseph Lash, who eventually published an award-winning biography of Eleanor. Lash, then in his early 30's, was Eleanor's close confidant and friend. They would walk, talk, and work together, often until late at night. According to several reports, Eleanor was closer to Lash than to her own children.

Sara Delano Roosevelt was also a frequent live-in guest, often entertaining her friends at luncheons or teas. The dictatorial Sara was still trying to boss her daughter-in-law, even when she was the guardian of the White House. When she criticized Eleanor for hiring "colored" servants instead of white help, as *she* did at Hyde Park, Eleanor replied, "Mother, I have never told you this before, but I must tell you now. You run your house, and I'll run mine."[4]

According to Lillian Parks, some things one would think might make Eleanor angry, didn't bother her at all. Once, when no guests arrived for a tea party, the First Lady discovered the invitations hadn't been mailed. Instead of being furious, she laughed and sent the food off "to the boys at Walter Reed (Hospital)."

It is also no surprise that Eleanor had other things on her mind than clothes. She liked to wear lace dresses for evening receptions, because they could be packed and unpacked for her many trips without wrinkling. She often had a favorite dress copied in three or four different colors or fabrics. And she was characteristically generous. Once she ordered blouses to be made for herself and three secretaries and instructed Lillian Parks to make the secretaries' blouses first.[5]

Eleanor Roosevelt was a rebel who did things her way, whether that meant running the elevator herself or moving the furniture around, and her caprices often threw the staff off balance. They soon learned, however, that one of her favorite routines was to cook Sunday night supper. She would request that a silver chafing dish be delivered to the State Dining Room and would cook such simple favorites as scrambled eggs and sausages, while she presided over a "salon" which included writers, artists, actors, actresses, painters, and sculptors, as well as her large family. (Aside from her Sunday night ritual, occasionally she would lapse in selecting daily menus. Once she ordered that sweetbreads be served six times in one week. FDR finally sent Eleanor a note about this fare: "I am getting to the point where my stomach rebels, and this does not help my relations with foreign powers. I bit two of them today.")

President Roosevelt had his own routines. He breakfasted in bed with customary, welcomed interruptions by his grandchildren, and his work day usually was solidly booked until cocktails were served in the Oval Study before dinner—the President personally mixed the martinis and old-fashioneds. Eleanor was a teetotaler, and although she joined her family and guests for cocktails, she never participated in this social rite, but she was always tolerant of other people's habits. (In the same way, she felt women had as much right to smoke as men, and at official parties, after dinner she would light up, thereby giving her stamp of approval to women smoking in public. It didn't take long for her to make her point, and when she did, she stopped smoking because she never really liked the habit.) What she did like was afternoon tea. Eleanor grew up in the age when young women knew how to serve tea, and it was her special time of the day for conversation.

Though "fancy entertaining" was not a major interest, she knew how elegant parties should be arranged, and was smart enough, too, to let others do the arranging. One of the social events during her time as First Lady drew about equal amounts of compliments and criticisms. When King George VI and Queen Elizabeth of England (the parents of the current queen) visited Washington, the White House was "briefed like a small army," according to Mrs. Nesbitt. "The women were...to contact the maids of Her Royal Majesty, and her ladies' maids' maids," and while the king and queen were pleased with the arrangements for their comfort, it is ironic that the maids, and maids' maids were not so pleased. During a typically steamy Washington summer, the White House staff was amazed by the English requests for blankets and hotwater bottles. The English king and queen however, enjoyed the State Dinner followed by entertainment by American folk and opera singers, and especially liked their visit to the Roosevelt family home at Hyde Park. Some members of the press ridiculed Mrs. Roosevelt for serving the royal couple a typical American picnic, with hot-dogs and hamburgers, corn on the cob, French fries, and fruit pies and strawberry shortcake. But the royals loved it.

On December 7, 1941, after the Japanese attack on Pearl Harbor, which FDR immortalized as "a day that will live in infamy," the New Deal became a New War, World War II. Just before Christmas, Winston Churchill came to stay at the White House for two weeks to map out strategies with his new ally. Churchill had unusual working habits, including napping during the afternoon (FDR did not), and then working late into the night. According to Eleanor, FDR experienced several unsettled days after Churchill left until he could resume his normal schedule. But the two leaders definitely had a strong rapport, a bonus during these rough times. When Churchill returned to England after Christmas, he received a message from the President: "It was fun to be in the same decade with you."[6]

The environment at the White House changed markedly with the onset of war. The gates were closed to visitors; a War Room with heavy security was established, and the Mansion was remodeled to provide additional office space. Some entertaining continued: the famous writer Alexander Woollcott became his own proverbial "Man Who Came to Dinner," and stayed for weeks at a time. But he amused FDR and distracted him somewhat from the troubles about the war. During this time, Russia's Prime Minister Molotov was also a visitor, as well as George II of Greece, Peter II of Yugoslavia, Queen Wilhelmina of Holland, and Madame Chiang Kai-shek, who brought, in addition to her entourage of forty, two nurses and two nieces and a nephew. The First Lady said somewhat testily, but quite accurately, "Madame Chiang could talk very convincingly about democracy...but hasn't any idea how to live it."

During the war, Eleanor was a stand-in for her husband, visiting war zones in England, New Zealand, Australia, Guadalcanal and other Pacific islands, as well as bases in Latin America and the United States. Servicemen responded to this warm, concerned lady, and applauded her visits. Another of her wartime efforts was to lobby—very *strongly*—for FDR to integrate the military racially, and she was far ahead of him in terms of these goals. The First Lady also tended to have a casual attitude about the material value of White House objects. At a tea for wounded servicemen, for example, she handed each of them silver teaspoons engraved "The President's House" as souvenirs. The Chief Usher felt he had to (gently) recommend that at future receptions she give them some token other than *silver* teaspoons. (Bess Truman's solution was to distribute ordinary buttons).

During their lives together—and certainly in the dozens of books published in the years since Eleanor and FDR died, observers wondered about the relationship between husband and wife: they seemed in so many ways to be mis-matched. But clearly, their marriage, their partnership worked. And, in its own way, it was an affectionate relationship. Doris Kearns Goodwin, in her comprehensive award-winning work, *No Ordinary Time*, provides ample evidence of their devotion to each other. In one anecdote she relates that FDR pointed out a portrait of Eleanor to Frances Perkins (Secretary of the Treasury), and told Perkins: "It's a beautiful portrait, don't you think so?...Lovely hair! Eleanor has lovely hair." Perkins was struck by the "light in his eyes, which to her mind signaled the light of affection."[7] The couple wrote warm notes to each other, and for some time, FDR tried to re-establish their physical relationship, but Eleanor never quite agreed, whether it was because she was too involved in myriad other responsibilities...or too insecure to take on that role again, we will never know.

FDR was re-elected to his fourth term in 1944, with a new running mate, Harry S. Truman. (By now, Presidential inaugurations were held in January, not on March 4th.) Unfortunately, after twelve years as President, FDR was totally exhausted, and in April, four months into the new term, he left for a brief stay at the "Little White House" in Warm Springs, Georgia. April 12, 1945 started out as an ordinary day: The President signed letters and studied papers, and planned to visit polio patients and attend a barbecue later that afternoon. While posing for preliminary sketches for a portrait, FDR complained of a "terrific headache," and fell unconscious. By 3:35 P.M. his doctors confirmed that he had died of a cerebral hemorrhage. Eleanor wasn't with him; she had been attending a charity tea in Washington. (It could not have been easy for her to learn that Lucy Page Mercer, who had been in and out of FDR's life for four decades, had been present at her husband's deathbed, and that their daughter, Anna, had implemented the tryst). As soon as Eleanor received the news of the President's death, she sent for Harry Truman, who was sworn in as the thirty-third President in the Cabinet Room in the Executive Offices. Later, she recalled, "I could think of nothing to say except how sorry I was for him [Truman], how much we would all want to help him in any way we could, and how sorry I was for the people of the country."

Before FDR was buried, Eleanor took a ring from her finger and placed it on his. Then she ordered the casket closed. At the funeral services, she stood before the flag-draped coffin with her daughter Anna and son Elliot; her other three sons were serving in the Armed Forces and had not been able to get home in time. Typically thinking of others, even in this grievous time, Eleanor Roosevelt instructed the staff to send the hundreds of wreaths and flowers to hospitals. Franklin Delano Roosevelt, who had served his country as President longer than any other man, was buried at Hyde Park.

After her husband's death, Eleanor at age 62 entered a new phase of her own life. She turned down pleas that she run for the Senate, continued with her writing, and became a delegate to the United Nations and Chairman of the United Nations Commission on Human Rights; her efforts on that commission resulted in ratifying the Covenant on Human Rights. In the past fifty years, she has been named, along with other First Ladies, as someone who would have been an effective President in her own right. When she died in 1962 Harry Truman said, "she had interest not only in the United States, but in the world." President Kennedy commented, "It is my judgment that there can be no adequate replacement for Mrs. Roosevelt."

And the American public seemed to agree. The Gallup Poll showed that for thirteen consecutive years, Eleanor Roosevelt was "the most admired woman in the world." One of her finest tributes came from her son James, who described his mother as a "sort of roving one-woman task force for social reform and international good will," and his father's "invaluable and trusted right arm."

THELMA CATHERINE "PAT"
RYAN NIXON

When Pat Nixon became First Lady in 1968, it was not a dream fulfilled, as it had been for many other Presidents' wives. It was more of a nightmare. She had worked long and hard for thirty years in support of her husband's political goals, but she had no wish whatsoever to live in the White House or to be the "First Lady of the Land."

As always, Thelma Catherine "Pat" Ryan Nixon carried out her responsibilities. (Her father called her Pat because she was born on the eve of St. Patrick's day; years later she legally changed the nickname to her first name.) Pat Ryan's mother died when she was 13 and her father just five years later. She and her two brothers supported themselves mentally and financially, but the going was rough. She worked at various jobs and in 1932 at age 20, had an opportunity to drive a couple from California to New York in their old Packard. Later she reminisced that during the trip she was "driver, nurse, mechanic and scared." In New York she worked as a secretary and X-ray technician and saved enough to return home and enroll at the University of Southern California, while earning extra money as a department store clerk and even a Hollywood extra. She graduated from USC *cum laude* in 1937, taught typing and shorthand at Whittier High School, and joined an amateur theater group to make new friends as well as satisfy a longtime interest in acting.

Pat Ryan was vivacious and attractive and soon became one of the most popular young women in Whittier. At the same time,

Richard Milhous Nixon, completed his law degree at Duke University and moved back to Whittier to start his law practice. He, too, joined the theater group. The first time Dick met pretty Pat, he asked her to marry him. "I thought he was nuts," she told reporters many years later. Although she didn't accept his proposal, he persisted. "He would drive me to meet other beaux and wait around to drive me home," she recalled. Finally after two years of dating him (and others), she agreed to marry him in June 1940. During World War II, while he served in the Navy, she worked in San Francisco as a government economist, and saved enough money to bankroll his first campaign for Congress in 1946.

One trait the couple shared was an attitude toward work. Pat Nixon once said, "I had to work. I haven't just sat back and thought of myself or what I wanted to do. I've kept working. I don't have time to worry about who I admire or who I identify with. I've never had it easy. I'm not like all you—all those people who had it easy." And she worked hard, even if she didn't agree with her husband's career choice.

When Richard Nixon was elected to Congress in 1947, it was a new experience for both Nixons. Daughter Julie Nixon Eisenhower writes in her book, *Pat Nixon: The Untold Story*, that during their first social season, they committed some gaffes because they were confused about "dress informal" (black tie, long gown) and "formal" (white tie/tails, formal gown).[1]

In 1952, Richard Nixon, the youngest Republican Senator, was touted as a running mate for General Eisenhower. Alice Roosevelt Longworth, a family friend, advised against the race. "If you're thinking of your own good and your own career you are probably better off to stay in the Senate and not go down in history as another nonentity who served as Vice President." But Nixon didn't heed the warning. At the July convention, a few hours after the Republicans nominated Eisenhower for President, Ike announced that Richard Nixon was his choice as a running mate to help fight the "Great crusade for freedom in America and freedom in the world."

A few months into the campaign, a reporter wrote about an $18,000 "slush fund" established for Nixon two years earlier for his senate campaign against Helen Gahagan Douglas. Critics viewed this fund (set up to cover printing costs and campaign trips) as an opportunity for the young senator to live in a grander style. This book is not the place to decide who was right and who was wrong. Nonetheless, fairly or unfairly, Nixon was called upon to explain the fund, and he got little support from Eisenhower, who chose to stay out of the fray. Instead, Nixon was advised to give a speech before a national television audience and explain the fund. His address, a little more than a month before the 1952 election became famous as the "Checkers Speech," so-called for the family dog which Nixon cited as the one gift he had ever accepted, sent by a Texan who had heard Mrs. Nixon say that she would love to have a pet for her daughters.

During the speech, Pat sat near her husband and was on camera only four or five times. *The Long Beach (California) Press Telegram* reported the next day; "Mrs. Nixon said not a word. One could hardly detect a movement in her face. But the character in her face, the picture of a loyal wife backing up her husband...made her a vital factor in the success of the appeal." This was perhaps the beginning of the public's misreading of Pat Nixon's expressions and body language. While she may have appeared stoic and stalwart, she later confided to friends that she was mortified and humiliated by the sentimentality and the public revelations of their private affairs. During the program, Nixon lauded Eisenhower, listed his own assets ($4,000 in life insurance and a two-year-old Oldsmobile), and pointed out that although his wife worked long hours in his senate office, she wasn't on the payroll. Then in a reference to a scandal in the Truman administration regarding a Presidential aide's gift of a $9,000 mink coat to a White House secretary, Nixon said, "Pat doesn't have a mink coat. But she does have a respectable Republican cloth coat." That mention of a "respectable Republican cloth coat" was to follow the Nixons for the rest of his political career.[2]

The telephone and mail reaction to the "Checkers Speech" (watched by an estimated 60 million viewers) was overwhelmingly positive, and the Republican ticket of Eisenhower and Nixon took off. On Election Day, 1952, they carried 39 states and just under 55 percent of the popular vote.

The years as Vice President's wife weren't easy for Pat. For one thing, in 1952, there was no official Vice President's residence, and since the Nixons were not independently wealthy, carrying out official entertaining was not only difficult, but costly: they had to hire facilities and caterers for dinners and receptions. In addition, Pat didn't have full-time help and was always lining up baby-sitters to take care of the girls during official events, as well as when she stood in at receptions Mamie Eisenhower couldn't attend.

The Nixons embarked on many goodwill tours during his eight years as Vice President. Most trips were highly successful, but a 1958 South American tour was disastrous. In Peru, for example, 2,000 Communist demonstrators shouted *"Muerte a Nixon"* (Death to Nixon) and blocked the entrance to San Marcos University when he was scheduled to speak. The mob threw fruit and rocks, smashed car windows, and there was personal danger for Nixon, who was standing in an open convertible. The secret service switched to closed limousines and the Nixons continued the tour. Even so, demonstrators spat at the Vice President and his wife while they were speaking, and then when the entourage tried to drive to the American embassy, the crowd used pipes, stones, rocks, and even baseball bats to destroy more car windows and terrorize the Americans. Later Pat recalled she was more angry than frightened until she saw that every window in her husband's car had been smashed.

In 1960, the Democrats nominated Senator John F. Kennedy of Massachusetts as their Presidential candidate, with Texas Senator Lyndon Baines Johnson as his running mate. The Republicans nominated Nixon and Henry Cabot Lodge for President and Vice President. During the campaign there was a great deal of gossip about how much the prospective First Ladies spent on clothes. Jacqueline Kennedy was pregnant and didn't campaign very much. She quipped that if she really spent $30,000 (or was it $50,000?) on clothing, "I would have to wear sable underwear" and guessed that Pat Nixon probably spent more on *her* clothes (not true by a long shot). Once again, Pat's "respectable Republican cloth coat" was used in defense.

The 1960 campaign introduced an innovation in Presidential campaigning—the televised debate—that Americans now take for granted. Four debates between the two candidates were scheduled. In the forty-plus years since then, few political commentators would argue the fact that JFK was one of those rare men (or women) the camera "loves," and Nixon, despite his favorable appearance during the "Checkers Speech" years before, looked unattractive, unfriendly, and unskilled. A new word, "charisma," took hold: John F. Kennedy had it; Richard M. Nixon didn't. And unquestionably, this new attitude carried over to the distaff side as well. Jacqueline Kennedy was young, beautiful, charming and pregnant; Pat Nixon seemed drab, dowdy, and stiff by comparison. The press began to dub her "Plastic Pat," and "The Robot."

Richard Nixon lost the election very narrowly to JFK, and while some advisers (including his wife) said he should challenge the results, especially those reported in Chicago and Texas, he conceded and seemed to be on the path back to private life in California. In 1961, Pat who passionately hated politics by then, asked her husband to sign a pledge that his political career was over, that he would never run for office again. To her despair, he broke the pledge in 1962, 1968, and again in 1972.

Private life in California was not a comfortable life for Dick Nixon, even as he vowed to switch careers. In 1962, again disregarding Pat's strong negative opinion (and the written pledge),

Nixon was persuaded to run for governor against the popular Pat Brown. Brown won the election. In his concession speech, Nixon not only thanked his supporters, but also sent a message to the press:

I leave you gentlemen now and you will now write it…just think how much you're gong to be missing. You won't have Nixon to kick around anymore, because, gentlemen, this is my last press conference…I hope that what I have said today will at least make (the media) recognize the great responsibility they have to report all the news and, second…if they're against a candidate, to give him the shaft, but also recognize if they give him the shaft, put one lonely reporter on the campaign who will report what the candidate says now and then.

It was a bitter, angry speech, and like a bad penny, came back to haunt Nixon six years later, when he made another bid for the presidency. After this disastrous loss and humiliating concession speech, Pat commented, "It takes heart to be in political life," and although she didn't approve of his goals and candidly said she hated politics, she loved her husband and believed in what he had to offer America. She never described their relationship as a partnership. She always said, "We're a team."

In 1968, the Democrats were in a weak position. Lyndon Johnson had bowed out of the race, and the man who might have been able to re-ignite that legendary Kennedy charisma, Robert Kennedy, was assassinated on the evening of his primary election success in California. (A few months earlier Martin Luther King, Jr. had also been assassinated.) Even though Vice President Hubert Humphrey was the party favorite, he was never able to dismiss the bitter memories of anti-war riots and disassociate himself from the now unpopular LBJ. Humphrey lost the election by a meager half million votes, perhaps poetic justice for the President-elect, Richard M. Nixon, who had lost to Kennedy eight years before by a similarly slim margin.

Pat Nixon had traveled all over the United States and to 53 foreign nations as the wife of the Vice President. By the end of her White House years she had visited 78 countries and had become the most widely traveled First Lady in history, even surpassing Eleanor Roosevelt's formidable record.[3] Her travels with the President included the historic visit to the People's Republic of China and summit meetings in the Soviet Union. Despite the disastrous trip in 1958, she returned to Peru on her own to take relief supplies to earthquake victims. Pat was also the first President's wife to tour a combat zone (Vietnam, where taking a cue from Eleanor Roosevelt, when she visited wounded soldiers in an evacuation hospital, she noted their names and addresses and wrote to their families when she returned to Washington). She was also the first First Lady to use the word "abortion," and advocate a pro-choice position, and according to her daughter, Julie, she energetically, but unsuccessfully tried to convince President Nixon to appoint a woman justice to the Supreme Court.

In addition to arduous traveling, Pat faced a task that confronts all First Ladies: refurbishing the White House. Seven million tourists in five years had visited the official rooms, and there had been hundreds of parties. Not only did guests ruin the carpet, souvenir hunters had cut snippets and bits of wallpaper and upholstery, and simple wear and tear were all too evident. Pat didn't have Jackie Kennedy's decorating zeal, or even Lady Bird's inclination to keep things as they were, but it was obviously necessary for her to do some redecorating.

Then, too, the Nixon family wanted the White House to be their *home*. Rooms were repainted, draperies and bedspreads replaced and the Nixons removed the army of telephones and special three-screen TV's that LBJ obsessively watched. One change caused criticism: Jacqueline Kennedy had had a plaque installed on the mantle in her bedroom noting the years she and JFK had resided in the room. Julie says this plaque was removed because it had nothing to do with a historic mantle; others believed removing the plaque was spiteful. In any case, by the time the Nixons left in 1974, Pat had almost finished Jackie's work: two-thirds of the furnishings in the Executive Mansion were authentic vintage pieces and included additions of 600 paintings and antiques.

As First Lady, Pat had a ten-woman staff, but she was still overbooked and overworked. Although her "cause" was never officially categorized as such and wasn't as glamorous as her predecessors', she established the "Vest Pockets of Volunteerism" and embarked on a nationwide trip to launch the program.

Another less touted accomplishment of Pat Nixon's was her work on the White House outdoor lighting, which Mrs. Eisenhower had first supervised, and then somehow was diminished or discontinued during subsequent administrations (including LBJ's efforts at economy). Pat used part of her redecorating funds to set up new lighting with the help of the National Park Service. In August, 1970, as the Nixons returned from a trip, the new lights were switched on and the delighted President asked the helicopter pilot to circle the White House several times so he could enjoy the spectacular view.

Julie Eisenhower cites other achievements:

By January of 1970, my parents had entertained 45,313 people as compared to the previous record of 28,000 in the Johnsons' final year in office. There had been 64 state and official dinners and 116 receptions. U.S. News and World Report *also pointed out that Mrs. Nixon entertained guests at tea at the rate of 26,000 a year.*[4]

(In fairness, during the Vietnam War, the Johnsons did not feel it was appropriate to have too many celebrations.) Although she was a Republican politically, Pat Nixon was a democrat personally. Shortly after the 1968 election she remarked that she would now entertain ordinary people in the White House. "The guests won't be limited to big shots!" she said. Her husband jokingly reminded her that most of their friends were "big shots," but she did succeed in having "ordinary" people in on Sunday mornings for an egalitarian religious service.

While Richard Nixon was President, the First Lady spent a great deal of time alone. Often the Nixons ate their meals separately in different parts of the White House. The President also spent many weekends with his friend Bebe Rebozo in the Bahamas, in Florida, or at Camp David, while his wife stayed in Washington. And whether the result of absent-mindedness or a lack of concern or feeling, many observers realized that Dick Nixon often ignored his wife during public appearances. At the Inaugural Ball in 1969, the President forgot to introduce Pat as First Lady at one ball; at another, he introduced his daughters and his son-in-law, Eisenhower's grandson, David, and *then* his wife. He was about to go off to the next ball when an aide reminded him that he had left Pat in the ballroom. On another occasion when he had an opportunity to congratulate his wife on her many talents, he instead praised her as a "wonderful stenographer."

January 1973 should have been a triumphant time for President Nixon, his family, and his administration. After months of negotiations the Vietnamese had accepted the terms that ended the war that had torn America apart. Instead of celebrating, the nation's attention was focused on the Watergate investigation. Years earlier, during the 1968 campaign, Pat was dismayed by the take-charge, high-handed attitude of Nixon's aide, Robert Haldeman. When Nixon won the election, Haldeman, along with key aides (John Erlichmann, John Dean, Attorney General John Mitchell, and others) put a distance between Nixon and some trusted advisers who had been with him for many years, despite his wife's warnings against so much reliance on and trust in the new team.

Although JFK, LBJ, and even FDR had taping facilities, Nixon made a mistake, in his daughter's view (and the opinion of millions of Americans), when he reinstated widespread taping with a purported aim of using the tapes for his memoirs. Thousands of hours of conversations—in the Oval Office, in the Lincoln Study, at Camp David—were recorded, and as the Watergate scandal unfolded, the existence of the tapes and what was on them became increasingly incriminating. Pat had begged her husband to confiscate them—she considered them his private diaries, not public information. She told Julie, and her opinion is a matter of record, that Nixon should have destroyed the incriminating tapes months, if not years, before. Now, not only would they not be used to help him write his memoirs, they had become the instruments of his disgrace. (Aside from any political insights the tapes may have afforded, they were so filled with words that shouldn't be repeated in polite company, that the term "expletive deleted" became part of our vocabulary). In retrospect, it seems so odd that Nixon, the consummate politician, exhibited such a tragic flaw by opting to keep them and therefore insure his own self-destruction.

After months of investigations and testimony, accusations and evidence became more and more devastating. By July 1974, for the first time in 106 years, a President faced impeachment.

The House Judiciary Committee had established five articles of impeachment against Nixon, including "Obstruction of the investigation of the Watergate case," "Abuse of the power of his office" and "Failing to comply with Judiciary Committee subpoenas" (for not turning over the tapes). The last two articles (bombing of Communist sanctuaries in Cambodia, and deductions the Nixons had taken on their Income Tax) were voted down by the Judiciary Committee. Even so, clearly Nixon could be impeached on the first three articles alone. There was little he could do to offset the charges, and while he was fighting them, the country would have been thrown into political limbo. At the same time, after Nixon lost congressional support, there was no point in continuing the fight.

When President Nixon announced his decision to resign, some family members and a few advisors tried to dissuade him. The valiant Pat wanted him to tough it out in a trial, or fight by producing other skeletons in the Federal closet. But he was more persuasive in his arguments to resign. No one was surprised ultimately by his decision. Just a day before the official resignation, Pat canceled the china she had ordered for the White House and began to pack the family's personal possessions

When President Nixon made his farewell speech, he talked about his family and his mother, Hannah Nixon, whom he called a "real saint," but he forgot to mention his wife. Julie Eisenhower writes, "That would have been asking too much of any man…When he spoke the words 'when sadness comes' much of the regret he felt at that moment, yet left unspoken was that he had let his family down."[5]

At that terribly sad and awkward scene as the Nixons and the Fords walked to the helicopter after leaving the White House, on the first leg of the trip back to California, Betty Ford, trying to make conversation, mentioned the length of the red carpet. Pat Nixon said wryly that after seeing so many red carpets, "you'll get to hate them." Pat Nixon was not a whiner, though. She once said "I hate complainers and I made up my mind not to be one." Still, she never talked about the Watergate events or her husband's resignation in public ever again.

A few months later, at La Casa Pacifica in San Clemente, Nixon almost died from recurring phlebitis; after weeks of touch-and-go medical reports, he recovered. Not long afterward, in 1976, the former First Lady suffered a stroke. Following her recovery, the family moved from California to New York City, and then to New Jersey, so that the Nixons—Pat in particular—could be near their four grandchildren.

In New Jersey, Pat Nixon enjoyed her home, her relaxed life, her grandchildren and her garden. Former President Nixon gave up his office in New York, and in a suburban office complex wrote several widely acclaimed books and his memoirs. Although some First Ladies—Eleanor Roosevelt, Lady Bird Johnson, Rosalynn Carter—continued their national and international activities after their service in the White House, Pat Nixon was more in the camp of Bess Truman, Edith Wilson and Lou Hoover, who preferred a restful return to quasi-anonymity.

In her book, *First Ladies*, Margaret Truman recalls how she had never thought much about Pat Nixon because she had always disliked Richard Nixon, who, during the 50's had accused her father, President Truman, of being a Communist. But she writes that with the passage of time she came to view Pat Nixon in her own light: "Lady Bird Johnson managed to transcend her husband's unpopularity. Pat Nixon was almost obliterated by the antagonism Richard Nixon generated. The result has been a blank in the public mind about one of the most gifted, hardest working First Ladies in the long history of the White House."[6]

But this view is not entirely valid. Millions of women recognized that behind the stiffness was heroism and strength, and recognized that she froze before cameras or in front of large audiences, not because of aloofness or a stubborn attitude, but because of shyness. For twenty years, beginning in 1953, she was named as one of the top ten Outstanding Homemakers of the Year.

Pat Nixon was also her husband's secret strength. Although he sometimes forgot to praise her while she was alive, after she died at home in 1993, at age 81, he told an interviewer, "Throughout our ordeals, Pat has been stronger than I." In his memoirs he gave her bittersweet accolades and regretted that his wife had "not received any of the praise she deserved. There (was) no round of farewell parties...no testimonials, no tributes. She had given so much to the nation and to the world." Her only reward, he wrote, was "to share my exile. She deserved so much more."[7]

Richard Nixon died ten months after his wife. Both are buried at the Richard Nixon Library and Birthplace in Yorba Linda, California.

ROSALYNN SMITH CARTER

James Earl Carter, Jr., our thirty-ninth President, who preferred to be known as Jimmy, once described his wife Rosalynn as "an almost equal extension of myself." Few would disagree; in fact, many historians consider the Jimmy/Rosalynn Carter duo a political partnership equal to that of Franklin Delano Roosevelt and his wife, Eleanor (and in some ways, a model for the Presidential partnership to come, that of Bill and Hillary Clinton).

There are other parallels: Both Eleanor Roosevelt and Rosalynn Carter were very shy young women who, because of necessity (their husband's political campaigns and elected offices) conquered shyness and became effective spokeswomen for their mates. Both had the major responsibility of raising children while their husbands were otherwise occupied (Carter in the Navy, FDR ill with polio). Rosalynn and Eleanor developed political skills while serving as governors' wives (Carter, Georgia; Roosevelt, New York).

And both women emerged from the shadow of strong mothers-in-law. Lillian Carter (like Sara Roosevelt), was always a force to be reckoned with, a headline grabber who joined the Peace Corps, spent her seventieth birthday in India, threw out the first ball in the 1977 World Series, toured Italy and West Africa when she was almost eighty, and was proud to say, "I'm *not* a long-faced square. I do the things I want to do."[1]

Aside from these similarities, Rosalynn Carter and Eleanor Roosevelt reached their positions as First Lady from very different directions. Rosalynn, the eldest of four children, grew up in rural

Plains, Georgia, where she is still remembered as "neat, pretty, clean, smart, reserved and not a blab-mouth or a high roller." Her father was ill with leukemia and died when she was 13; to support the family, her mother took in sewing and worked in a grocery store until she became the town's postmistress. Rosalynn worked hard, too—at after-school jobs and her schoolwork, and she graduated as valedictorian of her high school class.

Her best friend was Ruth Carter, whose handsome Naval Cadet brother, Jimmy, was considered the Number One Bachelor of Plains. One day, in true storybook fashion, the dashing officer noticed that his kid sister's friend had grown up. After one date, the story goes, he told his mother he had met the woman he was going to marry. (While we would hope our Presidents would be more cautious in foreign affairs, a majority of our leaders seem to have been victims of "love at first sight".) Rosalynn felt the same way. Shortly after Jimmy graduated from the Naval Academy in June 1946 and began his career in the Navy, they were married. The new Mrs. Carter "thought it would be exciting to...travel. At that age, I hadn't seen the world," she told writer Gail Sheehy, "and I thought there was more to it than Plains, Georgia."

Rosalynn did get to see the world, but most of her travels didn't take place until decades later. Following their wedding, she and Jimmy spent time in Norfolk, Virginia; Honolulu, Hawaii; and New London, Connecticut, and during those years they became parents of three sons, each one born at a different base. In 1953, however, Jimmy's father died, and he gave up his Navy career to supervise the family's peanut, fertilizer and seed business. Rosalynn fought this decision vigorously ("the only major disagreement of our marriage"), but Jimmy won the battle, and in 1954, they returned to Plains where they worked side by side to restore the failing business. Rosalynn served as the company's accountant.

When Jimmy decided to run for the state senate in 1962, Rosalynn handled all his campaign correspondence; when he was elected, she managed the business while he was away in Atlanta. In 1966, she took a far more active role in his campaign for governor of Georgia...but he was defeated. The next year brought a much happier event: the Carters were overjoyed when their only daughter, Amy Lynn, was born.

Neither Jimmy nor Rosalynn ever took defeat "lying down;" and they learned their lessons about losing-and-winning elections every step along the way. When Jimmy ran for governor again in 1970, Rosalynn was an energetic and effective campaigner, giving speeches, attending teas and receptions, shaking thousands of hands, and acting very much like an ideal politician's wife, even though she, like Eleanor Roosevelt, felt that public speaking was "an agony."

Hard campaigning by Jimmy and Rosalynn paid off: Jimmy won the election.

As the governor's wife, Rosalynn's main interest was mental health; to gain "hands on" experience with the problems of the mentally ill, she served as a volunteer at a hospital in Atlanta. She became adept at fulfilling her duties as Georgia's First Lady, helped establish 134 day-care centers in the state, and served as Chairman of the Georgia Special Olympics for retarded children.

In 1973, Jimmy decided to run for the presidency. When he announced his decision to his mother, Lillian responded, "President of *what?*" It was the wildest long shot, but after the Nixon Watergate scandal, and his subsequent pardon, Jerry Ford wasn't a strong candidate. Rosalynn persuaded Jimmy to enter every possible primary and campaigned for him and with him in an unprecedented *thirty-four* states over the course of fourteen months, accompanied at first, by just one friend. The shrinking violet became a "Steel Magnolia." After Carter won the nomination, she campaigned in ninety-six cities in thirty-six states, in the beginning, often having to answer the question, "Jimmy *who?*"

Unlike Pat Nixon, who always said she and Dick were a "team," Rosalynn Carter has consistently said of her husband, "Jimmy and I were always *partners*." One reporter who interviewed the Carters shortly after the inauguration came away puzzled after they often gave the same answers and finished each other's sentences. "I've just met two Jimmy Carters," he said. Rosalynn then and now has downplayed her influence in her husband's actions, but he has always acknowledged it, even going telling one interviewer, "I don't hesitate to discuss with her every major decision I make."

When Jimmy Carter was elected in 1976, and Rosalynn, at 50, became First Lady, she quickly put her 21-member staff to work on her primary interests: mental health programs, the needs of the aging, and the Equal Rights Amendment.

Many people think Hillary Clinton was the first President's wife to address Congress, but actually Ellen Wilson appeared before Congress to lobby for better housing for the Capitol's poor in 1914; Eleanor Roosevelt testified before a Congressional committee in the 1940's; and was followed three decades later by Rosalynn Carter who, as honorary chairperson of the President's Commission on Mental Health, addressed the Senate Resource Subcommittee on increasing government funds for mental health. During those hearings the intrepid First Lady battled a fierce adversary, Ted Kennedy, about how much was enough to include in the federal health budget.

Rosalynn was a major player in the historic meetings with Middle Eastern leaders at Camp David in 1978, and she was also the first President's wife since Sarah Polk to sit in on cabinet meetings, generating more than a little criticism. She went on a seven-nation tour of the Caribbean and Latin America in 1977, not as the traditional hospital-visiting, tea-drinking First Lady, but rather, as Jimmy Carter made it clear, in a substantive role in which she acted directly as his "personal emissary" in meeting with government leaders. In December 1977, Rosalynn accompanied the President to India and the Middle East and had her own itinerary of meetings with health officials on the status of women. Margaret Truman writes, "The Carter partnership had two components which made it unique. It was profoundly religious, and it was intensely ambitious. The religious component meant Rosalynn could simultaneously claim she had her own identity and freely submerge her personality and ideas in her husband's. The ambition was lofted on both religious and secular idealism to an almost dizzying height. The Carters came to Washington with the heady conviction that they could and would change America and the world."[2]

The Carters found time to entertain, too, but their style was much less formal than that of the Nixons or Fords, and Rosalynn never considered that side of the job her major priority. In her autobiography, *First Lady from Plains*, she gives short shrift to guests, menus, clothes, and the like in a very brief chapter on "People, Parties and Protocol." She explained that while earlier Presidents' wives were limited to roles as "official hostess" or "private helpmeet," in her view, "the public expectation has changed."

Jimmy and Rosalynn were undeniably an attractive and hard-working Presidential pair, but unfortunately, their luck did not hold in terms of world and national events. By 1979, Americans were concerned about their image abroad, the nation's ability to compete with Russia in nuclear capabilities, and most of all, that their former ally, Iran, now ruled by Ayatollah Khomeni, held over a hundred Americans hostage…and Jimmy Carter had not been able to get them released. Jimmy and Rosalynn Carter lost the 1980 election to an even more spectacular Presidential team—Ronald and Nancy Reagan.

After the White House, the Carters returned to Plains where they built a house (much of it with their own hands), and launched a program to renovate houses in slum districts which became the very successful "Habitat for Humanity." In 1982, Jimmy Carter founded the nonprofit Carter Center in Atlanta to promote peace and human rights worldwide, and Rosalynn Carter serves as vice chair, spearheading a program to diminish stigma against mental illness. The Center has initiated projects in more than 65 countries to resolve conflicts, prevent human rights abuses, build democracy, improve health, and revitalize urban areas. The former President has also worked to ensure fair elections and help promote peace in areas all over the world, including Haiti, Ghana, and Bosnia. Often his small staff includes just one or two aides...and Rosalynn.

The Carters, who still live in Plains, have also written more than a dozen books between them, and the forward or introduction to at least another dozen. And in 1987, they co-authored *Everything to Gain: Making the Most of the Rest of Your Life*, in which Rosalynn talks about their marriage. "Interestingly, as we passed our fortieth anniversary, we realized that the arguments have become more infrequent and less intense than in earlier years. Maybe we have exhausted most of the points of disagreement, or at least rounded off the rough edges of those that persist."[3]

We tend to think of the Carters as inseparable, as Jimmy-and-Rosalynn, and when Jimmy Carter speaks of his faith and his goals, one thinks of Rosalynn as sharing those goals. "I have one life and one chance to make it count for something," the former President told reporter Jim Wooten in 1995. "I'm free to choose what that something is, and the something I've chosen is my faith. Now, my faith goes beyond theology and religion and requires considerable work and effort...My faith *demands* that I do whatever I can, wherever I can, whenever I can, for as long as I can with whatever I have to try to make a difference. It isn't difficult."[4]

Several years ago, Rosalynn Carter indicated that she wasn't against running for public office on her own. She seemed to be thinking more in terms of the Senate or House, but the "Steel Magnolia" would have probably made an effective President. Instead, she has continued to write, focusing on assisting those in need. Three of her recent books include *Triumph Over Fear, Helping Someone with Mental Illness*, and *Helping Yourself Help Others* (which deals with caring for the elderly or ill).

In 1996, Rosalynn and Jimmy Carter celebrated their fiftieth anniversary...and Rosalynn's early dream has come true a hundred-fold: together, they have indeed seen the world...and helped to change it.

NANCY DAVIS REAGAN

During his last State of the Union Address, in January, 1988, President Ronald Wilson Reagan told members of Congress and his television audience that the nation was winning the battle against drugs, and he interrupted his speech to thank a leading soldier in that battle, Nancy Reagan, for her "Just Say No!" campaign. The visibly pleased First Lady took a bow on camera and enjoyed several minutes of a standing ovation.

It was the first time a President had praised his wife in a major address on the status of the country. But there were many firsts in Reagan's presidency, and this was just one of them. (Ronald Reagan was the first divorced man to be elected, and at seventy-seven he was the oldest President...the nation's fortieth).

The Reagans have always been very open about their affection for each other, but aside from the happily-ever-after love story, their devotion to each other was the secret weapon behind Reagan's political career. Although Nancy didn't sit in on cabinet meetings or make speeches about the President's policies, in her own way she was as strong a member of the Presidential team as two of her predecessors, Rosalynn Carter and Eleanor Roosevelt.

She was born Anne Frances Robbins, and soon after her birth her mother, Edith Luckett, and her father, Kenneth Robbins were divorced. For the first years of her life, maternal relatives cared for Nancy while her actress mother was on the road. When Edith married Loyal Davis, a prominent and wealthy Chicago neurosurgeon, the little girl's life changed markedly. Dr. Davis adopted her, changed her name to Nancy Davis, and she eventually became a prim, proper Smith-educated debutante. Her stepfather also provided an education in conservative political attitudes. After graduating from Smith (drama major) in 1943, Nancy studied acting in New York and appeared in minor roles in Broadway plays, but in 1951 she headed west to establish a movie career. At the time there was another actress named "Nancy Davis," which was not only confusing in itself, but the other Davis was known as a supporter of socialist causes—the opposite end of Nancy's political pole. She sought help from the head of the actor's union, Ronald Reagan (recently divorced from actress Jane Wyman), and the rest is history.

Nancy and Ronnie were married in 1952; seven-and-a-half months later their daughter Patti was born—in 1989 Nancy challenged reporters: "Go ahead and count." After the Reagans made a last film together, "Hellcats of the Navy," (which would be her final acting effort after 11 films) their son Ronald was born in 1958. She was on her way to fulfilling her lifelong ambition, publicly stated from the time she arrived in Hollywood: "to have a successful happy marriage." Nancy admittedly and proudly put her husband first in her life since then and frequently said, "My life didn't really begin until I met Ronnie." That statement may have infuriated feminists, but more important for all of us is that Nancy clearly helped shape his political views. Over the years Ronald Reagan made a complete swing from a liberal Democrat to a very conservative Republican.

In the late forties and early fifties, as Reagan moved up in the actor's union, had more and more contact with studio executives, and was increasingly influenced by his father-in-law, his sympathies began to switch from union members to producers and studio moneymen. The change became complete in 1954 when he was named a spokesman for General Electric, a corporation then known for anti-union attitudes. For his $125,000 a year salary, he acted as host of the "General Electric Theatre" and served as G.E.'s "goodwill ambassador," traveling all over the United States, giving dinner speeches and pep talks to employees. During his eight years with General Electric, he established a reputation as an effective speaker and was soon in demand for Republican fund-raisers and other political events, where he met key national GOP leaders. In 1964, the actor-turned-politician became the California chairman of conservative Republican Barry Goldwater's campaign against Lyndon Johnson. Goldwater lost, but as often happens in politics, Reagan's star was on the rise.

Prominent Californians formed a committee, collected a "war chest," and supported Reagan for governor against the popular incumbent, Pat Brown. Reagan vowed to cut the budget by 25 percent, reduce taxes, eliminate government waste and fraud, and touted a complete laundry list of law-and-order Republican causes. In 1966 he beat Brown, and even though most of his campaign goals never materialized, he was a popular governor.

Reagan also began dedicated work for national Republican causes. His newspaper column and weekly radio program, coupled with frequent speeches on behalf of Republican candidates, gave him more and more national prominence and recognition. In a 1975 poll naming most admired Americans, Reagan placed ninth. Despite Reagan's popularity and hard work for the party, President Gerald Ford was nominated in 1976, only to be defeated by Jimmy Carter. In 1980, however, the years of efforts paid off. Reagan became his party's candidate, and then, in a huge electoral victory, America's fortieth President.

During this climb up the political ladder, Nancy was always at her husband's side, charming important contributors, consistently in character as the perfect political helpmeet. And always acting as her husband's protector. That role came into sharp focus just 69 days after the 1981 inauguration when John Hinckley, Jr. shot and wounded the President (and his press secretary, Jim Brady). This may be an apocryphal story, but reportedly, Nancy who was at a ceremonial luncheon with Barbara Bush at the time Ronnie was shot, left the reception abruptly because her intuition told her something had happened to her husband. The First Lady returned to the White House much earlier than scheduled and immediately was informed about the shooting.

This was the beginning of a seesaw of public opinion unrivaled by any other First Lady in history, before or after. (Opprobrium or affection for Hillary Clinton, as discussed in the next chapter, did not swerve up and down so markedly. There was always a solid contingent of Hillary-lovers or Hillary-haters, no matter what the Clintons actually...or allegedly did). While Nancy scored high in the polls for her devotion to her wounded husband, at the same time the press began its attacks for what were seen as her extravagant and elitist habits. (This negative reputation began years earlier when she was First Lady of California and refused to live in the governor's mansion in Sacramento because, she said, "The place reminded me of a funeral parlor.") Her initial goal as First Lady was to follow in Jackie Kennedy's footsteps and restore elegance to the White House after the simple ways of the Carters. Her good intentions backfired, however, and were viewed as "an attitude," especially after she embarked on a redecorating plan which was to cost over $800,000, and it was rumored that she had spent over $1 million in designer dresses and gowns. The worst public relations gaffe occurred when the news that she had ordered 4,732 pieces of new china at a cost of

$209,000 broke about the same time Ron's administration announced plans to decrease nutrition standards for school lunches and made the infamous decision listing ketchup as a *vegetable*. (Actually, the Knapp Foundation donated the china and the $800,000 for redecorating the private rooms was contributed by a group of Republicans—but this never made much news.)

The media began to call her "Queen Nancy" and "Queen Bee," and by the end of 1981, Nancy had one of highest disapproval ratings of any modern First Lady. But Nancy, seeking damage control, decided to make jokes at her own expense. At the 1981 Al Smith Dinner in New York—where Republicans and Democrats alike give speeches with an emphasis on humor—she said, referring to her queenly status, "I'd never wear a crown. It musses up your hair." A few months later at the annual Gridiron Club dinner where journalists lampoon the President, First Lady, and other top government officials, one reporter sang "Second Hand Clothes," spoofing the Barbra Streisand/Fanny Brice hit. Reportedly surprising even the President, Nancy then appeared on stage and sang her *own* version of "Second Hand Rose," poking fun at herself. The appreciative media did a turnaround, and within a year, they were calling her the "comeback queen."

Nancy also made some drastic decisions about "her cause." Initially, she had decided to focus on a "Foster Grandparent Program," culminating in her 1982 book, *To Love a Child*. But this goal didn't resonate with the public. Advisors then came up with the campaign to fight drug use and the theme of "Just Say No!" Her public image soared...and drug use among young people declined. By 1985, after the second election, which Reagan won—49 states to one—Nancy scored higher than her husband in approval polls. She ranked 71 percent in popularity to his 62 percent, topping even Jackie Kennedy's highest ratings. She was on a popularity roll that peaked in April, 1985, when she invited the leading ladies of 17 countries to the White House for a First Ladies Conference to study the international drug problem. That was the good news...but a few months later when she met with Pope John Paul II to discuss the drug problem at the Vatican, she was criticized for her huge retinue—one news source called her staff an "entourage more appropriate to a visiting head of state."

Her popularity continued to nose-dive later that year when President Reagan was operated on for colon cancer. Since a reduced schedule was ordered following surgery, speculation arose about who actually was in charge during this time. The President added fuel to the fire in a radio address heralding the contributions of First Ladies, all of whom have been "heroes." Further, he thanked Nancy "for taking part in the business of the nation. I say to myself, but also on behalf of the nation. 'Thank you, partner. Thanks for everything.'" In response, *The New York Times* wrote that Nancy Reagan had "expanded the role of First Lady into a sort of Associate Presidency."[1]

In 1987 Nancy told a convention of newspaper publishers,

> *I don't get involved in policy, (but) it's silly to suggest my opinion should not carry some weight with a man I've been married to for 35 years. I'm a woman who loves her husband, and I make no apologies for looking out for his personal and political welfare. We have a genuine, sharing marriage. I go to his aid. He comes to mine.*

Nancy Reagan's protection of her husband has always been evident. In 1980 she said about him, somewhat cryptically, "He doesn't make snap decisions, but he doesn't tend to overthink, either."

Despite her statements, Nancy did try to influence Reagan and he would listen, but often she failed to convince him. One issue was abortion. She was pro-choice, but he wouldn't budge from his anti-abortion position. (Ironically, and to his credit, Ronald Reagan was the President who appointed the first woman justice to the Supreme Court, Sandra Day O'Connor, on July 7, 1981. Justice O'Connor has been an important factor in upholding the validity of Roe V. Wade in several opinions since then). So for the record Nancy was pro-life. In 1994, however, she told an interviewer her views on the subject were "somewhere in the middle," that while she was against abortion, she believed in a woman's right to choose.

Some of her stands were more controversial. Nancy was against the Equal Rights Amendment, and as a staunch believer in the "sanctity of marriage," opposed to easy divorce. One Reagan supporter described Nancy as "an anachronism (who) lives in the 1950's when it was a man's world and women were there to be perfect wives. She lacks compassion for the issues of the day because they have never been in her sphere of life."

During her husband's second term, however, she did take a stand on two contemporary problems: drug abuse with her successful "Just Say No!" campaign and AIDS. In 1987, perhaps after pressure from her son, Ron, who had become a spokesman for AIDS causes, she pushed the President to name a homosexual to his AIDS advisory committee, a logical request since a majority of AIDS victims at that time were gay men. Although advisers were against such an appointment, they knew they had an uphill battle. "Mrs. Reagan is just a tigress. When she gets her teeth into something she just does not let go," said one official.

Her tenacity and ability to get the President's ear on matters she felt strongly about were well known in Washington. When it was clear that several Reagan high echelon staffers were pushing the President toward decisions that were harming his image, she "waged a quiet campaign, planting a thought, recruiting others of us to push it along, making a case: foreign policy will be hurt, our allies will be let down," says Michael Deaver, a former White House aide, in his book *Behind the Scenes*. Deaver also reported that it was the First Lady who urged the President to meet with Gorbachev at the Geneva Summit. "She felt strongly that it was not only in the interest of world peace, but the correct move politically." And it was.

1987 was a crucial year for the Reagans, personally and Presidentially. Both Reagans battled cancer: the President, had prostate surgery and Nancy had a mastectomy. (Like Betty Ford, Nancy Reagan was very open about her bout with breast cancer, and her frank discussion of her illness prompted thousands of women to get mammograms.) But they were also battling dissension in the ranks (a good deal of it over how to handle the Iran–Contra crisis), the chain of command, and who was serving the President's best interests. Nancy also knew that her husband hated saying "No," or personally firing anyone. Most administrations have a person who takes on this role to spare the President the onerous task. Nancy was that "man" in the Reagan administrations.

During a wide-ranging interview with *The Los Angeles Times*, which appeared after the 1988 election, responding to questions about her influence on the President, Nancy said, "I don't feel his staff served him well, in general," and disclosed she was "hurt, surprised and disappointed" by their actions, especially regarding the Iran–Contra scandal:

> *I'm more aware if somebody is trying to end-run him and have their own agenda. I'm more aware of that than he is. It just never occurs to him that anybody is going to do that...A President's wife will hear things that he doesn't hear. And many times I get phone calls about one thing or the other, and I'd say: 'Please, go over and tell my husband.' But something happens to people when they walk into the Oval Office, and they freeze up, and they don't tell him. So then I end up telling him...somebody has to tell him.*[2]

Her interference, even behind-the-scenes, led to a great deal of criticism via the spate of "kiss-and-tell" books which surfaced in 1988, in addition to *Deaver's: Speaking Out*, by former White House Press Secretary, Larry Speakes; and perhaps the most damaging of all, former chief of staff Donald Regan's book, *For the Record*. Regan alleges that the First Lady arranged the President's schedule—when he should appear in public, when he should hold a press conference, when he should adopt a low profile—based on advice from a San Francisco "friend," who turned out to be socialite-astrologer, Joan Quigley.

According to Regan, Nancy's faith in her "friend's" predictions even led to the astrologer's naming the specific time to schedule matters as important as the signing of the nuclear weapons reduction treaty between Reagan and Gorbachev. Regan said he played along by color-coding his calendar: green for good days, red for bad, yellow for "iffy." He presented Nancy as a dragon lady and Reagan as a mental lightweight. After Regan's book was published, the President gallantly defended his Nancy, saying that Regan's and other "pay-back" books were, in effect, a "cheap shot." And allies of the President reminded the public that Don Regan had after all, been abruptly "terminated" from his job as chief of staff (perhaps as orchestrated by Nancy?) and suggested that his criticism of the Reagans must be viewed in that perspective.

Don Regan's book outraged Nancy. She told Margaret Truman, "I consulted her (Quigley) because I was looking for ways to find some comfort, to control my anxiety, every time Ronnie appeared in public. It made me feel better to be told that certain days were safer than others."[3]

Reportedly, the Reagans had consulted astrologists for many years, including the well-known "Astrologer to the Stars," Carroll Righter, and the equally famous "pop" astrologer Jeanne Dixon. Righter and Dixon were replaced after the 1981 assassination attempt when Nancy asked friend Merv Griffin (they often celebrated their July 6th birthdays together), for the name of an astrologer who could provide guidance to help protect Ronnie. The nation's press had a good laugh when the astrology story emerged via Regan's book. But in fairness to Ronald Reagan, did he make any major decisions based on advice from his astrologer? Was he doing anything so different from what millions of Americans do when they read their daily horoscope? (In fact, at the May 1988 Summit in Moscow, Gorbachev made a slight joke about reading *his own horoscope* every day). Other political figures who reportedly consulted the stars include Julius Caesar, Winston Churchill, Adolf Hitler and Indira Gandhi.

The pros and cons served up by the media about the Reagans' astrological dependencies were endless. Some very responsible publications reminded readers that this was not the first time a Presidential couple had relied on "outside help." *Time* magazine cited other First Ladies who had turned to seers and mediums for advice. The May 23, 1988 issue of *People* detailed the "heavenly approach to politics, past and present," and reported that Teddy Roosevelt kept an astrological chart pasted to the bottom of his chessboard, and the Founding Fathers based the signing of the Declaration of Independence on dates when the heavens were in "fortuitous alignment." Florence Harding and Edith Wilson consulted a Madame Marcia Champney for advice, Betty Ford asked Chicago's Laurie Brady about her husband's future, and Mary Lincoln held seances at the White House to track her husband's prospects.[4] In 1988, when the astrology news broke, *U.S. News and World Report* wrote that at least 25 percent of Congress turned to some sort of soothsayer for other-worldly guidance. (A few years after this heavenly storm, Hillary Clinton became the object of ridicule when she admitted she often "talked" to Eleanor Roosevelt—who had been dead more than three decades—for advice).

The astrological jokes generated by Regan's book were icing on the cake of criticism that had trailed Nancy for many years. The gossipy Washington press had always had their fun with this First Lady, picking away at her extravagance at receptions, ordering White House extras (such as the new china), her vanity (she lopped some years off her official birthdate), her clothes and weight (it was rumored that the size-four Nancy was anorexic), her fashion and status-fencing with Raisa Gorbachev, her lack of success as a parent, her coldness as a mother-in-law and a stepmother (she didn't see her stepson Michael's child until the baby was almost two), and her petty feuds.

In October, 1988, when it seemed as if the merciless spotlight would finally be off Nancy and on Kitty Dukakis and Barbara Bush, the wives of the Presidential candidates in the upcoming election, the media—again led by *Time* magazine—reported the damaging news that Nancy Reagan's extensive wardrobe of designer suits, dresses and formal gowns, as well as elegant jewelry, was worth as much as $1.4 million in "freebies." The claim was startling, inasmuch as in 1981, after similar gifts were revealed, the First Lady had promised to decline future presents from designers and jewelers because they were an embarrassment to President Reagan. (The next year, however, the White House had concluded that Nancy wasn't covered by provisions of the Watergate-inspired Ethics in Government Act prohibiting such gifts or loans, and she resumed her practice of borrowing).[5]

In her November, 1988 interview with *The Los Angeles Times*, Nancy insisted she would discuss her wardrobe and other topics (including astrology, her relations with her children, and her reactions to some of the President's advisers) in the autobiography she would write to "set the record straight on a lot of things." But she did tell her interviewer that the bottom line is "A First Lady is a wife, first of all. I don't care. That comes first for me. I'm sure with everybody that comes first. And I certainly felt that for Ronnie's interest—it was to his interest."[6] When *My Turn: The Memoirs of Nancy Reagan* was published in 1989, it became a best seller, but it did not quash all the rumors.

By the time the Reagans left the White House in 1989, Nancy's popularity had once again bottomed-out. It should be noted that the First Lady was an early victim of the endless search for headline-news, generated by the emerging presence of the cable newscasts hungry for 24/7 material, along with the increasingly evident tabloid mentality, served by the plethora of chatty (and inexpensively-produced) tell-all programs on network and local broadcast outlets, and exploited in ink by the supermarket scandal sheets as well as some of the "traditional" print media.

One of Nancy's problems on the way out had been there to plague her on the way in: the criticism that her unabated devotion to her husband led her to neglect her children and created future family feuds. For example, although Reagan was named "West Coast Father of the Year" in 1976, daughter Patti was not allowed to bring her live-in boyfriend home. The Reagans were also not pleased when son Ron left Yale to become a dancer. (They never saw him dance until after Ronnie became President). Ron, Jr., eventually abandoned his dance career to become a journalist (following in the footsteps of his half-brother, Michael, a conservative talk show host), with valuable connections provided by his famous family. In 1986, Patti published a thinly disguised *Mommy Dearest*-type novel in which she was particularly cruel to her mother. When her grandmother died in 1987, the rebellious Patti didn't attend the funeral, nor was she present a few weeks earlier when Nancy had her mastectomy. You can view the family photos, with all the smiling faces, taken at the ranch or the White House, but by the time the Reagans left Washington, it was clear that family ties had unraveled...and so, once again, had Nancy's image.

In a 1994 poll of 125 history professors, Nancy Reagan came up next to last on the list of 37 First Ladies, just ahead of poor neurotic (psychotic?) Mary Todd Lincoln. But this was a professorial, historic and limited view of Nancy's impact and popularity as a First Lady. Not long afterwards, President Reagan released the poignant statement that he had been diagnosed with Alzheimer's disease, and was about to embark on "the journey that will lead me into the sunset of my life." Every American—whether Democrat, Republican, Independent, or for that matter, Communist or Socialist—was moved by this open, honest declaration by the Great Communicator, bravely signaling, and accepting, his ultimate fate.

We all knew, too, that Nancy Reagan would be right there with him, sharing that fate. Once again, her public image soared...but there would be no more peaks and valleys—if we could, we would give her a medal for courage and devotion.

At first the President continued to go to his office several times a week, and then eventually did not appear in public at all. At the 1996 GOP convention, Nancy gave a brief speech, and reminded her audience that she was not the speechmaker in the family. A few years ago, Maureen Reagan, (Ron's daughter from his marriage to Jane Wyman) said of her stepmother, "I can say that as my father has weakened, Nancy has gotten stronger. She has gotten beyond denial and is facing this full-on." Maureen was also a spokeswoman for the Alzheimer's Association and visited her father frequently—Michael, Patti and Ron, Jr. do not. (In 1996, Maureen was diagnosed with malignant melanoma; several years later, the cancer had metastasized and she died on August 8, 2001)

By 1997, the woman who had once been known as "The Dragon Lady of the White House," was now nationally commended for her steadfast—and lonely—role as the one person President Reagan still recognized. By 2000, even that ability had diminished; in 2001 the former President fell and broke a hip, but his body, still strong and fit at 90 recovered. In July, 2001, Nancy Reagan, along with hundreds of others, personally implored President Bush to sanction and fund stem cell research, which scientists believed could help find cures for such diseases as lzheimers, Parkinsons, diabetes and scores of other illnesses.

In the fall of 2000, *I Love You, Ronnie* by Nancy Reagan was published, which included Ron's love letters to his wife and her comments. In a letter dated February 14th, 1977, their twenty-fifth anniversary, he wrote:

Dear St. Valentine,

I have a request to make of you but before doing so feel you should know more about her. For one thing she has 2 hearts - her own and mine. I'm not complaining. I gave her mine willingly, and like it right where it is...

My request of you is—could you on this day whisper in her ear that someone loves her very much and more and more each day? Also tell her, this "Someone" would run down like a dollar clock without her so she must always stay where she is.

And she has. March 2002 will mark the fiftieth wedding anniversary for Nancy and Ronald Reagan.

HILLARY RODHAM CLINTON

The last First Lady of the twentieth century generated more attention—newspapers, magazines, books, radio and television, cable, films, lectures, rallies, and person-to-person buzz—than any other First Lady in history; possibly, if such coverage could be documented, *more* publicity than all the other First Ladies of the twentieth century *combined*. Not only did Hillary Rodham Clinton face the public head-on during the heightened demand for 24/7 "news," but the tumultuous events during William Jefferson Clinton's tenure as forty-second President of the United States powered a relentless spotlight on her political role, her past history, and the ongoing state of her marriage.

For the past ten years (yes, even now), it seemed as if every American had a vociferous opinion to offer about Hillary. Unlike Nancy Reagan, whose popularity rose and fell according to circumstances (high for her drug program, low for her extravagances and reliance on astrology, high again for her protection of Ronnie), Hillary was—and is—like spinach or liver. You either hate it...or you love it. The opinions of media pundits and your next door neighbors seldom changed regarding Hillary. They only became more entrenched, one way or the other.

Although Hillary Rodham Clinton had a public life before her husband began his Presidential campaign, they were "Bill and Hillary Who?" to most of us until January 1992, when 100 million Americans met the Clintons in an interview on "60 Minutes" which aired just after the Super Bowl game. The TV "moment" was a brilliant strategical response to the first Clinton scandal, which almost destroyed his nascent bid for the Democratic Presidential nomination: the Gennifer Flowers supermarket tabloid tell-all about her alleged twelve-year affair with Bill. The couple, seated side-by-side, presented an earnest and attractive image. Bill acknowledged "bringing pain" to their relationship, but admitted nothing more...and Hillary answered a few questions, and, displaying the skill at damage control which would be employed many, many times in the years ahead, told viewers if they did not like what they had seen or heard, then "heck, don't vote for him." Overnight she became just "Hillary."

During the 1992 campaign, Hillary's background was examined more closely than any other candidate's wife to date...she had done more, on her own, after all; she was the only candidate's wife until then who had had a full-time professional career. And she presented a distinct contrast to the motherly, always-popular Barbara Bush. When Barbara made a blunt statement she was praised for her honest talk. When Hillary spoke too quickly, she spent weeks (and in some cases, years) back-pedaling energetically to get her foot out of her mouth. There is the widely-quoted "cookie" comment uttered during the 1992 primaries: "I suppose I could have stayed home, baked cookies, and had teas..." The statement was mis-quoted and truncated, because, after all, that made more interesting news. What she actually stated, as reiterated in her 1996 book, *It Takes a Village*, was in response to a question about the "ceremonial role" of a governor's wife.

> *I replied I had chosen to pursue my law practice while my husband was governor rather than stay home as an official hostess, serving cookies and tea to guests...I never thought that my cookie-baking or tea-serving abilities made me a good, bad, or indifferent mother, or a good or bad person. So it never occurred to me that my comment would be taken as insulting mothers (I guess including my own)...Nor did it occur to me that the next day's headlines would reduce me to an anti-cookie—and therefore anti-family—"career woman"...I learned (from the episode) that when I am asked a question that relates to me personally, I have to be aware that my answer may be measured by how people feel about the choices they've made in their own lives.[1]*

Hillary Clinton had a great deal to learn about politics, but she has always been a fast learner and in time became a crack campaigner. Like every other First Lady in history, however, she never dreamed of a path that would lead to the White House.

She was born in Chicago on October 26, 1947, and grew up in the suburb of Park Ridge, Illinois, with two younger brothers. Her father, Hugh, owned a fabric store and her mother, Dorothy, a full-time housewife, encouraged her only daughter to go to college. Hillary had a typical, busy, upper middle-class childhood and adolescence, enjoying tennis, swimming, ballet, softball, skating, the Girl Scouts and Methodist youth group activities, while getting high enough grades all through school to gain acceptance to prestigious Wellesley College in 1965.

She entered Wellesley as a Goldwater Republican and eventually became a McCarthy Democrat (In contrast, her successor, Laura Bush, entered college in Texas as a Democrat and became a conservative Republican). When Hillary graduated with honors in 1969, her Wellesley classmates chose her to give the commencement address. Instead of the traditional pep talk about going out into the world, or even idealistic takes on Wellesley's motto (*non ministrari, sed ministrare*—"not to be ministered unto, but to minister"), Hillary spoke out against the establishment ideas that hers was a do-nothing generation. She said she and her peers "attempt to forge an identity in this particular age...the prevailing acquisitive and competitive corporate life is not for us. We're searching for a more immediate, ecstatic and penetrating mode of living." During the course of her talk, she even attacked Senator Edward Brooke, the guest speaker, for underestimating her generation. This valedictory address resulted in Hillary's first 15 minutes of fame—her picture in *Life* (along with other prominent graduates who had given provocative commencement addresses).

At Yale Law School (which she chose over Harvard with its "boys' club mentality") she began to plan a career in public service, focusing on children's rights. Marian Wright Edelman became a friend and one summer Hillary worked at Edelman's Children's Defense Fund, doing research on the welfare of children. After returning to her studies at Yale Law, she assisted professors in writing a Carnegie Council book, *All Our Children: Families under Pressure in the United States*. Her stellar grades also earned her a post on the Board of Editors of the Yale Review of Law and Social Action.

However, Hillary was not all work and no play during her Yale Law School days. A university library has always been a great place to meet kindred spirits, and that's where she met William Jefferson Clinton, whose background was very different from hers...but they were in sync in many other ways, including ideological goals and principles.

Their relationship didn't proceed as smoothly as that of Nancy and Ron, or Rosalynn and Jimmy, or even Eleanor and FDR. After graduation in 1973, Bill returned to Arkansas, and Hillary returned to Washington, working first as a staff attorney for the Children's Defense Fund, and then with the House Judiciary Committee, investigating President Nixon's involvement in the Watergate break-in and subsequent developments. She was one of three women on a staff of 41 lawyers. When Nixon resigned in 1974, her job was over; rather than take any of the offers she had from major law firms, she decided to follow her heart—and her Bill—to Arkansas, where she accepted a position teaching law at Arkansas Law School in Fayetteville (Bill also taught there). They were married October 11, 1975 and her close-knit family (mother, father, and brothers Hugh and Tony) accompanied the newlyweds on their honeymoon to Acapulco.

When he was elected attorney general in 1976, they moved to Little Rock, the state capital, and she became the first female lawyer (and then, partner) ever hired by the old guard Rose Law Firm. In 1978, Bill was elected governor of Arkansas, and at age 32 was the nation's youngest governor.

If you look at photos of Hillary during these years—or even earlier as a Wellesley student and then, later in Washington—you see a rather dowdy young woman, with thick glasses, no visible make-up, hair held back casually by a band (as if to get it out of her way). She says of that time that not wearing make-up was a "statement." And it certainly was a puzzling statement to Bill's mother, Virginia Kelley, who didn't quite know what to make of this plain "hippie" from the "North." A few years ago I visited the Nixon library in Yorba Linda, California, and viewed a display of First Lady wedding gowns. Hillary's dress, bought "off the rack" in a quick shopping expedition to an Arkansas department store, was a simple, long, off-white cotton dress. But then, fashion had never been one of Hillary's major interests. Over the years though, she definitely improved her look and her looks, wore more fashionable clothes, got contacts, and then…despite her efforts, was constantly criticized for her hairdos, her hats…or any other way she changed her appearance.

In Arkansas, she also had to change her name. Until 1982, she used her maiden name, Hillary Rodham, but this expression of "feminism" didn't go over well in that conservative turf, and when it seemed as if the name game was one of the reasons her husband wasn't re-elected as governor in 1980, she became Hillary Rodham *Clinton*.

This was a busy time for the young First Family of Arkansas. Her career was successful—she was twice named one of the "100 Most Influential Lawyers in America"—and their marriage was enriched when Chelsea Victoria Clinton was born on February 27, 1980.

(During her years as the nation's First Lady, among the plethora of disparaging rumors was the one that she had only wanted one child. Disputing that in one interview she sadly commented that she and Bill had "tried and tried unsuccessfully to have more children, but it never happened." In *It Takes a Village*, she discussed this very personal matter once more: "Bill and I had wanted to start a family immediately after we married, in 1975, but we were not having much luck. In 1979, we scheduled an appointment to visit a fertility clinic right after a long-awaited vacation. Lo and behold, I got pregnant during that vacation. (I have often remarked to my husband that we might have had more children if we had taken more vacations!)[2]

Her role in those days may not have included baking cookies and serving tea, but many reports by those journalists polarized one way or the other credit Hillary with saving Bill's career after he was defeated for re-election as governor in 1980. In addition to becoming "Mrs. Clinton," she sharpened his political goals, "edited" his coterie of friends, and re-shaped his entire political campaign. Then, after he was re-elected in 1982 and went on to win re-election three more times, Hillary Rodham Clinton became a key player in getting the ball rolling for his national run, helping to choose the team that developed the strategy for the primaries, captured the nomination for President, and finally won the election.

As the Democratic candidate's wife, she was fair game, and after working for 20 years she had represented some clients whose own pasts had been suspect. She had also taken some stands that were not popular—such as work for the Legal Services Corporation, which was supposed to provide nonpartisan aid to poor people—but her critics complained that she had directed funds toward well-known liberal groups. She was even accused (inaccurately) of encouraging children to sue their parents in abuse cases. During the campaign she was called "The Lady Macbeth of Little Rock" by enemies, and applauded as having a mind of her own (and enough courage to speak her mind) by feminists and liberal groups and media.

The campaign was spirited and youthful. Bill and Hillary (along with Al and Tipper Gore) after all, could have been poster kids for the baby boomer set. They were photographed, almost like two couples on a double date, cavorting in their campaign bus; Bill and Al often appeared at rallies in casual clothes and their wives in pant suits...and campaign speeches were often bracketed by popular music of *their generation*, such as Fleetwood Mac's "Don't Stop Thinking About Tomorrow," or Aretha Franklin's "Respect."

William Jefferson Clinton won the 1992 election with 370 electoral votes (and a plurality of 43 percent with 44,908,233 popular votes) to 168 electoral votes for Bush, who had a popular vote of 39,102,282 (38 percent). That was the year Texas billionaire Ross Perot, who captured *no* electoral votes, garnered an astounding 19,741,048 popular votes for his Reform party.

Right after the election, a proud Bill Clinton gave new meaning to the First Lady's job when he stated, only half joking, that with the Clintons, America "bought one and got one free." It was said, and this may be apochrophyl, that the new President considered naming Hillary to a cabinet post; however, in 1967 Congress had passed a law prohibiting such an appointment. But in keeping with his campaign pledge to provide health insurance for every American, he named his wife head of the Task Force on Health Care Reform.

Hillary plunged into this monumental assignment with typical gusto and energy, ultimately developing a staff of more than 500, traveling to nine different states, speaking to dozens of groups, and participating in over 50 meetings with various congressional committees.

But before her work on the Task Force took off, she was marking her own territory as First Lady in some traditional—as well as not so traditional—ways. First she set up her office in the *West Wing*, the heart of Presidential action, instead of the East Wing, the office choice of most of her predecessors. (As noted, one of Laura Bush's first actions as First Lady was to move her office *back* to the East Wing). Hillary also hired Margaret (Maggie) Williams, whom she had met when both worked for the Children's Defense Fund, as her chief of staff.

Early on, she fired the French chef who had served during the Bush administration and hired an American, Walter Scheib III, who specialized in lighter fare—perhaps with an eye on Bill's waistline and his penchant for Big Macs—but more likely in keeping with the current trend toward sensible eating, good nutrition, healthier food. She, realized, too, how dramatically her own life had changed one evening when Chelsea was sick and Hillary went to the small family kitchen to cook scrambled eggs for her daughter. Before she could crack one egg, a steward suddenly appeared offering to prepare an *omelet!*). Hillary redecorated the family quarters in the informal style the Clintons favored, with wicker furniture and rocking chairs, while initiating more formal, traditional redecorating in other rooms.

Hillary Clinton has always had a reputation for thoroughly researching any new project. (It is said that she read every book ever written about First Ladies when she became one, and when embarking on her refurbishing of the White House, she undoubtedly read every book on that subject as well—with an eye on authenticity.) One of her favorite projects was restoring the "Map Room," which had been the center of WWII strategy sessions during the Roosevelt years. One of the focal points of the renovated room was a map of Europe, showing the "Estimated German Situation," prepared for the President in April 1945. It was the last map seen by Roosevelt at the White House before he died a few days later on April 12th.

Another decorating project of special interest was the "Treaty Room," which President Clinton used as an upstairs office (also the choice for President Nixon, and our current President Bush). Hillary decided to return to the decorating scheme of the 19th century when this hideaway was used as the "Cabinet Room."

Even with all her reading and researching, there were problems settling into the new role, for her and her family. Henry Lou Gates, Jr., writing in the *New Yorker, reported,* "Susan Porter Rose, who was the director of scheduling for Mrs. Nixon and Mrs. Ford and the chief of staff for Mrs. Bush, is a savant on the subject and she addresses the question (about Hillary's adjustment to White House life) with Jeeves-like discretion. 'The place has its own sociology, and it's filled with banana peels and land mines.'"[3]

These early months, during the spring and summer of 1993, were the halcyon days for both Hillary and Bill Clinton, when admiration was more evident than opprobrium. Hillary probably graced more magazine covers during this time than her husband...or even the highest paid *uber* models (including *Vogue,* virtually all the women's magazines, and news weeklies and pop magazines from *Newsweek* to *People*) And she was the subject of countless photo essays and features. There she is, in a February 1993 feature in *The New York Times,* looking glamorous in an elegant gown while inspecting a formally set table for a state dinner. As flattering as this photo was (and others taken by such famous photographers as Annie Liebowitz), other publications, such as Rupert Murdock's ardently conservative *New York Post,* began a policy of printing the most *unflattering* shots of the First Lady.

Admirers were coining such phrases as "the icon of America womanhood." Detractors gave her such names as "Empress Hillary." The Conservative Union began publishing a newsletter called "Hillary Alert," which listed her latest power plays. The old gray lady, *The New York Times,* in some instances couldn't quite decide which way to go. A cover story in the Sunday magazine on May 1993, depicted a happy, rather serene looking Hillary dressed in a demure white suit and pearls, and the headline: "Hillary Rodham Clinton and The Politics of Virtue." The article itself is headlined "Saint Hillary," and the writer Michael Kelly attempts to present a balanced picture of the fledgling First Lady. "The public debate over her that swirled throughout the 1992 Presidential race centered on two lesser questions—how left wing was she and how hungry for power—but failed to consider the larger point of her life," the message of values and religion." Kelly explains Hillary Clinton's political theories:

> *"They are, rather than primarily the politics of left or right, the politics of do-goodism, flowing directly from a powerful and continual stream that runs through American history from Harriet Beecher Stowe to Jane Addams to Carry Nation to Dorothy Day; from the social gospel of the late 19th century to the temperance-minded Methodism of the early 20th century to the liberation theology of the 1960's and 1970's to the pacifistic and multiculturally correct religious left of today."*[4]

Do-goodism or not, by the summer of 1993, rumors were swirling that did no good for Hillary's reputation...about Vince Foster, Deputy White House Counsel and Hillary's old Rose Law Firm pal, who committed suicide in July (had they been lovers?)...about the $100,000 Hillary made from a $1,000 investment in cattle futures... about Filegate and Travelgate...and information or documents that were doled out bit by bit or mysteriously lost...and whether or not Hillary had actually thrown a lamp (or was it a bible?) at Bill.

During that time, however, the First Lady's popularity rating was almost as high as her husband's: 55 percent favorable to his 61 percent. Ninety-one percent of those polled by *Time/CNN* described her as intelligent and 63 percent thought she was a good influence on the President. Also, while 63 percent felt her prominent role in government was appropriate, one third of those queried did not approve.

In the meantime, Hillary was preparing her report on health care...and in so doing managed to offend many important factions. She later admitted she had made serious mistakes in launching her task force and one of the worst was to shut out physicians who wanted some role in the discussions. Instead, she held meetings in private, literally behind "closed doors," which got her into more trouble. Spokesmen for the doctors said meetings should be open to the public since they were using public funds and she wasn't a government official. One judge ruled for open meetings; a decision that was later reversed by a federal appeals court, but by this time the task force had finished its work so the decision was moot...but it certainly added to the criticism of the First Lady.

All during that fall of 1993, Hillary appeared before Congress to talk about the Task Force recommendations—one week she spoke before five different committees. Regarding her many trips to the Hill, *The New York Times* earmarked them as "the official end of an era when Presidential wives pretended to know less than they did and to be advising less than they were." Initially she wowed congressmen of both parties, but it didn't take long for Republicans to realize the impact of the Clinton health plan: this major initiative was directly contrary to the GOP ideal of minimizing government's role in private lives, and even more significant than this ideological impasse, the plan was anathema to mega bucks Republican contributors. As syndicated columnist E.J. Dionne, Jr., wrote, conservative Republicans vehemently rejected the plan, and "Republican leaders *lobbied* the business *lobbyists*," following through with very creative *negative* advertising against the plan.

The program was torpedoed, and thus sank one of Bill Clinton's major goals...as well as his wife's reputation. While Hillary has always admitted that she made mistakes in presenting her program (even when running for Senator in 2000, by poking fun at herself), she reminds us that fifty years ago, Harry Truman brought up health care during every session of congress, and he never got a program through.

Perhaps Hillary had a premonition of the criticism that would be leveled at her for her health care recommendations when she told Michael Kelly for his *New York Times* article, "I know that no matter what I did—if I did nothing, if I spent my entire day totally disengaged from what was going on around me—I'd be criticized for that. I mean, it's a no-win deal, no matter what I do, or try to do."[5]

What she tried to do was maintain a lower profile and stick to more traditional First Lady activities. This was difficult for two reasons. First, as she told a class on the role of the First Lady sponsored by George Washington University in 1994, "That would not be at all in my nature or my background. I, for better or worse have spoken out on public issues for 25 years. Some kind of 'First Lady amnesia' would not have been credible." Secondly, facts and rumors and charges were beginning to emerge that made it impossible for her to stay behind the scenes.

1994 got off to a bad start for the Clintons and continued to get worse. Questions about their involvement in the Whitewater Development Corporation (events dating back to 1979) kept surfacing and under increasing Republican pressure, the President asked Attorney General Janet Reno to appoint a special prosecutor. Paula Jones, whose allegations first appeared in a conservative magazine, filed sexual harassment charges against the President. And Hillary Clinton, under fire for her commodities profits as well as her legal work on the Whitewater project and a bankrupt savings and loan, felt compelled to explain these situations at a press conference in April. (Interestingly, Hillary was not the first

Presidential spouse to make a huge profit in the stock market. In 1869, Julia Grant allegedly made $25,000 in a scheme to corner the gold market).

Wearing a pink sweater set and a headband, she addressed the press in the State Dining Room of the White House, fielding question after question in a session that lasted more than an hour. She told the media representatives that Eleanor Roosevelt had given more than 300 news conferences during 13 years in office, but had only invited women. "I don't think you'd let me get away with that, she joked. Explaining why she had decided to "go public," the First Lady stated: "I've always believed in a zone of privacy (but) I've been re-zoned." She credited her astounding $100,000 profit on a $1,000 investment in cattle futures to "luck and good advice," and revealed that James Blair, an executive of Tyson Foods in Arkansas advised her and placed her trades. She also denied any knowledge of illegal transfers of funds during her husband's 1984 gubernatorial campaign, and said, "We went into Whitewater to make money, not to lose it. It keeps getting beat like the deadest horse it is, over and over."

And the horse would continue to be beaten during endless investigations and testimony for the next five years until finally she and Bill were cleared of any wrongdoing...but that, as we know, was not the worst of the problems to come. By the summer of 1994, the First Lady's approval ratings had fallen by 20 points.

Nonetheless, she still was our nation's First Lady, the hostess at the White House, and she tried hard for high marks in "social diplomacy." Among several notable state dinners that spring and summer was one held in June under a massive tent on the White House lawn for the Emperor and Empress of Japan. She also orchestrated gala banquets for Russia's Boris Yeltsin and South Africa's Nelson Mandela.

On the investigative front, however, both the House Banking Commission and the Senate Banking Committee (chaired by New York's Senator Al D'Amato) began separate hearings on Whitewater, and Kenneth Starr replaced Robert Fiske as the independent prosecutor. In August, Webb Hubbell, Hillary's former Rose Law Firm partner and a deputy White House Counsel, was convicted of fraud charges (he falsely billed clients and used the funds for personal expenses). That fall the Democrats were defeated in the 1994 midterm elections, which led to Republican control of Congress for the first time in 40 years.

Hillary Clinton continued to puzzle—and annoy, even irritate the media. Although she treated reporters and interviewers respectfully, as one writer observed, "You can't really fool the press with politeness. Their antennae are up—they can sense hostility and resentment." In his column in *The New York Times*, Frank Rich discussed the different degrees of Hillary coverage, both pro and con, concluding, "She can't win for losing." In his view, one possibility might be that she doesn't know who she is, and that's why she changes her look or her hairdo so often. "But it's just as plausible that this First Lady is a complex mixture of many traits—some appealing, some not—and that she has provoked so much hostility because she exercises the full power of her personality, not just political power. She refuses to censor or pigeonhole herself to fit any stereotyped image, pre-or post-feminist, that might freeze her image for easy mass consumption."[6] Another *Times* columnist, Bill Safire, didn't mince words. He called Hillary a "congenital liar," a comment that made Bill Clinton threaten to punch him out, echoing the sentiments expressed by President Truman decades earlier when a critic disparaged his daughter Margaret's singing.

Hillary scored some positive press with her trip to Beijing in September 1995 to attend the United Nations' sponsored Fourth World Conference on Women. Delegates and guests from 180 countries attended (visas for some 10,000 delegates were declined and another 30,000 delegates were "quarantined" in slipshod facilities in the suburb of Huairou, about 30 miles from Beijing). China made very few efforts to provide comfortable accommodations for those who attended, and one wonders why the United Nations chose China for this conference on the plight of women world wide to begin with. According to *Time*, "the food was unpalatable, the toilets stank. Bathrooms flooded, and accommodations were cramped...Confusion prevailed...even the heavens glowered, sending forth rain that churned up mud, mud everywhere."[7]

Hillary wasn't even going to go until China released Harry Wu, a U.S. citizen and a harsh critic of China's human rights abuses. When she gave her first talk in Beijing, she spoke forcefully about China's one-child policy (without mentioning China specifically). "It is a violation of human rights when women are denied the right to plan their own families and that includes being forced to have abortions or being sterilized against their will." Her theme: "If there is one message that echoes forth from this conference it is that human rights are women's rights and women's rights are human rights, once and for all...Let me be clear," she said. "Freedom means the right of people to assemble, organize and debate openly. It means respecting the views of those who may disagree with the views of their governments."

But when she traveled to Huairou to speak to the sequestered delegates, it was a disaster. Because of the rain, the meeting had been moved inside to a movie theater that only held 1,500 people. Three thousand delegates packed the theater. But thousands more waited outside in the rain and were forcibly detained from entering the cinema, including Lisa Caputo, Hillary's press secretary, and feminist icon Betty Friedan. Loudspeakers outside the hall announced that the jam was America's fault for changing venues...but clearly the fault lay with the Chinese. Donna Shalala, Clinton's Secretary of Health, later said, "They will never get another international conference again." (However, short memories prevail, and at this writing, China has been named as the site for the 2008 Olympics. We can only hope that their hospitality—and bathrooms—have improved).

The positive spin for the First Lady was short-lived. Hillary was supposed to start the new year off with a publicity tour for her new book, *It Takes a Village And Other Lessons Children Teach Us,* but the nationwide spin-fest, "meant to be cuddly, has degenerated into an inquisition on Mrs. Clinton's behavior," wrote Maureen Dowd in *The New York Times* on January 14th. The same week, some of Hillary's long-lost billing records were found in the White House. Carolyn Huber, who handled personal letters for Bill and Hillary Clinton and had been office manager at the Rose Law Firm, discovered computer printouts of fees billed to the failed Madison Guaranty S & L mixed in with a stack of personal letters and memorabilia.

Another problem surfaced because Hillary declined to give the conventional acknowledgment of thanks to a contributor of *It Takes a Village*. Barbara Feinman, who had worked on part of the original manuscript not only didn't get a "thank you" for her efforts...for a time it appeared as if she wouldn't get paid for her work. (She eventually was paid). Feinman had many friends among the Washington Press Corps and this story spread, unfavorably linked to the book's publication, as well as the ongoing questions about Whitewater, "Travelgate," and "Filegate."

In a story headlined "Life in the Wiggle Room," for example, *Time* magazine commented, "The more the First Lady tries to explain things, the more questions she raises."8

Newsweek had agreed to publish an excerpt of *Village*, and in its January 15th issue featured Hillary on the cover, but the cover-line posed the question "Saint of Sinner?" And in addition to the excerpt, there were two separate stories about Hillary, one about her background on ongoing investigations, the second about the surfacing of the billing records.9

A few writers defended Hillary. Suzanne Garment, a resident scholar at the American Enterprise Institute, wrote in a newspaper "commentary," "There seems to be a special pleasure in the twisting of the knife on this one. When columnist William Safire (in *The*

New York Times) called the First Lady a 'congenital liar,' the phrase was reported everywhere—and there was silence from some quarters where there should have been protest." Regarding her proposals for universal healthcare, although she was criticized, ridiculed, castigated...(as too liberal, too left, too socialistic, too radical), Garment noted, "Most of all she was moralistic—excoriating people for making profits off the medical system while exploring the politics of meaning." Ironically, some of Hillary Clinton's "radical" recommendations re-surfaced in various "Patients' Bill of Rights" programs under discussion in Congress during 2001.

Unfortunately, the ongoing onslaught of all the issues—past and present—concerning Hillary in these first months of 1996, diminished what Hillary was trying to *say* in *It Takes a Village*. The book reflects her lifelong concerns about the welfare of children, which can be summed up by one of her favorite comments: "There is no such thing as other people's children."

Aside from the research and reports on studies involving children, in her book Hillary also shares many insights into her own life, her marriage, and motherhood. She talks about her "strong feelings about divorce and its effects on children (which) have caused me to bite my tongue more than a few times during my own marriage and to think instead about what I could do to be a better wife and partner."[10] Of course, this was written before Monica Lewinsky, but after Paula Jones and Gennifer Flowers. Some observers who took the time to read *It Takes a Village* concluded that Hillary Clinton is liberal politically, but personally, on many moral or religious issues, she is strongly conservative.

During these early months of 1996, still another crisis confronted Hillary. She had the dubious honor of becoming the first "sitting" First Lady to be subpoenaed to testify before a grand jury. Her testimony shed no light on any of the issues under investigation, but it did lead to a great deal of speculation about what she wore and what that meant. On her way in and out of the Grand Jury, Hillary was photographed wearing a black coat with a swirl of beading on the back. Dozens of reporters said that "swirl" was a dragon, a *dragon*..."The Dragon Lady with an Emblem," and of course that stirred up the media gossip-pot. But Robin D. Givhan, writing about the "black coat" in the *Washington Post* set the record straight and summed up the fashion quandary that Hillary, perhaps more than any other First Lady, had to face. "It wasn't a dragon," she wrote. "It is an abstract design that resembles an art deco rendering of seashells...(the coat) is three or four years old...(A remembrance of happier times?)." But perhaps, as Givhan noted, "we would have gone with a black cashmere duster sans beading. Or maybe a nice camel hair balmacaan? The issue of the dragon was about subtext, semiotics...wishful thinking. A dragon! Dragon lady! Monster!" She mentions the criticism over the pink sweater Hillary wore at her press conference months earlier:

> *Political wags figured that the First Lady was trying to change her tough, lawyerly image and to come across as soft, sweet and innocent...What should Mrs. Clinton have worn? What would have happened if she had chosen something purple. She probably would have been accused of trying to put on royal airs. White would have meant she was trying to claim purity and innocence. Red would have signaled that she was conjuring up the don't-mess-with me aura of Nancy Reagan. Bar Blue? Going for Barbara Bush's lovability, of course. Yellow? Clearly she'd be pulling the Little Miss Sunshine ploy. Black? Stone the witch...No matter what the First Lady wears, it means something. And when approval ratings are down, it undoubtedly will mean something bad.[11]*

Hillary's "bad press" was reflected in a major way in a special double issue of *The New Yorker*, published in late February, which included the comments of some viper-tongued ladies. Peggy Noonan, ace Republican speechwriter ("a thousand points of light" for the first President Bush) said, "I truly feel she did not have the wit to understand that the prosecutorial atmosphere that she and her friends unleashed and encouraged would engulf them, too." (referring to the Democrats' investigation of President Nixon during Watergate). Sally Quinn, columnist for the Washington Post, called Hillary "book-smart and street-stupid." Marilyn Quayle, wife of Bush's Vice President Dan Quayle, said of Hillary, in what might be described as a case of *very* sour grapes, "You're not breaking ground by being appointed by your husband to a quasi-Cabinet-level position—that's just getting an office through your husband."

Gloria Steinem, seeking to explain Hillary-hatred in the *New Yorker* article concluded, "She and the President are presenting, at a very high, visible level, a new paradigm of a male-female relationship. And that is very much resented." Perhaps Hillary herself summed it up in a very understandable way when she told the writer, Henry Louis Gates, Jr., "I apparently remind some people of their mother-in-law or their boss, or something."[12]

Whatever she wore or said, by mid-1996, a Gallup poll showed that 57 percent of those surveyed believed that Hillary was involved in a cover-up of Whitewater.

In June, Hillary once again drew extra attention, but this time the prevailing reaction was laughter and ridicule: In his new book,

The Choice, the *Washington Post's* Bob Woodward reported that Hillary had consulted spiritual advisers when she was working on *It Takes a Village*, and had imaginary conversations with her personal hero, Eleanor Roosevelt. Critics said she had held "séances"; the White House said the First Lady merely held "brainstorming sessions" at Camp David with Jean Houston (Co-Director of the Foundation for Mind Research), Mary Catherine Bateson (anthropologist and daughter of anthropologist Margaret Mead), and Doris Kearns Goodwin, who shared her thoughts about Eleanor Roosevelt. Woodward wrote that "Astrology only changed timing and it was a kind of pseudo-science that could be fun or worth a laugh. Yet the Reagans had been ridiculed. Hillary's sessions with Houston reflected a serious inner turmoil that she had not resolved." Hillary gave her own response in her nationally syndicated column on June 4, 1996: "I occasionally have imaginary conversations with Eleanor Roosevelt to try to figure out what she would do in my shoes. She usually responds by telling me to buck up or at least to grow skin as thick as a rhinoceros." (In July 2001, our current President Bush proudly displayed a bust of *his hero*, Winston Churchill and said he was "proud to have Churchill visiting with him…sometimes he (Churchill) will talk back, but sometimes he won't.")

Actually, Eleanor Roosevelt was not keen on any type of psychic connection. Some sixty years ago, when the visiting Queen of the Netherlands tried to interest Eleanor in spiritualism, the First Lady said "Since we're going to be dead such a long time anyway, it's rather a waste of time chatting with all of them before we get there."

The brouhaha over "conversations with Eleanor" soon subsided as the nation began to compare the wives of the Presidential candidates for the fall 1996 election, Hillary and Elizabeth (Liddy) Dole. In the July 1st issue, with "Hillary vs. Liddy" on the cover, *Time* observed, "There are those who argue that both women would make better candidates than their husbands; unlike Elizabeth, Hillary can give the impression that she thinks she would be a better President as well. Both are more disciplined, more demanding, much less forgiving. Both are excellent speakers, though their styles are different. Hillary can speak in perfect paragraphs for an hour without notes and changes her speech with ease to suit different audiences…Elizabeth never gets a word or pause or chuckle out of place, but she can no more ad lib than levitate."[13]

During the campaign, Hillary and Bill were still viewed as *partners*, while Bob and Elizabeth Dole stressed that theirs was a marriage, *not* a partnership. Senator Dole called Elizabeth his "secret weapon," his "Southern strategy." And she was. Elizabeth Dole's credentials were as strong as—if not stronger than—Hillary's. She was the only woman who ever served in two different cabinet posts for two different Presidents and her Ivy League law degree (from Harvard) was as prestigious as Hillary's. An election choice between Liddy Dole and Hillary Clinton would have been exciting for the country...but 1996 was not their time. Americans, angered by Republican efforts to balance the budget, cut spending, and reduce taxes which led to a shutdown of the government, sided with Clinton and led to election victory, with figures higher than his 1992 win: 46 percent of the popular vote (47,401,185 and 379 electoral votes) compared to Dole's 39,197, 469 popular votes and 159 electoral votes (Perot supporters gave him over 8 million votes).

As 1996 drew to a close, Hillary tried to downplay her role in the administration and become a more traditional First Lady. *Time's* Eric Pooley reported in December: "Very often in public she is smiling but remote, her eyes concealed by dark sunglasses. Even when she is having fun...there is an unmistakable sadness to her, a pensive, fragile air that reflects four bruising years in Washington and the bone-deep weariness that campaigning brings."[14] Little could she dream of the four years that were ahead.

While President Clinton worked with the Republican Congress to achieve a balanced budget in 1997, the Office of the Independent Counsel (O.I.C.), Congress and a platoon of Washington attorneys worked on Whitewater, charges of questionable fundraising activities during the 1996 campaign and the Paula Jones Case. Here's a brief timetable of what happened in 1997:

- *May: O.I.C. investigates Webb Hubbell's $400,000 in "consultant" payments from Clinton allies.*

- *June: O.I.C. questions troopers about Clinton's alleged affairs while he was Arkansas governor.*

- *July: Linda Tripp informs Paula Jones' lawyers about Kathleen Willey.*

- *October: Monica Lewinsky tells Linda Tripp about her affair with the President; Tripp shares this information with literary agent Lucianne Goldberg, who instructs Tripp to tape her conversations with Monica.*

- *November: Tripp tapes over 17 hours of conversations with Monica.*

- *December: an "anonymous" caller alerts the Jones' lawyers to Monica Lewinsky; they issue a subpoena for Monica to testify. Later in December, Clinton pal Vernon Jordan meets with Monica and arranges a job for her with Revlon (he serves on their board).*

In January 1998 in what *Time* described as "A Fateful Convergence" of three intertwined scandals (Whitewater, the Paula Jones case, and the Monica Lewinsky revelations), circumstances—and fate—collided head-on:

- *January 12: Tripp contacts Starr about the Lewinsky tapes.*

- *January 13: Tripp is wired by the FBI for a meeting with Monica, a few days after Monica had given Starr an affidavit denying any relationship with the President.*

- *January 14: Starr expands his probe to investigate perjury and obstruction of justice in the Jones case.*

- *January 26: President Clinton gives his famous "I did not have sexual relations with that woman...I never told anybody to lie" denial.*

The next day, Hillary appeared on NBC's "Today" and told Matt Lauer, "the great story here for anybody willing to find it and write about it and explain it, is this vast right wing conspiracy that has been conspiring against my husband since the day he announced for President." That statement generated a new torrent of ridicule and contributed fodder to the dozens of offensive anti-Hillary web-sites already on the Internet. In fairness, right-wing Republicans had backed many initiatives to discredit the Clintons. The wealthy and ultra-conservative Scaife family bankrolled ($2.4 million) *The American Spectator*, which first reported about Paula Jones, the trooper gossip and other scandals in its ongoing "Arkansas project"; gave more than $5 million in as many years to conservative foundations and think tanks which lent lawyers and spokespersons to spar against the Clintons; and over several decades gifted Pepperdine University in California with more than $13 million. When Pepperdine offered Ken Starr a deanship, the Independent Counsel announced his resignation from the O.I.C., but public opposition to his "retirement" (and charges of conflict of interest) forced him to stay at his post. And the rest is history. As Marie Brenner wrote in *Vanity Fair*, "It was all too evident that the O.I.C.

had become the roving dragon...during the Monica Lewinsky scandal, legal experts would observe that the main concern of the O.I.C. had shifted from the detection of impropriety, if not real crimes, in the Whitewater matter to sex."[15]

The investigations and testimony continued and the scandalous headlines proliferated until it became all-Monica, all-day, all-week. Whatever one's particular political point-of-view, these years, and these revelations were not a proud time for America...even though President Clinton's performance reviews remained high, while his personal popularity dipped below 50 percent. And many Americans felt his private life should have remained just that—*private*.

Here is the rest of the 1998-1999 countdown:

- *September 11: Ken Starr delivers his massive report to Congress, revealing all the salacious details of Clinton's White House trysts.*

- *December: The House Judiciary Committee approves four articles of impeachment.*

- *December 13: Clinton settles the Paula Jones case for $850,000—without offering an apology.*

- *January 7: The Impeachment trial begins.*

- *February 12: The President is acquitted of impeachment and perjury charges. Soon after, he is found in contempt of court and fined $90,000 for giving false testimony in the Paula Jones case in 1998, thereby becoming the first President to be cited for contempt.*

The national nightmare had ended, with the country bitterly divided over whether or not impeachment proceedings should have been brought against President Clinton to begin with. Scholars and pundits now discussed his legacy, which not only positioned him ignominiously as the second President in our history to be impeached, but forever identified him with the Monica/Paula Jones sex scandals. (Andrew Johnson, you may remember, was impeached because he tried to fire his Secretary of State).

But this book is about the Presidents' First Ladies. Hillary Clinton remained at Bill's side, sometimes photographed, however, with Chelsea *between* the two of them, and in 1999 began to drop some hints about where the Clintons' would live after Bill left office (New York)...and what her own plans for the future might include. A week after the President's acquittal, on February 18th, Associated Press reported that three of her confidants said Hillary was "thinking" about running for the U.S. Senate seat which would be vacated in 2000 by the retiring Senator Patrick Moynihan of New York (who had held the post for 24 years). She also went house hunting and settled on property in Chappaqua, in New York's tony Westchester County.

In July, 1999, making a more definite announcement of her plans at Senator Moynihan's country retreat, she embarked on a "Listening Tour" which took her to every county in New York state, and then, in November, despite nasty charges of being a "carpetbagger," she formally announced she would run for the Senate. Initially, her opponent was the formidable Rudy Giuliani, mayor of New York City, but in May, 2000, Giuliani stepped down after his diagnosis of prostate cancer, and Rick Lazio, a four-term Republican congressman from Long Island, took Rudy's place. The campaign, heavily bankrolled by both parties, was spirited—and sometimes negative—on both sides—but in the end, Hillary drew heavy support, not only from Democratic faithfuls, but also from soccer moms and working women to beat Lazio by a margin of 55 percent to 43 percent.

She returned to Washington for the last days of the Clinton administration, a bittersweet time, since her husband, soon to be the former President Clinton, had been relegated to the sidelines during the Presidential election, and its long, drawn-out resolution of the Florida count and recount.

The Clintons did not leave the White House under the most auspicious circumstances. First, in December, there was the charge that they had received expensive gifts from wealthy contributors—a hopechest? "bridal shower?—to be used to furnish their Chappaqua home. Another charge was that they were furnishing the Chappaqua home with items from the White House which were meant to be permanent gifts for residents of the Mansion...not personal gifts for the Clintons. Eventually, these charges were dismissed or settled and many pieces were returned.

Most troubling, however, for Bill Clinton, (and once again, his actions bounced on to his wife), were the zero hour pardons he made just before the Bush Inauguration. While none were illegal, the worst was his pardon of Mark Rich and his partner Pincus Green who left the United States in 1983 to evade charges of tax evasion and illegal trading with Iran. Rich's ex-wife Denise contributed hundreds of thousands of dollars to the Democratic National Committee, hostessed many fund-raising galas, and donated at least $450,000 toward Clinton's library-to-be. In addition to other questionable last-minute pardons, it was alleged that Roger Clinton, Bill's wayward brother, had taken money with the promise of putting in the good word with brother Bill for pardons (none of which were granted), and that Hillary's own brothers, Tony and Hugh (Hughie, as he's called, especially) had tried to peddle their influence. All of these charges are still under investigation at this writing, but Senator Hillary Clinton, the first and only First Lady ever elected to national office, is trying to shake off the criticism and do a good job for her new home state.

She has even gained some friends in unlikely places. The venerable Senator Strom Thurmond was said to be charmed by the new Senator. Recently Hillary and Trent Lott (former majority leader who became minority leader in May 2001 when Vermont Senator Jim Jeffords switched his party affiliation from Republican to Independent and gave the Democrats a majority of one) have started a "bad hair club" in the Senate and they are earnestly scouting for new members.

Although Hillary has a new life, undeniably, her eight years as First Lady left their mark. In an interview with Margaret Truman she made a statement which President Truman's daughter described as "one of the most profound—and touching—things I have heard from any First Lady." Hillary said, "It's more than being a political partner. I don't think there's any job like it in the world. You have to be a partner in the fullest sense of the word—someone who's trying to support the President in a personal way that's not available to him elsewhere."[16]

Even while Hillary Clinton was campaigning for her Senate seat, reporters and columnists were beginning to speculate whether or not this was her first step toward becoming President herself. *During* the campaign she repeatedly said she intended to serve out her term. *After* the campaign she repeatedly said she intended to serve out her term. She continues to say so, and has been quoted as ruling out a run for President, not just in 2004, but in 2008 and beyond. I wouldn't take bets on that because the political world is changing in terms of women and their leadership potential for the United States, as discussed in the next chapter.

How will Hillary be remembered as a First Lady? On July 22, 2001, the Harris Poll reported that our current First Lady, Laura Bush received a rating of "excellent" to "pretty good" from almost 70 percent of those surveyed. As to the best ratings, dating back to Jacqueline Kennedy, Mrs. Kennedy garnered 50 percent, followed by Laura Bush, Hillary Clinton and Nancy Reagan. When asked who they thought was the *smartest* President's wife, the overwhelming answer was: *Hillary Clinton.*

DEFINING THE ROLE

Has the traditional role of First Lady become obsolete? Does it still make sense in the twenty-first century to have a ribbon-cutting figurehead First Lady who gives grand parties and wears great clothes? On the other hand, has the President's "partner" become too powerful? In our nation's history, whenever a First Lady assumed too much authority, she was denigrated as an "un-elected official" with no right to interfere in the judgments of *our* chief elected official, *The President*. The confusion about the First Lady's "job" reached its peak during the Hill-and-Bill years, and then settled down as Laura Bush reverted to more traditional duties. As Hillary Clinton and others before her discovered, it is difficult for a First Lady to know where to draw the line, and which lines should not be crossed. Some have been more successful at toeing that line than others.

It often seems as if we Americans want it both ways: we want a charismatic, attractive wife and mother we're proud of whether she's hostessing gala receptions at the White House or presiding ("co-presiding?") at official events here and abroad. And, we expect our First Lady to be a spokeswoman on issues important to other women—and men—and families. A nice fringe benefit (not new to the twenty-first century) is a wife who is not afraid to give her husband—even if he is the President—a strong nudge in the right direction.

This dichotomy causes many problems for the lady "in office" during any particular administration. As Felicity Barringer wrote in

The New York Times, just after the 1992 election, "The First Lady's office has evolved into a quirky but efficient engine consisting of 20 or 25 people (the number depends on whether you count the calligraphers and social secretaries). But while Mrs. Clinton has come to symbolize the strong, independent woman of the late 20th century, the office from which she will shape her tenure is born of two traditions. It was created to serve the needs of gentility and elegance, but since the days of Eleanor Roosevelt has often served as a bully pulpit for smart women with something to say."[1]

Our double-edged expectations may account for some of the seemingly inexplicable choices we make when queried about favorite First Ladies. In 1988, for example, when this book was first published, the Gallup Poll released results of a survey asking Americans to rate First Ladies on such qualities as background, value to the country, integrity, leadership, intelligence, accomplishments, public image and value to the President. The winner on all levels was Eleanor Roosevelt, followed by Lady Bird Johnson, Rosalynn Carter, Betty Ford, Edith Wilson and Jacqueline Kennedy. Lowest on the list of seventeen First Ladies was Florence Harding, and not much higher up were Pat Nixon and Nancy Reagan. It is interesting to note that the top five were women who had political input as well as ceremonial recognition, and that some Presidential wives with the lowest ratings worked their way up the scale *after* they left office. In 2001, a similar poll, as reported earlier, revealed that among modern First Ladies (that is, in the last half century), Jacqueline Kennedy received the highest rating of 50 percent, followed by Laura Bush, Hillary Clinton, and Nancy Reagan. But Eleanor Roosevelt remained the all-time favorite.

Why has the public responded so favorably to some First Ladies and reacted so negatively to others? Eleanor Roosevelt dressed dowdily, was not known for major entertaining, but showed great style when she served hot dogs and soda pop to the king and queen of England; her down-to-earth comments in her newspaper column gave her the affectionate cachet of the nation's "aunt" or "grandmother," a fond sobriquet often applied to Barbara Bush. Some First Ladies were initially disliked or ridiculed, until a tragedy endeared them to the country. The media poked fun—and worse—at Jacqueline Kennedy for her debutante whisper, her fabulous, expensive clothes and her aristocratic bearing—until JFK was assassinated and she became a heroic model of grace and dignity. Nancy Reagan, who had been publicly criticized for her protectiveness of "Ronnie," and her excessiveness in spending the nation's money, experienced several dramatic turnarounds in public opinion. Hillary Clinton, who probably generated the strongest opinions about any First Lady since Eleanor Roosevelt, has ranked first as the most admired woman in the *world* every year since 1993, even during the height of the impeachment proceedings and allegations about her involvement in Whitewater. In a December 29, 2000 Gallup Poll, she was still number one with the highest percentage among those polled. We should add that according to this survey, the second most admired woman in the world is Oprah Winfrey.

Through the years, quite a few Presidents have praised their wives publicly—JFK in France, Reagan and Clinton in state of the union addresses, George W. Bush in his campaign speeches. Some Presidents, including John Adams and George Washington chose to praise their wives privately in their letters. And unfortunately, other Presidents expressed their feelings posthumously, as did Richard Nixon, Theodore Roosevelt and Woodrow Wilson—Harry Truman, who always let his "Boss" know how he felt during their lives together (we'll never know, because the very private Bess Truman burned their letters), summed it up for all the women who served in this unpaid and often exhausting job: "I hope some day someone will take time to evaluate the true role of the wife of a President, and to assess the many burdens she has to bear and the contributions she makes."

Unquestionably, the trend seems to be toward "partnership presidencies," as opposed to the devoted wife entertaining the President's guests. Which leads to the next question. Will America ever have a female President? Although Abigail Adams was referred to derisively as "Mrs. President," and Edith Wilson acted as our "First Lady- President," someday perhaps we will have a President who happens to be a woman. We can't even agree on the terminology. Would a female President's husband be known as the "First Man?" Consider this: If a male President's wife is called the First Lady; then a female President's wife should be called "The First Gentleman." If one decides to call such a person the "First Man," then the current version of the President's spouse should be called "The First Woman." Will our First Man or First Gentleman be able to pull off this role with as much grace as Prince Philip of England (and even he gets cranky about walking six dutiful steps behind), or more significantly, the low-profile husband of the former British prime minister, Margaret Thatcher?

When Geraldine Ferraro ran as a Vice-Presidential candidate with Fritz Mondale in 1984, her husband's finances were subjected to much closer scrutiny than those of Barbara Bush, whose husband was then running as vice President on Reagan's ticket. Pat Schroeder, a congresswoman and former leader of NOW, the National Organization of Women, abandoned her Presidential run because it was too tough on her family and some of the campaign

267

developments and criticisms frankly made her cry. When Elizabeth Dole became the first serious female candidate for President by running in the primaries in 2000, her credentials were excellent, but it was awkward for her husband, former senator Bob Dole who had lost to Clinton in his own bid for the presidency in 1996. (It didn't help Liddy's image that while she was campaigning her husband appeared in some widely televised ads for Viagra).

Some years ago, Edmund Muskie gave up his Presidential dreams after snide comments about his wife made him cry. President Clinton often told us "I feel your pain," but we didn't actually see him cry. Are Presidents, whether they are male or female, allowed to cry? (This question actually became moot after the disastrous terrorist attack on the World Trade Center and the Pentagon on September 11, 2001. Everyone wept - from the President to Dan Rather to the rescuers...and the victims. Tears are no longer the province of the female gender)

Would we critique the First Man's clothes? Would we expect him to espouse an official cause? Would we allow him to continue his own career and give him room for individual interests and a private life? Or would we expect him, in effect, to act as the President's "host," become her official caretaker and unofficial advisor?

In December 1996, after Bill Clinton was re-elected, Hillary Clinton addressed 400 women at the Sydney, Australia Opera House. During a Q & A session she was asked why she had so much trouble with her image. She acknowledged that stereotyping was one of the problems for all first ladies, but then went on to say, "This position is such an odd one. In our country we expect so much from the woman who is married to the President - but we don't really know what it is we expect." She noted that the only way to "escape the politics" would be to "totally withdraw and perhaps put a bag over your head, or somehow make it clear that you have no opinions and no ideas about anything - and never express them, publicly or privately." As the audience cheered her on, Hillary became even more candid. "There is something about the position itself which raises in Americans' minds concerns about hidden power, about influence behind the scenes, about unaccountability. Yet if you try to be public about your concerns and your interests, then that is equally criticized. I think the answer is to just be who you are and do what you can do and get through it - and wait for a First Man to hold the position."[2]

Opinions about whether the United States will ever elect a woman as President are often divided along generational lines. According to an informal survey, the split seems to occur more or less neatly at the age of forty. The older respondents felt there would never be a "lady President," and they were somewhat embarrassed about the First Man's role if this unlikely event should occur. Those under forty believed in the likelihood of a woman President, and believed that her husband would be able to do his own thing and succeed in his own career. Until that scenario becomes a reality, the unanswered question remains: Who will monitor the President's waistline, re-do the White House, cut the ribbons, and launch the ships?

THE PRESIDENTS
AND
THEIR FIRST LADIES

1	George Washington Martha Dandridge Custis Washington	1789–1797
2	John Adams Abigail Smith Adams	1797–1801
3	Thomas Jefferson Martha "Patsy" Jefferson Randolph	1801–1809
4	James Madison Dolley Payne Todd Madison	1809–1817
5	James Monroe Elizabeth Kortright Monroe	1817–1825
6	John Quincy Adams Louis Johnson Adams	1825–1829
7	Andrew Jackson Emily Donelson Sarah Jackson	1829–1837
8	Martin Van Buren Angelica Singleton Van Buren	1837–1841

9	William Henry Harrison Anna Symmes Harrison	1841
10	John Tyler Letitia Christian Tyler Julia Gardiner Tyler	1841–1845
11	James Knox Polk Sarah Childress Polk	1845–1849
12	Zachary Taylor Margaret Smith Taylor Elizabeth Taylor Bliss	1849–1850
13	Millard Fillmore Abigail Powers Fillmore	1850–1853
14	Franklin Pierce Jane Means Appleton Pierce	1853–1857
15	James Buchanan Harriet Lane	1857–1861
16	Abraham Lincoln Mary Todd Lincoln	1861–1865
17	Andrew Johnson Eliza McCardle Johnson	1865–1869
18	Ulysses S. Grant Julia Dent Grant	1869–1877
19	Rutherford Birchard Hayes Lucy Webb Hayes	1877–1881
20	James Abram Garfield Lucretia Rudolph Garfield	1881
21	Chester Alan Arthur Mary Arthur McElroy	1881–1885
22	Grover Cleveland Rose Elizabeth "Libby Cleveland Frances Folsom Cleveland	1885–1889

23	Benjamin Harrison Caroline Scott Harrison	1889–1893
24	Grover Cleveland Frances Folsom Cleveland	1893–1897
25	William McKinley Ida Saxton McKinley	1897–1901
26	Theodore Roosevelt Edith Carow Roosevelt	1901–1909
27	William Howard Taft Helen "Nellie" Herron Taft	1909–1913
28	Woodrow Wilson Ellen Axson Wilson Edith Bolling Galt Wilson	1913–1921
29	Warren Gamaliel Harding Florence Kling Harding	1921–1923
30	Calvin Coolidge Grace Goodhue Coolidge	1923–1929
31	Herbert Clark Hoover Lou Henry Hoover	1929–1933
32	Franklin Delano Roosevelt Anna Eleanor Roosevelt	1933–1945
33	Harry S. Truman Elizabeth Virginia "Bess" Wallace Truman	1945–1953
34	Dwight David Eisenhower Mamie Doud Eisenhower	1953–1961
35	John Fitzgerald Kennedy Jacqueline Bouvier Kennedy Onassis	1961–1963
36	Lyndon Baines Johnson Clauda Alta "Lady Bird" Taylor Johnson	1963–1969
37	Richard Milhous Nixon Thelma Catherine "Pat" Ryan Nixon	1969–1974

38	Gerald Rudolph Ford Elizabeth Ann "Betty" Bloomer Ford	1974–1977
39	James Earl "Jimmy" Carter Rosalynn Smith Carter	1977–1981
40	Ronald Wilson Reagan Nancy Davis Reagan	1981–1989
41	George Herbert Walker Bush Barbara Pierce Bush	1989–1993
42	William Jefferson "Bill" Clinton Hillary Rodham Clinton	1993–2001
43	George W. Bush Laura Welch Bush	2001–

NOTES

THE PIONEERS

Martha Dandridge Custis Washington

1 Frank Donovan, *The Women in Their Lives: The Distaff Side of the Founding Fathers*, 120
2 Francis Russell, *Adams: An American Dynasty*, 113
3 Marianne Means, *The Woman in the White House*, 8
4 Ibid., 10-11
5 Ibid., 13
6 Ibid., 17

Abigail Smith Adams

1 Russell, 29
2 Means, 35
3 Russell, 32
4 Donovan, 153
5 Ibid., 150-161
6 Ibid., 166
7 Ibid.
8 Ibid., 176
9 Ibid., 187

THE PIONEERS (CONT.)

Abigail Smith Adams (cont.)

10 Ibid., 198

11 Amy La Follette Jensen, *The White House and its Thirty-Four Families*, 10

12 Means, 29

Martha "Patsy" Jefferson Randolph

1 Donavan, 221

2 The Report of the Monticello Research Committee on Thomas Jefferson and Sally Hemings,

3 Jensen, op. cit., 14

Dolley Payne Todd Madison

1 Means, 52

2 Donovan, 308

3 Means, 54

4 *Time*, Sept. 18, 2000

5 Means, 59

6 Ibid., 63

Elizabeth Kortright Monroe

1 Jensen, 23

2 Ibid., 38

Louisa Johnson Adams

1 Russell, 157

2 Ibid., 161

3 Donovan, 233

PRIVATE LIVES

Anna Symmes Harrison

1 Jensen, 61

PRIVATE LIVES (CONT.)

Lucy Webb Hayes

1 Jensen, 72
2 Esther Singleton, *The Story of the White House*, 155

Caroline Scott Harrison

1 Singleton, 222
2 Jensen, o138
3 Singleton, 229

Elizabeth Virginia "Bess" Wallace Truman

1 Means, 239
2 Ibid., 241
3 Lillian Roger Parks, *My Thirty Years in the White House*, 33
4 Ibid., 281
5 Ibid., 38
6 West, 77
7 Means, 214
8 West, 121
9 Means, 241
10 Margaret Truman, *First Ladies*, 352–353

PRIVATE PAIN

Margaret Smith Taylor and Elizabeth Taylor Bliss

1 John Fiske, *The Presidents of the United States, Volume II*, 140
2 Ibid., 141
3 Irene Hazard Gerlinger, *Mistresses of the White House*, 41

Abigail Powers Fillmore

1 Gerlinger, 44
2 Fiske, 167

PRIVATE PAIN (CONT.)

Jane Means Appleton Pierce

1   Fiske, 201

Mary Todd Lincoln

1   Singleton, 33
2   Means, 97
3   Ibid., 96
4   Ibid., 98
5   Ibid., 101
6   Jensen, 83
7   Ibid., 86
8   Ibid., 93

Eliza McCardle Johnson

1   Fiske, *Volume III*, 18-20
2   Means, 56
3   Jensen, 96
4   Singleton, 106
5   Jensen, 97

Lucretia Rudolph Garfield

1   Singleton, 172
2   Jensen, 120

Ida Saxton McKinley

1   Gerlinger, 78-79

Grace Goodhue Coolidge

1   Parks, 185
2   Ibid., 183

THE ELEGANT ENTERTAINERS

Letitia Christian Tyler and Julia Gardiner Tyler

1 Jensen, 62
2 Ibid., 63
3 Ibid., 67

Julia Dent Grant

1 Fiske, *Volume II*, 103
2 Jensen, 105
3 Singleton, 129
4 Ibid., 145

Rose Elizabeth Cleveland and Frances Folsom Cleveland

1 Jensen, 136
2 Ibid, 137

Edith Carow Roosevelt

1 Singleton, 267
2 Ibid., 280

Lou Henry Hoover

1 Gerlinger, 84

Mamie Doud Eisenhower

1 West, 145
2 Parks, 34
3 Ibid., 316
4 *New York Times*, Nov. 17, 1996
5 West, 131

THE SUPPORTIVE STAND-INS

Emily Donelson and Sarah Jackson (for Andrew Jackson)

1 Russell, 209
2 Ibid., 212
3 Ibid., 213
4 Jensen, 47
5 Ibid, 51
6 Ibid., 53
7 Ibid., 53-55

Angelica Singleton Van Buren (for Martin Van Buren)

1 Jensen, 56
2 Ibid., 59

Harriet Lane (for James Buchanan)

1 Fiske et al, Volume III, 237

Mary Arthur McElroy (for Chester Alan Arthur)

1 Fiske et al, Volume III, 237
2 Singleton, 174
3 Ibid., 188

THE SPOKESWOMEN

Jacqueline Bouvier Kennedy

1 Means, 267
2 West, 195
3 Ibid., 196
4 Ibid., 253
5 Means, 268
6 Ibid., 271
7 *Time*, May 30, 1994
8 Oleg Cassini, *In My Own Fashion*, 7-8
9 *Time*, April 30, 2001

THE SPOKESWOMEN (CONT.)

Claudia Alta "Lady Bird" Taylor Johnson

1 West, 283–285
2 Jensen, 299
3 Ibid., 304

Elizabeth Anne "Betty" Bloomer Ford

1 David Wallechinsky and Irving Wallace, *The People's Almanac,* 334
2 Ibid., 339

Barbara Pierce Bush

1 *People* magazine, Nov. 21, 1988
2 Ibid.
3 *New York Times*, Dec. 11, 1988
4 *Life*, Nov. 1988
5 Ibid.
6 *New York Times*, op. cit.
7 *People*, op. cit.

Laura Welch Bush

1 *Los Angeles Times*, Feb. 19, 2001
2 *People*, Jan. 29, 2001
3 *Washington Post*, Jan. 20, 2001
4 Ibid.
5 *Washington Post*, April, 3, 2001
6 CNN., July 30, 2001
7 *People*, June 18, 2001
8 *Los Angeles Times*, op. cit.
9 *New York Times*, Sept. 30, 2001

EYES, EARS, VOICES

Sarah Childress Polk

1 Fiske, 118
2 Means, 76
3 Fiske,118
4 Means, 76

EYES, EARS, VOICES (CONT.)

Helen "Nellie" Herron Taft

1 Means, 118
2 Parks, 108
3 Jensen, 195
4 Means, 130

Ellen Axson Wilson and Edith Bolling Galt Wilson

1 Means, 161
2 Edith Bolling Wilson, *My Memoirs*

Florence Kling Harding

1 Means, 164
2 Ibid.
3 Ibid, 168

Anna Eleanor Roosevelt

1 Doris Kearns Goodwin, *No Ordinary Time*, 628
2 *People's Almanac*, 301
3 Parks, 68
4 Ibid., 27
5 Ibid., 47
6 Goodwin, 313
7 Ibid., 629

Thelma Catherine "Pat" Ryan Nixon

1 Julie Nixon Eisenhower, *Pat Nixon: The Untold Story,* 94
2 Ibid., 123
3 Ibid., 254
4 Ibid., 260
5 Ibid., 428
6 Margaret Truman, *First Ladies*, 188
7 Ibid., 189

EYES, EARS, VOICES (CONT.)

Rosalynn Smith Carter

1 *Current Biography*, 1978, 69

Truman, 147

Jimmy and Rosalynn Carter, *Everything to Gain*, 184

New York Times, Jan. 29, 1995

Nancy Davis Reagan

1 *New York Times*, July 13, 1986

2 *Los Angeles Times* News Service, Nov. 13, 1988

3 Truman, 167

4 *People*, May 23, 1988

5 *Time*, Oct. 1, 1988

6 *Los Angeles Times* News Service, op. cit.

Hillary Rodham Clinton

1 Hillary Rodham Clinton, *It Takes a Village And Other Lessons Children Teach Us*, 211

2 Ibid. 8

3 *New Yorker*, Feb.—March 1996

4 *The New York Times*, May 5, 1993

5 Ibid.

6 *The New York Times*, Jan.15, 1995

7 *Time*, Sept.18, 1995

8 *Time*, Jan. 22,1996

9 *Newsweek*, Jan.15, 1996

10 Clinton, op. cit., 43

11 *The Washington Post*, Feb. 4,1996

12 *The New Yorker*, op. cit.

13 *Time*, Jul. 1,1996

14 *Time*, Dec. 2, 1996

15 *Vanity Fair*, June, 2001

16 Truman, op. cit. 332

DEFINING THE ROLE

1 *The New York Times*, Dec. 6, 1992

2 *Time*, Dec. 2, 1996

BIBLIOGRAPHY

Butt, Archibald W., *Taft and Roosevelt: The Intimate Letters of Archie Butt*, Garden City, New York, Doubleday, Doran Company, Inc., 1930.

Carter, Jimmy and Rosalynn, *Everything to Gain: Making the Most of the Rest of Your Life*, New York, Random House, 1987.

Carter, Rosalynn, *First Lady From Plains*, Boston, Houghton-Mifflin, 1984.

Cassini, Oleg, *In My Own Fashion*, New York, Simon & Schuster, 1987.

Clinton, Hillary Rodham, *It Takes a Village And Other Lessons Children Teach Us*, New York, Simon & Schuster, 1996.

Colman, Edna M., *Seventy-five Years of White House Gossip: From Washington to Lincoln*, Garden City, New York, Doubleday, Page & Company, 1926.

Donovan, Frank, *The Women in Their Lives: The Distaff Side of the Founding Fathers*, New York, Dodd, Mead & Company, 1966.

Eisenhower, Julie Nixon, *Pat Nixon: The Untold Story*, New York, Simon & Schuster, 1966.

Fiske, John et al, Wilson, James Grant, ed., *The Presidents of the United States—1789-1914*, New York, Charles Scribner's Sons, 1914.

Ford, Betty (with Chris Chase), *Betty: A Glad Awakening*, Garden City, New York, Doubleday & Company, Inc., 1987.

Gallagher, Mary Barelli (Leighton, Frances Spatz, ed.), *My Life with Jacqueline Kennedy*, New York, David McKay Company, Inc., 1969.

Gerlinger, Irene Hazard, *Mistresses of the White House*, Freeport, New York, Books For Libraries Press, 1948.

Goodwin, Doris Kearns, *No Ordinary Time, Franklin and Eleanor Roosevelt: The Home Front in World War II*, New York, Simon & Schuster, 1994.

Hoover, Irwin H., *Forty-two Years in the White House*, Boston, Houghton-Mifflin Company, 1934.

Jaffray, Elizabeth, *Secrets of the White House*, New York, Cosmopolitan Book Corp., 1927.

Jensen, Amy La Follette, *The White House and its Thirty-Four Families*, New York, McGraw-Hill, 1958.

Keckley, Elizabeth Hobbs, *Behind the Scenes*, New York, G.W. Carleton & Company, 1868.

Longworth, Alice Roosevelt, *Crowded Hours*, New York, Charles Scribner's Sons, 1933.

McCullough, David, *John Adams*, New York, Simon & Schuster, 2001.

Means, Marianne, *The Woman in the White House*, New York, Random House, 1963.

Nesbitt, Victoria Henrietta, *White House Diary*, Garden City, New York, Doubleday & Company, 1948.

Parks, Lillian Rogers (with Leighton, Frances Spatz), *My Thirty Years in the White House*, New York, Fleet Publishing Corporation, 1961.

Reagan, Nancy (with William Novak), *My Turn: The Memoirs of Nancy Reagan*, New York, Random House, 1989.

Roosevelt, Eleanor, *This I Remember*, New York, Harper & Brothers, 1949.

Russell, Francis, *Adams: An American Dynasty*, New York, American Heritage Publishing Co., Inc., 1976.

Singleton, Esther, L., *The Story of the White House*, New York, The McClure Company, 1907.

Smith, Margaret Bayard (Hunt, Gaillard, ed.), *The First Forty Years of Washington Society*, New York, Charles Scribner's Sons, 1906.

Taft, Helen Herron, *Recollections of Full Years*, New York, Dodd Mead & Company, 1914.

Truman, Margaret, *First Ladies*, New York, Random House, 1995.

Wallechinsky, David, and Wallace, Irving, *The People's Almanac*, Garden City, New York, Doubleday & Co., 1975.

West, J.B. (with Mary Lynn Kotz), *Upstairs at the White House*, New York, Coward McCann & Geoghegan, 1973.

Wilson, Edith Bolling, *My Memoirs*, Indianapolis, The Bobbs-Merrill Company, 1939.

INDEX

A

Abell, Bess, 164
Adams, Abigail "Nabby" (child of Abigail), 18
Adams, Abigail Smith, 2, 10, 12, 15, 17-23, 26, 42-43, 53, 79, 85, 153, 155, 174, 189, 267
Adams, Charles (son of Abigail), 18
Adams, Charles (son of Louisa), 44-45
Adams, Charles Francis (grandson of Abigail), 18
Adams, George Washington (son of Louisa), 23, 41, 43-44
Adams, Henry (grandson of Louisa), 45
Adams, James (cousin of John), 18
Adams, John (son of Louisa), 44
Adams, Louisa Catherine (daughter of Louisa), 44
Adams, Louisa Johnson, 10, 23, 35, 39, 41-45
Adams, President John, 2, 9, 13, 17-23, 26, 43, 174, 267
Adams, President John Quincy, 10, 18, 23, 39-45, 112, 137-139, 174, 192
Addams, Jane, 250
Agnew, Vice President Spiro, 168
Ailes, Roger, 173
Albert I and Elizabeth, King and Queen of Belgium, 204
Albert, Edward, Prince of Wales
    See Edward VII, King of England
Alexander, Czar of Russia, 44
Alzheimer's Disease, 241-242
American Spectator, The, 259
Arden, Elizabeth "Maine Chance", 129
Arthur, Ellen "Nell" Herndon, 147
Arthur, President Chester Alan, 69, 94-95, 135, 147-148
Arthur, Prince, (son of Queen Victoria), 114
Astrologers
    Astrologer to the Stars, Righter, Carroll, 239
    Brady, Laurie, 240
    Champney, Madame Marcia, 240
    Dixon, Jeanne, 239
    Quigley, Joan, 239

B

Baldridge, Letitia "Tish", 157
Barnham, P.T., 86
Barringer, Felicity, 265
Bateson, Catherine, 257
Beauharnais, Hortense de (mother of Napoleon III)
    See Hortense de Beauharnais, Quuen of Holland
Bell, Alexander Graham, 95
Betty Ford Center for Substance Abuse, 169
bin Laden, Osama, 181
Blair, James, Tyson foods, 252
Bliss, Colonel William, 77
Bliss, Elizabeth Taylor (daughter of Margaret Taylor), 75, 77
Bones, Helen, 200
Booth, John Wilkes, 87
Boston Tea Party, 18
Boudin, Stephane (White House decorator), 158-159
Bouvier, John Vernou III (father of Jacqueline Kennedy), 158, 178
Brady, Jim (Press Secretary to President Reagan), 235
Brenner, Marie, 259
Britton, Nan, 207
Brooke, Senator Edward, 245
Brown, Governor Pat, 221, 234
Buchanan, President James, 82, 84, 109, 135, 145-146, 148
Buck, Pearl, 157
Burr, Vice President Aaron, 34
Bush, Barbara (daughter of Laura), 177, 180
Bush, Barbara Pierce, 154, 171-176, 178, 180-181, 235, 240, 244, 249, 256, 266-267
Bush, Jeb (son of Barbara)
    See Bush, John Ellis "Jeb"
Bush, Jenna (daughter of Laura), 176, 180
Bush, John Ellis "Jeb" (son of Barbara), 172
Bush, Laura Welch, 3, 109, 154, 175-178, 180-182, 245, 262, 265

288

ABOUT THE AUTHOR

R ae **Lindsay** has written, ghost-written or edited 21 non-fiction books including *Left is Right: The Survival Guide for Living Lefty in a Right-Handed World, Alone and Surviving: A Guide for Today's Widow, Sleep and Dreams, The Pursuit of Youth, How to Look as Young as You Feel, Job Discrimination* (and *Job Discrimination II*) and an earlier edition of *The Presidents' First Ladies*, published in 1989.

For ten years, Ms. Lindsay wrote the syndicated column "First Person Singular" for Associated Press Newsfeatures, and during her career has contributed dozens of articles to national magazines. She has also taught English and Journalism courses at Seton Hall University, St. John's University, and William Paterson University.

Ms. Lindsay is a graduate of Wellesley College and currently serves as vice-president of her class; she is also a member of the National Press Club.